M000086738

Shampa Biswas, Bruce Magnusson, and Zahi Zalloua

University of Washington Press
Seattle and London
IN ASSOCIATION WITH
Whitman College
Walla Walla, Washington

This series aims to pursue the challenges that globalization poses, and the possibilities that it offers, in an interdisciplinary setting. Each volume seeks to promote a more nuanced understanding of timely issues while providing critical dialogue with prior scholarship and new ways of shaping how these issues are envisioned and framed. The series probes to what extent our vision of globalization both alters and is altered by the singularity and complexity of the topic at hand, compelling, in turn, perpetual re-visions.

Torture: Power, Democracy, and the Human Body
edited by Shampa Biswas and Zahi Zalloua

Contagion: Health, Fear, Sovereignty
edited by Bruce Magnusson and Zahi Zalloua

TORTURE

POWER,
DEMOCRACY,
AND THE
HUMAN BODY

EDITED BY
SHAMPA BISWAS
ZAHI ZALLOUA

UNIVERSITY OF WASHINGTON PRESS

PO BOX 50096, SEATTLE, WA 98145, USA

WWW.WASHINGTON.EDU/UWPRESS

WHITMAN COLLEGE

345 BOYER AVE.

WALLA WALLA, WA 99362

WWW.WHITMAN.EDU

LIBRARY OF CONGRESS CATALOGING-IN-PUBLICATION DATA

Torture : power, democracy, and the human body /

edited by Shampa Biswas and Zahi Zalloua.

p. cm. — (Global re-visions)

Includes bibliographical references and index.

ISBN 978-0-295-99122-1 (pbk. : alk. paper)

1. Torture—Moral and ethical aspects—Congresses. 2. Human body—
Moral and ethical aspects—Congresses. 3. Psychiatric ethics—Congresses.
4. Mind and body—Congresses. I. Biswas, Shampa. II. Zalloua, Zahi Anbra, 1971–
III. Title: Power, democracy, and the human body.

HV8593.T6627 2011

364.6'7—dc23   2011029716

CONTENTS

ACKNOWLEDGMENTS   vii

INTRODUCTION
Torture, Democracy, and the Human Body
Shampa Biswas and Zahi Zalloua   3

1   **TORTURE AND DEMOCRACY**
What Now?
Darius Rejali   25

2   **NOW THAT WE'VE TORTURED**
Image, Guilt, Consequence
Mark Danner   46

3   **"WE ARE ALL TORTURERS NOW"**
Accountability after Abu Ghraib
Timothy V. Kaufman-Osborn   67

4 **DYING IS NOT PERMITTED**
Sovereignty, Biopower, and Force-Feeding at Guantánamo Bay
Lauren Wilcox   101

5 **THE TORTURE DEVICE**
Debate and Archetype
Stephanie Athey   129

6 **SPECTERS OF THE *MUSELMANN***
Guantánamo Bay Penalogial Theme Park and the Torture of Omar Khadr
Joseph Pugliese   158

7 **THIS FRAGILE BODY**
Susan Crile's *Abu Ghraib: Abuse of Power*
Julia A. Ireland   188

8 **SRI LANKA**
Landscapes of Massacre
Suvendrini Perera   215

BIBLIOGRAPHY   245
NOTES ON CONTRIBUTORS   265
INDEX   269

ACKNOWLEDGMENTS

This volume emerged out of the symposium "Torture and the Human Body" held at Whitman College, Walla Walla, Washington, on February 27, 2009. Organized by the Global Studies Initiative, the symposium was developed to stimulate an interdisciplinary conversation on a topic of contemporary relevance. It appears to us that too many of our most important conversations happen within the relatively narrow confines of academic disciplines or specialist communities. Inspired by the liberal arts model of colleges like Whitman, we believe that it is both possible and valuable to generate discussions across different kinds of epistemic communities without sacrificing intellectual rigor. Our hope is that this volume, much like the symposium, will continue what we consider to be an absolutely necessary public debate on the question of torture and will do so in a way that is both sophisticated and accessible to various reading publics. Stephanie Athey, Mark Danner, Julia Ireland, Timothy V. Kaufman-Osborn, and Darius Rejali participated in the symposium and contributed revised versions of their presentations to this volume.

Our foremost gratitude goes to the many faculty, administrators, students, and staff who have helped make Whitman College the vibrant intellectual community that makes possible projects such as these. We would like to thank President George Bridges, former provost and dean of faculty Lori Bettison-Varga, and current provost and dean of faculty Timothy V. Kaufman-Osborn for all their encouragement and support. The Global Studies steering committee, composed of Gaurav Majumdar (English), Bruce Magnusson (Politics), Jim Russo (Chemistry), and Elyse Semerdjian (History), was the intellectual force that helped conceptualize and implement this project. Susan Bennett, administrative assistant to the provost and dean of faculty, provided crucial logistical support all along the way. And most important, none of this would have been possible without the enthusiasm and interest of the smart and dedicated students of Whitman College. Among these, we owe particular thanks to several individual students whose contributions are reflected in many ways in this volume. Philosophy major Adam Chapman (2009), Politics major Nadim Damluji (2010), and English major Valerie Lopez (2009) were all participants in the symposium, and many of the chapters in this volume were enriched by their sharp commentary. Politics majors Ali Edwards (2010) and Tristan Grau (2011) provided invaluable research and editing support. We cannot emphasize enough how instrumental these and other students were in posing probing questions, challenging the contributors to sharpen their analyses, and in general elevating the quality of the symposium and the resulting volume through their active engagement. As teachers at Whitman College, we consider ourselves fortunate to be in the midst of such thoughtful and supportive colleagues and students. Finally, we would like to thank Pat Soden, Marilyn Trueblood, and Jacqueline Ettinger for all their encouragement and help with this volume and Laura Iwasaki for her superb copyediting of the manuscript.

We would like to express our gratitude for permission to reprint Timothy V. Kaufman-Osborn's "'We are all torturers now': Accountability After Abu Ghraib," *Theory & Event* 11, no. 2 (2008), and Joseph Pugliese's "Apostrophe of Empire: Guantánamo Bay, Disneyland," *borderlands* 8, no. 3 (2009): 1–26, which appears here in slightly modified form.

TORTURE

INTRODUCTION

Torture, Democracy, and the Human Body

Shampa Biswas & Zahi Zalloua

Given the events of the last decade, the topic of torture, democracy, and the human body hardly needs any justification. Yet it
is its apparent obviousness that makes the topic all the more
urgent. What is torture? Who defines it? What are its immediate and long-
term effects on the human body, on the social body, and the political
bond that ties these bodies together, that is, democracy? These questions
resist easy answers. Torture, like any other contentious concept, has its
own twisted history. In this respect, we might do well to keep in mind
Friedrich Nietzsche's observation that "only that which has no history is
definable."[1] The challenge at hand, however, is not simply to recognize
that the interpretation of torture becomes an endless task and battle
of interpretive wills, something that we never define once and for all.
Rather, a genealogical perspective on the subject displaces the essentialist
question "What is torture?" in order to ask instead "What meaning have
we given to torture?" or "What is the function and purpose of torture
today?" In other words, torture as such cannot be defined in isolation but
refers back to systems of belief, social networks of power, and ideological

worldviews that invariably ascribe to torture a certain meaning. The nature of that meaning is precisely what is in question in contemporary debates on torture, and the authors in this volume approach that question from diverse angles.

Torture as Political Violence: Interrogating the Relationships among State, Violence, and Democracy

The question of torture, as it has been posed in our contemporary moment, has renewed debates about what is or is not legitimate political violence when the goal is state security. Political violence usually brings to mind war, genocide, and terrorism, and it is not uncommon for discussions of these topics to center around killing and death. It is no doubt true, as Judith Butler points out, that the deaths resulting from these sorts of political violence register on our public consciousness almost entirely through nationalist frames, and so some deaths are mourned while others go unaccounted.[2] Nevertheless, whether in policy circles or scholarly studies, the most significant measure of the habits of war, genocide, and terrorism is the number of dead, both soldiers and civilians. This focus on killing and death is true also of conceptualizations of political violence inspired by Marxist political economy—accounts of "structural violence" that take stock of the less direct, but equally brutal and always untimely deaths brought by institutionalized structures of poverty and inequality. Johan Galtung's now famous argument that the unequal distribution of global resources truncates the lives of many innocents simply because of an accident of birth has helped complicate considerably our dominant understandings of political violence. Yet the insight that structures themselves "kill," too, leaves intact our sense that what is most risky and fraught about political violence is the loss of life.[3] The question, then, is how do we understand the conscious and brutal infliction of bodily pain and damage that is called "torture" but that does *not* lead to death, and in which, indeed, the preservation of life is absolutely crucial?

In chapter 4, "Dying Is Not Permitted: Sovereignty, Biopower, Force-Feeding at Guantánamo Bay," Lauren Wilcox draws our attention to the strenuous efforts made by the U.S. government to *prevent* the deaths of tortured prisoners at the Guantánamo Bay detention facility. She describes the invasive and sometimes painful technologies mustered, often with the help of medical professionals, for the purpose of force-feeding desperate and humiliated prisoners who, seeing no end to their suffering, refuse food as a form of protest. While preserving these "useful" bodies from which torture is meant to extract valuable information, administration officials claim to be acting humanely in keeping these bodies alive. This poses a paradox for our common understandings of political violence. Legally ambiguous "enemy combatants" detained in legally ambiguous geography, Guantánamo Bay detainees can indeed be killed (or tortured) with impunity.[4] Or, to draw from Michel Foucault's understandings of power, as Wilcox does, these are bodies on whom the sovereign power *to kill* can presumably be exercised with abandon, yet these prisoners are not just allowed to live but are forced to live, their lives closely monitored, regulated, preserved, even nurtured.[5] In remarking on the comfortable conditions of life at Guantánamo Bay compared to their abject lives in the third world, U.S. senators and policy makers even implicitly acknowledge the structural violence from which these detainees, they argue, are being rescued! In her chapter, Wilcox attempts to make sense of this uneasy conjuncture of the sovereign power to kill and torture, the disciplinary power to regulate, and the biopolitical power to preserve and nurture life in a place like Guantánamo.

Tortured bodies are kept alive because they have been deemed useful, and there has, indeed, been much recent debate on the "usefulness" of torture. Since much of this debate has revolved around the question of what constitutes "legitimate violence" for achieving the goals of national security, it may be helpful to understand how legitimacy is bestowed on violence, what makes any kind of violence legitimate, and who authorizes violence that is deemed legitimate. If we were to accept the classic Weberian definition of the state as the entity that wields monopoly over legitimate violence, then the extensive efforts of the George W. Bush administration to make a case for the acceptability of torture as legitimate state violence might begin to make some sense. The recent torture debate as it occurred in the United States in the context of the war on terror hinged around two central questions: First, *if and when* should we torture and, second, *how and to what extent* can and should we torture? The administration expended considerable energy on the second question through its extensive efforts to define torture and distinguish it from "enhanced interrogations."[6] But sanctioning torture itself as a form of legitimate political violence deployed by the state hinges primarily on the first question, the "if and when" question. Are there instances when torture can be considered legitimate and, if so, under what conditions?

We now know, thanks to the release of the infamous "torture memos," that Department of Justice lawyers developed fairly elaborate arguments for who could be tortured and in what ways.[7] One might see these memos as essentially an attempt by the state to make a legal case for why and on whom the use of torture constitutes legitimate violence. As Mark Danner points out in chapter 2, "Now That We've Tortured: Image, Guilt, Consequences," these memos were written at least partly because officials in the intelligence community sought legal protection. But Danner also reminds us, in case we have the impression that these are entirely secret machinations going on within a politicized justice department,[8] that laws written and approved by Congress, such as the Military Commissions Act of 2006, permitted and made these sorts of practices possible.[9] In other words, to understand the use of torture as legitimate political violence requires us to interrogate more attentively the institutions of political democracy that sanction and justify its uses. The question of culpability for the torture practices of the Bush administration lies at the very heart of Danner's chapter. Seeing these practices as a failure of democracy, he lays the onus for the revival of these practices quite squarely on calculating politicians, Republicans and Democrats alike, feeding on the post–September 11, 2001, culture of fear. Pushing even further, however, Danner argues that democratic publics who yield to fear and turn a blind eye to the torture occurring in the name of securing their safety bear some responsibility as well. This collusion, in any final accounting, means that "we are all torturers now."[10]

In chapter 5, "The Torture Device: Debate and Archetype," Stephanie Athey, too, takes up this question of public complicity, albeit in a different manner. She does so by drawing our attention to the extensive speculative debate in the media on the question of whether and when one should torture, a debate eagerly consumed by reading and viewing publics. This debate, as she points out, began emerging in mid-September 2001, *before* any of the memos or executive orders were drafted, and acquired significant density before the 2004 Abu Ghraib photos created the first noticeable public outcry against torture. Identifying dozens of feature stories, news analyses, and commentaries in the mainstream press that debated the utility of torture in the war on terror, she lays out in descriptive detail the seductive logic through which torture was made acceptable to the U.S. public. Offering a so-called ticking-time-bomb scenario, the articles draw the reader into identifying with the morally vexing predicament of a well-meaning interrogator, always a professional working in a controlled environment and engaged in a rather simple utilitarian calculus—if and how much pain should be inflicted on a single terrorist in attempting to extract information that might save the lives of thousands of innocents. David Luban has argued that utilitarian torture for intelligence gathering is the only one that can find justification within a liberal democracy that finds all other reasons for torture—producing pleasure for the victor, terrorizing into submission, meting out punishment, and extracting confessions—abhorrent and illiberal.[11] These speculative stories on torture, Athey argues, do the work of "imagining and projecting a unified community that believes it has a stake in torture," and it is the utilitarian logic of the exercise that makes it both compelling and seductive to people who think of themselves as simultaneously ethical and pragmatic.[12] If one is to really push the question of democratic complicity, one might argue that it is the image of torture in these speculative stories that did as much, if not more, to legitimize the use of torture in society than the much more maligned torture memos.

Reports and stories of torture, some descriptive, some speculative, had been emerging since September 2001. What really captured the U.S. public's imagination, however, were the now infamous images from Abu Ghraib prison in Iraq, released in late April 2004, first aired on the CBS news program *60 Minutes II*, published in the *New Yorker*, and then widely disseminated through various media. As both Athey and Danner point out, much of what became publicly known after those photos were revealed had already appeared in several previous news stories, including some startling remarks from administration officials about the use of torture, but it was the *visual* evidence of torture in the Abu Ghraib photos that led to the first sustained press investigations as well as horror and moral outrage among the general public. There is no question that part of the reason these photographs so horrified people, as Susan Sontag pointed out in a widely read essay published in the *New York Times Magazine* soon after the scandal, was that the torture had been visually recorded, by gleeful perpetrators celebrating their "trophies."[13] But what appears to be so offensive about these photos is not just the hubris Sontag points to but also the obvious humiliation being inflicted on the prisoners. Indeed, in the most discussed of these photographs, such as those that include Lynndie England, it is the humiliation much more than the pain of torture that is most viscerally unsettling. Returning to the eager consumption of the speculative debate on torture that Athey discusses, one might argue that the infliction of humiliation is so striking and troubling because it appears gratuitous, or, indeed, the opposite of utilitarian. There seems to be no purpose to the torture—no rational but tormented professional infliction of calculated amounts of pain in the most efficient manner, no softening up of detainees for the purpose of yielding urgent and necessary information—in fact, no sense of urgency and necessity at all in that recreational economy of desire that might suggest that a bomb might be ticking somewhere.

But buying into that very distinction between *good, rational, utilitarian torture* and *bad, sadistic, gratuitous torture* is what makes it possible to be persuaded by the indictment of the "few bad apples" responsible for the Abu Ghraib abuses.[14] This is a matter not just of exonerating those officials and policy makers higher up in the military and civilian chain of command, as many have pointed out, but also of keeping alive the fiction of a controlled form of painful torture practiced by more upright torturers that is separate and distinct from the infliction of humiliation by more depraved torturers. That this separation does not hold water is clear from the fact that all interrogation manuals, including the Army Field Manual 34-52, that officially governed the treatment of those imprisoned at Abu Ghraib, quite explicitly recognize the infliction of humiliation as a method of extracting information, and these methods were used not just on prisoners in Abu Ghraib but on high-value detainees at Guantánamo as well as in CIA black sites around the world.[15] There is no reason to think that this abuse was an aberration or gratuitous when perpetrated at Abu Ghraib but was utilitarian and controlled when used on high-value detainees elsewhere.[16] But then again, consider waterboarding—one of the most famous enhanced interrogation methods approved by the Department of Defense and one that ostensibly has nothing to do with humiliation—which is widely recognized as torture by most legal experts. In chapter 4, Wilcox puzzles over the marginal value of the information yielded by the 183 waterboardings of Khalid Sheik Mohammed. When in that process, one might wonder, did utilitarian torture end and gratuitous violence begin?[17] And most reports indicate that, unlike the so-called high-value detainees allegedly tortured for critical information, 70 to 90 percent of those being held at Guantánamo (and an even larger percentage at Abu Ghraib) were simply common criminals and bystanders caught up in the sweep of military attacks. Yet again, one wonders how much of what occurs in these places was really even meant to be utilitarian torture for the extraction of information and how much was simply gratuitous violence?

The point here is that the seductiveness of the powerful utilitarian and rationalist logic of torture masks the fact that "interrogation" or "intelligence gathering," according to Elaine Scarry, is an "alibi" or "false motive" for torture. One must then ask with Athey, what else is going on with torture that is not about information extraction? In thus distracting us from torture's inherently violent nature by focusing on what appears as the excess of violence, the Abu Ghraib images may not have been particularly helpful in aiding our understanding of the role of political violence in a democracy. To the extent that we consume the fiction of utilitarian torture, done in the name of "our security," however, we become complicit in perpetuating and legitimizing what in effect becomes popularly sanctioned uses of violence.[18]

This brings us back to the question of democracy and accountability. As Darius Rejali notes in chapter 1, "Torture and Democracy: What Now?" we think of democracy as the remedy for torture and expect that more democracy, transparency, and political accountability mean less torture. But, he argues, democracies have had a fairly intimate relationship with torture; no less likely to use torture than authoritarian states, democracies just resort to different kinds of torture, torture that does not leave visible marks, such as waterboarding, sleep deprivation, and forced standing. One might even argue, as Danner does in chapter 2, that if democracy has something to do with majoritarian rule, widespread fear of the kind that followed the events of September 11, 2001, can even lead to overt public support of torture. But Rejali disagrees with Danner on this point, finding that torture was sanctioned even though a majority of the U.S. public fairly consistently opposed its use during the years of the Bush presidency. Rejali believes that preventing torture's recurrence requires holding public officials accountable through political will and processes of public reckoning, although he is pessimistic that this will happen in the United States.

However, this debate about democratic and public accountability misses the point, writes Timothy V. Kaufman-Osborn in chapter 3, "'We Are All Torturers Now': Accountability after Abu Ghraib." The question of public complicity, he contends, is moot in a context in which the substance of democracy has been effectively evacuated from the empty institutions that still carry its name. Drawing from Iris Marion Young, Kaufman-Osborn examines the historical transformation of the United States into a "security state," beginning in the early decades of the twentieth century and gathering momentum particularly in the years of the Cold War. The enhancement of executive power that emerges when the imperatives of national security trump other political demands and desires renders the institutional structures and processes of democratic checks largely ineffective and turns citizens from willing and active participants in a Lockean social contract into mere passive recipients of state protections. There is no doubt that the Bush administration, according to Kaufman-Osborn, was both "heir" and "an innovative contributor" to the development of that security state, but public complicity in the torture used in the war on terror is of a more complex kind that requires more substantial institutional remedies than can be effected through "politically correct hand-wringing." The question of public accountability is an institutional one, then, and preventing torture, if the public really does oppose it as Rejali maintains, requires restoring the institutional and procedural matrix through which public officials can be held democratically accountable.

But one could go further and probe the imaginaries through which we think of democracy and its legal and ethical articulation with a territorial nation-state structure. In posing the question of democratic accountability, it might also be worthwhile to ask what and whom democratic accountability is meant to protect. This returns us to Judith Butler's discussion of nationalist framing.[19] Moving beyond the question of democratic proceduralism, one might ask if the very premises of a security state are inscribed in a (nation-)statist logic that pits and privileges the safety and well-being of the state's citizens against and above those of others. Butler argues for the adoption of a vocabulary and imaginary that embrace common vulnerability as the premise of a shared humanity. But to the extent that democracy in practice requires us to subscribe to the illusion of invulnerable security, delivered by a statist apparatus (democratic or not), do we not yield to the possibility of legitimizing and using the kind of political violence we call "torture" in the name of that security? In other words, when we think that democracy is the solution to torture, what we mean, as many of the authors in this volume remind us, is that democracy just transfers torture to those we consider to be others, those we have deemed less than human, in spaces that we consider distant. It is to that question of alterity that we turn next.

Challenging the Politics of Torture: Ethical and Aesthetic Interventions

Questioning this logic of othering, exposing the mechanisms by which individuals or groups become designated and accepted as torturable bodies, goes hand in hand with challenging the politics of torture. Since the tragic events of 9/11, a dominant narrative that captures an American imaginary of torture in a global era seems to have emerged.[20] Its effectiveness lies in part in its simplicity. It runs something like this: they (the bad guys) torture, but we (the good guys) don't do it, and if we did do it, it would be under the strictest of conditions. Fostering a Manichean worldview of good and evil, an uncomplicated political reality pitting us against them, this one-dimensional discourse on torture contains and converts cultural, religious, and political differences into monolithic identities. In the war on terror, those deemed enemies of the United States are framed as unworthy, lacking human dignity, and driven negatively by pure hate ("They hate our freedom and democratic way of life" is by now a familiar refrain). These enemies also fall outside what Butler terms "frames of recognition," which define those whom Western publics commonly acknowledge and recognize as human, that is, as beings worthy of respect, saving, and mourning.[21] Labeling opponents of U.S. policies as "Islamo-fascists," for example, enacts both senses of the word "framed": they are presumed guilty in advance *and* they are nothing like us.

This Manichean narrative of good and evil takes on ideological force once the "norms of recognition"[22] that it helps institute are naturalized, that is, once their contested origins are erased and presented to the American people as a self-evident reality. Examples of attempts at this type of erasure, to smooth over torture's disputed history and definition, lie close at hand. Consider the comment of U.S. Representative from Colorado Tom Tancredo, responding to a question during a 2007 Republican presidential primary debate: "We're wondering about whether water-boarding would be a—a bad thing to do? I'm looking for Jack Bauer at that time, let me tell you."[23] Jack Bauer is the fictional hero of the Fox television network's hit show *24*. He is the American patriot who tortures right, who tortures despite himself for the greater good of the United States, and usually when compelled to do so by the highly charged and paradigmatic ticking-time-bomb scenario.

It would be somewhat misleading, however, to see Tancredo's conflation of reality and fiction simply as a *distortion* of torture, as only a *mis*representation of torture. It is that and more. What a critique of this conflation needs to make more visible is torture's underlying social fantasy or phantasmatic structure, the way in which the murky "reality" of torture is organized and mediated by comfortable narratives about democracy and its others. Athey's intervention aims precisely at unsettling the captivating image of torture that still holds so much sway in the public eye. She meticulously traces how arguments on both sides of the torture debate return time and again to a view of torture as ultimately reducible to a dyadic relation, that of the torturer and the tortured. Opponents of torture (wanting to preserve America's pre-Lapsarian moral self, so to speak) condemn the practice as antithetical to the ideals of liberal democracy, while its proponents argue for its necessity for American security. The latter lay out a realpolitik, moving away from a rhetoric of what America *ought* to do as a beacon of Western civilization (a rhetoric deemed to reflect a pre-9/11 mentality) to what it *must* do to preserve its actual way of life, even if it has to do it unilaterally. For Athey, however, this formulation defines the parameters of torture much too narrowly, failing to account for the social networks and structural conditions of torture: torture always has a communal dimension that the face-to-face encounter between the interrogator and the victim invariably distorts. Shifting from the dyadic model of torture to one that views torture as taking place within a community of participants (including not only the interrogator but military guards, security contractors, and other observers) also enables Athey to scrutinize more effectively the alleged purpose of torture, which is to gather information in order to foil future attacks.

Athey contests what torture's proponents proclaim it achieves: the gathering of reliable information. The false tie between interrogation and torture was perhaps most forcefully exposed by the Abu Ghraib photographs, which reveal the dubious link between humiliation (one form of interrogation) and intelligence. The photos provide jarring evidence that torture at the prison was an undesirable technique being deployed not simply for a noble end (American security) but as *an end in itself*, attesting to the imbrication of America's war on terror and the country's racism, misogyny, and religious persecution of the Islamic other.

Athey does not dismiss the need for counterintelligence; instead, she shows that torture and the culture associated with it prove ineffectual if not outright harmful to American interests.[24] But what about the seemingly less controversial claim that the tragedy of 9/11 forced the United States to enter a new era in its relation to torture? To be clear, the newness associated with the United States and torture refers here to both torture as new weapon in the war on terror and the new post-9/11 climate that makes possible a public discussion of torture. Athey rejects both senses of the newness of torture. Its first sense can be easily dismissed by exposing the continuity of the United States' actual use of torture in its history. In the aftermath of the 9/11 disaster, the U.S. government underwent nothing short of an ideological make-over, effacing its pre-9/11 record of abuse and torture and transforming itself into a pure (and innocent) victim for whom torture was something truly foreign, something that it needed to consider for the first time, initiating the turn to the "dark side," as Vice President Dick Cheney put it. The second sense of the newness of torture proves more complicated. Athey takes issue with Slavoj Žižek's warning that positing torture as a legitimate subject of public discourse can have the dangerous effect of normalizing it. For Žižek, torture as such is an elusive notion that always runs the risk of exceeding its original intent, typically, a (morally justified) response to a ticking-time-bomb scenario: "The idea that, once we let the genie out of the bottle, torture can be kept at a 'reasonable' level is the worst liberal illusion."[25] There is even something perverse, argues Žižek, about making torture a topic of intellectual debate. Against the backdrop of an "open" discussion on the war on terror, in which everything—we are repeatedly told—should be on the table (including the definition of torture), Žižek makes his point by drawing a parallel between rape and torture, rape often being an example of torture:

"For example, a clear sign of progress in Western society is that one does not need to argue against rape: it is 'dogmatically' clear to everyone that rape is wrong. If someone were to advocate the legitimacy of rape, he would appear so ridiculous as to disqualify himself from any further consideration. And the same should hold for torture."[26] Disturbed by the public's willingness to discuss torture, Žižek yearns for the days when torture was something that shamed a nation, something it sought to suppress, making him "nostalgic for the good old days of the colonial war in Algeria, when the torture practiced by the French Army was a dirty secret."[27]

Žižek and Athey are perhaps not so far apart. While Athey underscores the danger of thinking of torture as something new for the United States, because doing so necessarily obfuscates its past practices, Žižek highlights the different ideological face that torture is assuming in contemporary society. Like many commentators on torture, Žižek takes an interest in the show *24* but focuses on what can be called the "phantasmatic ethics" that *24* effectively produces and promotes. Žižek, like Athey, is more interested in the ideological system of *24* than in the particular instantiations of dyadic torture scenes. In his provocative article "*24*, Or Himmler in Hollywood," Žižek locates the show's "fundamental lie" in the belief that despite their repeated acts of torture, Jack Bauer and his counterterrorist patriots "remain 'warm human beings,' loving, caught in the usual emotional dilemmas of us, 'normal' people. . . . They are something like the psychological equivalent of decaffeinated coffee: doing all the horrible things the situation necessitates without paying the subjective price for it."[28] For Žižek, Jack Bauer succeeds in doing "the necessary dirty job" without turning into an ethical monster. How is it possible? What allows the agent of torture to remain immune to the horrors of torture? This is where the lessons of Heinrich Himmler, the leader of the Nazi SS, come into play. Confronting the ethical dilemma of convincing moral subjects to act in a way that is contrary to their natural inclination, Himmler instituted a heroic ethics of self-sacrifice. The Nazi murderers came to see themselves as enduring—rather than perpetrating—a horrific condition for the greater good of the nation:

Instead of saying: "What horrible things I did to people!," the murderers would be able to say: "What horrible things I had to watch in the pursuance of my duties, how heavily the task weighed upon my shoulders!" In this way, they were able to turn around the logic of resisting temptation: The temptation to be resisted was the very temptation to succumb to the elementary pity and sympathy in the presence of human suffering, and their "ethical" effort was directed toward the task of resisting this tempta- tion *not* to murder, torture, and humiliate.[29]

On Himmler's account, it is too easy—and childish, reflecting liberal naïveté—to follow one's natural feelings, to opt for the psychological comfort of moral absolutism (as expressed in the commandment "Thou shall not kill"). The exemplary subjects of Himmler struggle and over- come. They find their ethical resolve, and truer being, in the transcen- dence of the immediate (feelings of pity or sympathy) for a higher end (the greatness of their Nation's cause). Their duty to their country thus not only safeguarded their human dignity but gave these Nazis, and by extension today's proponents and practitioners of torture, a "tragic-ethic grandeur."[30] Thus, *24*'s ideological lie resides in the perpetuation of this ideal or possibility. It is ideological because it both proposes an ideal that falsifies the reality of torture (people are indeed affected psychologically by the suffering of others) and suppresses the ethical ramifications of the ideal, which is that the "moral catastrophe" lies not in the failure but in the success of the heroic ideal, that is, in one's psychic capacity to sepa- rate one's public self, the self who must torture and murder, from one's private self, the normal self who loves others and is able to take pleasure in everyday life.[31]

To be sure, any parallel between Nazi Germany and the United States in the war on terror must be drawn with great care, requiring interpretive self-restraint so as to avoid overgeneralization in comparing historical conditions that are fundamentally incommensurable. Upholding such hermeneutic vigilance, however, does not preclude critically engaging with the ethics and politics of the Holocaust and the current war on terror along with its culture of torture. Quite the contrary, to expose the traces of Himmlerian ethics in a contemporary blockbuster TV show like *24* is precisely the kind of analytic work that needs to be done.

Holocaust and trauma studies in particular have provided invaluable insights into the ethics and politics of representation: How does one give an account of the victims of torture when those individuals' very human- ity has been systematically denied? The last three chapters in this volume offer distinct responses to this fundamental challenge. In chapter 6, "Specters of the *Muselmann*: Guantánamo Bay Penalogical Theme Park and the Torture of Omar Khadr," Joseph Pugliese discusses the Muslim prisoner of Guantánamo as a contemporary embodiment of the *homo sacer*, a life dispossessed of dignity and value that can be sacrificed with no consequences, revisiting and building on Giorgio Agamben's analysis of the dehumanizing transformation of Jews into *homines sacri* under the Third Reich.[32] As an alternative to ahistorical or abstract accounts of the other, the legal concept of the *homo sacer* has proved a productive means of understanding the abject condition of victims of torture. In ancient Roman jurisprudence, the term *homo sacer* designated the excluded or exiled other par excellence, someone who was cast out of the community, who could be killed with impunity by anyone, and whose life no longer possessed any worth and thus lacked sacrificial value. Prior evocations of similarities between the camps at Auschwitz and the detention center at Guantánamo Bay have used the concept of *homo sacer* to shed light on the prisoners' ambiguous legal status. Žižek argues, for instance, that the Guantánamo Bay detainees are caught "between two deaths," because, according to the government and its media apologists, "'they are those who were missed by the bombs.'"[33] As such, these prisoners are *homines sacri*, dwelling in zones of exclusion, tortured with impunity and perpetually robbed of their dignity, reduced to "bare life," and made to appear to an international public as less than human—that is, barbaric, irrational, and evil.[34] Pugliese's exploration of the concept of *homo sacer* probes instead its most extreme manifestation in the paradoxical figure of the *Muselmann*. For Agamben, the *Muselmann* is a limit-figure, residing between life and death, neither fully human nor wholly inhuman: he is the "non-human who obstinately appears as human" and "the human that cannot be told apart from the inhuman."[35] The origins of the term are disputed, but at its most basic, literal level, the word *Muselmann*—Auschwitz camp slang for prisoners who had fallen into a vacuous, corpselike state—simply means "Muslim," "the one who submits unconditionally to the will of God." Taking up the Islamophobia and Arabophobia associated with this term, Pugliese explores the logic underpinning the transformation of the Guantánamo Bay prisoner into "Muslim *Muselmann*," a figure of alterity whose convoluted composition marks its historical singularity and transhistorical abject commonality with past victims of state violence.

Into this exploration of the structural similarities and distinctions between Guantánamo Bay and the Nazi concentration camps Pugliese interweaves another, less commonly drawn parallel, that between the prison and another American icon, the Disneyland theme park in Anaheim, California. The disturbing homologies between the two are made visible in Pugliese's analysis of the guerrilla artist Banksy's installation of a Guantánamo prisoner doll at Disneyland. While the installation highlights the narratives of U.S. imperial conquest that underpin these two radically different camps, Banksy's use of a doll as a translation or mirror of the tortured body also functions as an apostrophe, an address to the public. Yet in so doing, Pugliese argues, the installation reveals its own difference from the *homo sacer*, who is excluded by definition from discourse, deprived of the means of articulating this very exclusion or demanding redress.

The need to sustain the difference between the observer-witness and the victim of torture can be articulated as a kind of double bind: the critic, artist, or writer is compelled to give an account of the tortured other, yet, at the same time, he or she must resist the desire to speak for — in place of — that other, an act that would efface the distance between the self and the other through an interpretive mastery of the latter's pain or trauma. Reactions to the 2004 Abu Ghraib torture photographs underscore the stakes of this double bind. The photos shocked the American psyche, calling into question the country's image as morally unique and historically exceptional. Narratives aimed at attenuating the damage quickly followed. The U.S. soldiers appearing in the photographs were dismissed as "a few bad apples" who could not be considered emblematic of any larger culture of torture. George W. Bush made this point emphatically: "These pictures didn't understand the true nature and heart of America."[36] For those who did not want to compromise or apologize for the photographs, the events depicted represent simply a case of "excessive" hazing (whose elements of sexual humiliation resemble those typically found in high schools, on college campuses, or in military rites of passage).[37] On this account, the gap between the self and the other (between the U.S. soldiers and the Iraqi prisoners) is perversely effaced to the extent that it *de*politicizes the actions of the prison guards. "The Iraqi prisoners were in effect *initiated into American culture*," Žižek states, not without irony.[38]

In chapter 7, "This Fragile Body: Susan Crile's 'Abu Ghraib: Abuse of Power,'" Julia A. Ireland analyzes the way in which the Abu Ghraib photographs reproduce this effacement and asks how the recognition of difference between witness and victim, as well as a sympathetic response to pain, can possibly be reestablished. As Ireland puts it, "How can we recuperate a sympathetic response to the immediate suffering of the bodies in the photographs *against* the photographs' own structuring of a complicit seeing?" If the photographs work to negate the affective potential or dimension of these scenes of humiliation and abuse, Susan Crile's drawings of the original photographs reorient the viewer to the Iraqis' humanity, made visible (restored through art) in his or her recognition of the prisoners' shared condition of vulnerability. By foregrounding the body as "the site of a common humanity," Crile radically alters the perception of the viewer, moving him or her to consider the dehumanized other of the photographs as a grievable other/self.[39] In this respect, the tortured body of the victim solicits what Dominick LaCapra has called "desirable empathy," an empathy that "involves not full identification but what might be termed empathic unsettlement in the face of the traumatic limit events, their perpetrators, and their victims. . . . It involves a kind of virtual experience through which one puts oneself in the other's position while recognizing the difference of that position and hence not taking the other's place."[40]

In chapter 8, "Sri Lanka: Landscapes of Massacre," Suvendrini Perera pursues the inquiry into art's relation to politics and ethics through a discussion of Sri Lanka's thirty-year war. She approaches the complex relationships between violence, bodies, and nationalized landscapes by navigating among history, politics, and literature. Adapting Achille Mbembe's notion of necropolitics, which refers to a sovereign state's "power and . . . capacity to dictate who may live and who must die,"[41] Perera examines the Sri Lankan government's exercise of sovereignty through its disturbing management of the visibility and invisibility of wounded, slain, or disappeared bodies during the war. Perera turns next to Michael Ondaatje's novel *Anil's Ghost* and other literary texts as telling examples for thinking about Sri Lanka's traumatic past. Yet what Perera reveals in her symptomatic reading of *Anil's Ghost* is the novel's discursive blindness, its complicity and (unavoidable) implication in the ideology of territorial myths, an ideology that the text purports to be criticizing. For the most part, the ethical desire to unearth, name, and/or give voice to the wounded and slain proves to be a complicated task indeed, fraught with reactionary impulses, such as those of restoration and repair. What emerges is a gap between the need to mourn a collective trauma, reflecting the nationalist desire to move on and heal the sociopolitical body, *and* the need to bear witness to the singularity of each nameless, voiceless tortured body. Failure to account for the second need risks condemning those tortured bodies to a kind of second death.

19

Outline of the Volume

As Robert Jackson, the U.S. Supreme Court Justice who served as chief U.S. prosecutor at the Nuremberg trials, stated in 1945: "If certain acts in violation of treaties are crimes, they are crimes whether the United States does them or whether Germany does them, and we are not prepared to lay down a rule of criminal conduct against others which we would not be willing to have invoked against us."[42] His words make clear the United States' lack of exceptionality when it comes to following international law. Yet much of the current revival of torture by the United States has been made in the name of such exceptionality, the conviction that the United States is an exceptionally moral power facing exceptional circumstances that require exceptional measures. Chapters 1 to 3 in this volume, by Darius Rejali, Mark Danner, and Timothy V. Kaufman-Osborn, intervene in this question of U.S. exceptionality, debating its premises, albeit in very different ways and sometimes in disagreement with one another. Each chapter is engaged with thinking through the structures and practices of democratic accountability and their ability to restrain the exercise of executive power in the name of exceptionality. The next two chapters, by Lauren Wilcox and Stephanie Athey, move this debate in a somewhat different but related direction by complicating our understandings of both state power and torture itself. While Wilcox examines the multiple and contradictory state technologies through which contemporary regimes of torture damage as well as nurture human bodies, Athey demystifies the dominant narratives through which torture is represented and made acceptable in order to reveal its multiple functions. Both chapters are especially attentive to the historical, social, and political economies within which torture works to mark some bodies as "torturable." The final three chapters, by Joseph Pugliese, Julia A. Ireland, and

Suvendrini Perera, continue this discussion by interrogating further the interpretive and narrational media through which we apprehend tortured bodies and push us to consider the ethical limits of that exercise. Pugliese and Ireland continue the discussion of contemporary torture as related to the war on terror, seeing in art the possibility to disrupt the ideological narratives that insidiously manage our exposure as well as curtail any ethical responses to the trauma of an all-too-distant other, while Perera leaves us with the haunting echoes of another war, the long and now ostensibly concluded Sri Lankan civil war, reminding us how a tortured past continues to make our present and future. All three compellingly demonstrate that the attempt to do justice to the victims of torture (past and present), to give an account of their suffering through an aesthetic lens, comes with no assurances and abounds with difficulties: the dangers of abstraction and the effacement of historical specificities, the instrumentalization of the other for an ethico-aesthetic end, the desire for peace and reconciliation at the expense of those dismembered bodies and tortured voices obliterated from history. Yet it is in the face of such interpretive, ethical, political challenges that the reader or critic gains a sense of urgency.

NOTES

1   Friedrich Nietzsche, *On the Genealogy of Morals and Ecce Homo*, trans. Walter Kaufmann (New York: Random House, 1989), 2:13, 80.

2   See Judith Butler, *Precarious Lives: The Powers of Mourning and Violence* (New York: Verso, 2004); and Judith Butler, *Frames of War: When is Life Grievable?* (New York: Verso, 2009).

3   Johan Galtung, "Violence, Peace and Peace Research," *Journal of Peace Research* 6, no. 3 (1969): 167–91.

4   A wide literature draws from Giorgio Agamben's formulation of the concept of *homo sacer*—bodies whose killing would not be considered murder—to understand places like the Guantánamo Bay detention camp as "states of exception" or "zones of indistinction." See Giorgio Agamben, *State of Exception*, trans. Keven Attell (Chicago: University of Chicago Press, 2005); Derek Gregory, "The Black Flag: Guantánamo Bay and the State of Exception," *Geografiska Annaler: Series B, Human Geography* 88, no. 4 (2006): 405–27; and S. Reid-Henry, "Exceptional Sovereignty? Guantánamo Bay and the Re-colonial Present," *Antipode* 39, no. 4 (2007): 627–48.

5   Foucault's reflections on different kinds of power are scattered over many
     of his writings. Here are a select few: Michel Foucault, *The History of Sexuality: Volume 1: An Introduction*, trans. Robert Hurley (New York: Random
     House, 1978); *Discipline and Punish: The Birth of the Prison*, trans. Alan
     Sheridan (New York: Vintage Books, 1979); *"Society Must Be Defended": Lectures at the Collège de France*, trans. David Macey (New York: Picador, 2003);
     Security, Territory, Population: Lectures at the Collège de France, 1977–78, trans.
     Graham Burchell Basingstroke (Hampshire: Palgrave Macmillan, 2007);
     and *The Birth of Biopolitics: Lectures at the Collège de France*, trans. Graham   **21**
     Burchell Basingstroke (Hampshire: Palgrave Macmillan, 2008).

6   As its title suggests, the United Nations Convention Against Torture and
     Other Cruel, Inhuman, or Degrading Treatment or Punishment prohibits
     not only torture but also what might be considered less serious offenses.
     Michael Dorf points out that the United States ratified the convention and
     enacted federal legislation establishing criminal liability for Americans
     who torture abroad. However, under a reservation adopted during the ratification process, the federal statute does not impose criminal liability for
     cruel, inhuman, or degrading acts; instead, these acts are seen as unconstitutional under the Fifth, Eighth, and Fourteenth Amendments. Seizing upon
     this distinction between torture and cruel, inhuman, and degrading acts,
     "the basic strategy became to define all but the most horrific acts as insufficiently severe to constitute torture"; thus, the threshold for torture was set
     at "excruciating and agonizing" pain or pain "equivalent in intensity to the
     pain accompanying serious physical injury, such as organ failure, impairment of bodily function, or even death" (Michael C. Dorf, "Renouncing
     Torture," in *The Torture Debate in America*, ed. Karen J. Greenberg [New York:
     Cambridge University Press, 2006], 249). Eventually, as Dorf points out, a
     2004 Office of Legal Counsel memo repudiated this narrow definition after
     the Abu Ghraib scandal broke. We now know, as many authors in this volume point out, that Secretary of Defense Donald Rumsfeld explicitly authorized or signed off on a series of brutal techniques such as painful stress
     positions, frigid temperatures, sleep deprivation, and waterboarding.

7   The most famous of these were two memos, a January 2002 memo by John
     Yoo that argued that Taliban and Al Qaeda fighters were in the category
     of "unlawful combatants" to whom the Geneva Convention protections
     did not apply and an August 2002 memo by Jay Bybee from the Office
     of Legal Counsel in the Justice Department that provided a rationale for
     using torture to extract information from Qaeda operatives. These were
     approved by White House Counsel Alberto Gonzales. In Gonzales's words:
     "In my judgment, this new paradigm renders obsolete Geneva's strict
     limitations on questioning of enemy prisoners and renders quaint some

of its provisions" (quoted in Danner, *Torture and Truth,* 84). See David Cole, ed., *The Torture Memos* (New York: New Press, 2009), for a collection of the memos that have been released.

8   It is important to note that there was some opposition to these memos from within the Justice Department and especially from Department of State lawyers (fairly strenuous in the case of William H. Taft IV) as well as military lawyers.

9   The Military Commissions Act is a bill that effectively grants the president the power to decide who could be tortured by accepting the category of unlawful combatants not subject to Geneva Convention protections and shields perpetrators from prosecution under the War Crimes Act of 1996.

10   Danner made this case quite pointedly in the op-ed "We Are All Torturers Now" (*New York Times,* January 6, 2005, section A, late edition) and repeats it in chapter 2 in this volume. Timothy V. Kaufman-Osborn discusses and critiques this point in chapter 3.

11   David Luban, "Liberalism, Torture, and the Ticking Bomb," in *The Torture Debate in America,* ed. Greenberg. Luban examines and critiques how the Bush administration made the case for this "liberal ideology of torture."

12   Yet, as Darius Rejali points out in chapter 2, all of the evidence, including testimonies of military interrogators, shows that torture is notoriously ineffective in intelligence gathering and also undermines organizational discipline and soldier morale.

13   Susan Sontag, "Regarding the Torture of Others," *New York Times Magazine,* May 23, 2004. It is this representation of torture through the voyeuristic eyes of the perpetrator, in a way that occludes the victim's suffering, that Julia A. Ireland finds so troubling in these photos and which she believes is remedied in Susan Crile's sympathetic re-presentation of the Abu Ghraib photos (see chapter 2 in this volume).

14   Senior administration officials, including President George W. Bush, Secretary of Defense Donald Rumsfeld, and Lieutenant General Ricardo Sanchez, commander of the U.S.-led military coalition in Iraq from June 2003 to July 2004, repeatedly attributed the abuses at Abu Ghraib to a few lower-level miscreants acting entirely on their own.

15   Timothy V. Kaufman-Osborn makes this point in an article that conducts a feminist analysis of the humiliation tactics used at Abu Ghraib. See Timothy Kaufman-Osborn, "Gender Trouble at Abu Ghraib?" *Politics and Gender* 1, no. 4 (2005): 597–619.

16   It bears repeating here that even though the Geneva Conventions were supposed to apply to detainees in Iraq because they were members of a recognized sovereign state, practices approved for Guantánamo Bay migrated to Abu Ghraib after General Geoffrey Miller, the commander

at Guantánamo, visited Abu Ghraib and made particular recommendations, especially with respect to the use of the military police to soften up targets for interrogation. This is what has been called the "Gitmoization of Abu Ghraib" (Seymour M. Hersh, "The General's Report: How Antonio Taguba, Who Investigated the Abu Ghraib Scandal, Became One of Its Casualties," *New Yorker*, June 25, 2007).

17 Legal scholar Michael Dorf reminds us of the perils of the slippery slope when torture is allowed, even if only for extreme cases: "Categorical prohibitions against torture like the one contained in the U.N. Convention and federal law are based on the sensible assumption that if torture is condoned in the extreme case of the known terrorist who has certainly planted the ticking time-bomb, security officers will come to believe that they hear bombs ticking everywhere, and will use torture against people merely suspected of posing a security threat. Only by prohibiting torture under all circumstances, such laws assume, can we prevent an extremely limited authorization, for torture in extreme circumstances, from becoming a license for routine torture" (Michael C. Dorf, "Renouncing Torture," in *The Torture Debate in America*, ed. Karen J. Greenberg, 250).

18 The killing of Osama bin Laden revived the narrative of utilitarian torture; indeed, media speculation concerning whether or not the "enhanced" interrogations of Khalid Sheik Mohammed yielded any actionable information all but concedes the debate to the proponents of torture.

19 See Butler, *Precarious Lives*, and Butler, *Frames of War*.

20 For an illuminating account of the difficulties involved in naming the attacks that took place on September 11, 2001, see Giovanna Borradori, ed., *Philosophy in a Time of Terror: Dialogues with Jürgen Harbermas and Jacques Derrida* (Chicago: University of Chicago Press, 2003), 86–94.

21 Judith Butler plays with this double sense of "frame": to structure and to plant evidence (*Frames of War*, 5–8).

22 Ibid., 5.

23 Justice Antonin Scalia has also expressed his support for the Bauer approach to the ticking-time-bomb situation. At a legal conference in Ottawa in June 2007, he defended the actions of Jack Bauer, raising doubt that the fictional agent could be successfully prosecuted for his admittedly illegal behavior: "Are you going to convict Jack Bauer? Say that criminal law is against him? 'You have the right to a jury trial'? Is any jury going to convict Jack Bauer? I don't think so. So the question is really whether we believe in these absolutes. And ought we believe in these absolutes" (quoted in Colin Freeze, "What Would Jack Bauer Do?" in *Secrets of "24,"* ed. Dan Burstein and Arne J. de Keijzer [New York: Sterling, 2007], 145).

24 U.S. Army Brigadier General Patrick Finnegan, the dean of the United

States Military Academy at West Point, explicitly made this point in a meeting with the creative team of *24*, which, in his judgment, was having a damaging effect on the West Point cadets. Many of the students became resistant to the prohibition against torture, saying "'If torture is wrong, what about '24'?" Cognizant that the show's producer was not about to alter a winning formula, Finnegan made the following modest request, asking the team to "do a show where torture backfires" (quoted in Jane Mayer, "Whatever It Takes: The Politics of the Man Behind *24*," in *Secrets of "24*," ed. Burstein and de Keijzer, 27).

25   Slavoj Žižek, *Welcome to the Desert of the Real* (New York: Verso, 2002), 104.

26   Slavoj Žižek, "Knight of the Living Dead," *New York Times*, March 24, 2007.

27   Slavoj Žižek, *Iraq: The Borrowed Kettle* (New York: Verso, 2004), 53.

28   Slavoj Žižek, "*24*, Or Himmler in Hollywood," in *Secrets of "24*," ed. Burstein and de Keijzer, 204.

29   Ibid., 204–5.

30   In the final season of *24*, the U.S. president herself orders torture for a female suspected traitor in order to procure information not about an impending bomb but about the location of a video file that could compromise and derail a Middle East peace treaty. Torture is thus depicted not just as guaranteeing U.S. security but as preserving the liberal ideal of world peace.

31   Žižek, "*24*, Or Himmler in Hollywood," 205.

32   See Giorgio Agamben, *Homo Sacer: Sovereign Power and Bare Life*, trans. Daniel Heller-Roazen (Stanford, Calif.: Stanford University Press, 1998).

33   Slavoj Žižek, *The Parallax View* (Cambridge, Mass.: MIT Press, 2006), 371.

34   Giorgio Agamben argues that the legally "unclassifiable and unnamable" detainees of Guantánamo Bay have effectively become the paradigmatic subjects of "bare life" (*State of Exception*, 3–4).

35   Giorgio Agamben, *Remnants of Auschwitz*, trans. Daniel Heller-Roazen (New York: Zone Books, 1999), 81–82.

36   Quoted in Sontag, "Regarding the Torture of Others."

37   See ibid.

38   Žižek, *The Parallax View*, 370.

39   For a slightly different account of the vulnerable body, see Butler, *Frames of War*.

34   Dominick LaCapra, *Writing History, Writing Trauma* (Baltimore: Johns Hopkins University Press, 2001), 102, 78.

41   Achille Mbembe, "Necropolitics," trans. Libby Meintjes, *Public Culture* 15, no. 1 (2003): 11.

42   Quoted in Müge Gürsoy Sökmen, *World Tribunal on Iraq: Making the Case Against War* (Northampton, Mass.: Olive Branch Press, 2008), 6–7.

1

TORTURE AND DEMOCRACY

What Now?

Darius Rejali

On January 21, 2010, Matthew Alexander, a former U.S. Air Force officer, wrote in the *New York Times* that American interrogation policies under President Barack Obama remain "both inhumane and counterproductive."[1] Alexander led the team that, without torture, found Abu Musab al-Zarqawi, the leader of al Qaeda in Iraq. He has been a strong proponent of sound interrogation policies without torture.[2] Alexander affirms what I argued less than two months after Obama signed an executive order ostensibly outlawing torture, namely that the changes Obama introduced were not as great as many thought and that we were entering a time of forgetfulness about torture. And this is now the consensus across the human rights community and well beyond that: the continuities are greater than the differences.[3]

But at the time I made these points, many sidestepped what we know about torture, and for two, seemingly contradictory, reasons. On the one hand, some believed that Congress would investigate the torturers. I recall a panel member at a conference waving the front page of the *New York Times* and mocking any pessimistic views, noting that Senator

Patrick Leahy was investigating torture. Democracy was at work! On the other hand, some believed nothing could be expected of Obama, since the United States was not a Lockean democracy and had not been so for some time. Democracy was dead; long live the national torture state!

What both sides share is the curious belief that "more democracy" cures torture. The only question is, who is characterizing American politics more accurately? But both sides are mistaken. "More democracy!" is neither necessary nor sufficient for preventing torture.

I begin by setting aside some inevitable misunderstandings of how torture functions. Then I turn to some basic points about the development of modern torture and its alleged efficacy.[4] Next, I present what we know about preventing torture, explaining why Obama's failure was predictable. In that context, I look at how Americans are forgetting both political and social facts about their country's torture crisis.

The good news is that preventing torture is well within our grasp if we understand what it is and how to fight it. Americans have done it before. We eliminated organized torture from domestic policing in the 1930s, and there is no reason we cannot do it again.

Yet I don't believe Americans will address torture concretely, and not because I think we live in a national torture state that resists change. Rather, Americans are deeply invested in dangerously mistaken beliefs about torture. We live in a time of self-willed amnesia. The left wants to fight torture in the wrong places in the wrong ways. The right embraces mistaken beliefs about torture in order to shelter itself from judgment. And the center lacks the will for pedestrian political reasons. No national coalition will emerge to stop torture in the United States, and so torture will live to come back another day. And that is a grim prospect.

Torture Is Not a Policy

Let me clarify what I mean by torture. By torture, I mean the systematic infliction of physical torment on detained helpless individuals by state officials for police purposes: that is, for confession, information, or intimidation. No doubt one could slice torture in other ways,[5] but whatever one wants to call these practices, they have a long history in the world's democracies, from ancient Greece and Rome, to the Renaissance republics of Venice and Florence, to the great modern democracies.

We are inclined to think that torture changes as governments change. We also think, as Alexander implies, that torture is a *policy,* and so that when governments issue a new interrogation policy, torture changes—depending on how sincerely we try. The war ends and so torture won't be needed any more. The detention centers at Guantánamo Bay close, torturers retire, and scholars like myself will go out of business.

But that is not the way it works. Torture changes least when governments change. It changes most during periods of relative stability, when governments are secure and can experiment with alternatives. Times of instability are not periods of innovation. When governments are insecure, they will reach for what the guys before them used.

Torture is not a government policy. It is a social practice, and it lives in society. Once it appears, it does not fade easily. It casts a very long shadow. And the fight against torture is a fight in society. Government may authorize torture, but it is society that runs forward with the demand and supplies the required techniques. Techniques do not hide in a vault at the CIA.

Now when governments legitimate this social practice, they set in motion deeply corrosive practices. Torture does not simply destroy the lives of victims and torturers alike. It triggers powerful corrupting forces that destroy the judicial, intelligence, and military institutions that use it. And its presence in social institutions lingers for decades.

Social amnesia can greatly enhance this corrosion. For example, at the end of World War II, Americans made sincere and often effective efforts to prevent torture at home and to encourage human rights abroad—the Universal Declaration of Human Rights was adopted in 1948. But Americans also came to believe that no one on our side ever was a torturer. Being a winner was all about being morally pure. Torture came from the Nazis and the Stalinists; it was the method of the enemy.

But this was not the case. Before World War II, the English, Americans, and French all practiced torture—the French and British in their colonies, and the Americans in the Philippines and in their own cities, large and small—including electrotorture and water torture. Sometimes this was done in collusion with locals and sometimes with quiet, if not explicit, approval from governments. And all this before the CIA ever existed.

So at the end of World War II, we forgot our past. And torture lived on to come back another day. We don't need to make the same mistake twice.

If we are to avoid past mistakes, then we must learn to speak intelligently about cruelty. And this critical evaluation has to begin by setting aside any notion that winners are morally pure or that democracies have no history of torture. Democracies just have a different history. And let me be clear, the democratic record is not as bad as that of authoritarian states. Nazis and Stalinists deserve their terrible reputation. But what requires explanation is not *whether* torture is compatible with democratic life but how it is compatible, what factors allow it to persist in democracies, and why democracies have been such torture innovators.

We can better understand the dangers ahead, and the kinds of mistakes to avoid if I simplify the history of torture. To this end, I'll focus on two aspects, what I'll call the "supply side" and the "demand side" of torture.

The Demand for Torture

Where does the demand for torture come from? We may think that demand for torture arises mainly out of national emergencies when there is a genuine or perceived threat, the so-called ticking-time-bomb cases. But those probably add up to no more than a third of the cases scholars have documented in democratic states.

Torture can also arise locally, as a quiet arrangement between police, local businessmen, and homeowners. The latter two want safe streets and good house values and quietly look the other way. This is clearly what torture was like in Chicago between 1973 and 1991. It involved more than fifty detectives, with most incidents implicating former Chicago police commander Jon Burge. And this is how torture appears today in Johannesburg, São Paulo, Mexico City, and Chicago.

Torture can also arise in permissive judicial systems. When judges favor confessions, the police will get confessions any way they can, including by torture. When judges allow indefinite detention without charges, torture is almost inevitable. This is what triggered Japan's torture crisis in the 1980s, one that involved ordinary criminals, not terror suspects.

The demand also arises from decommissioned soldiers coming back from war. Military police who have completed their service often get jobs in policing and private security, and they want to get ahead, so they use techniques they know. This has happened twice in U.S. and French history.

Everyone now is familiar with the word "waterboarding," a loose term for a group of water tortures. American soldiers brought these techniques back with them from war in the Philippines in 1905, and by the 1920s, waterboarding could be found in police stations large and small across the United States, especially in the American South. The techniques of Commander Burge in Chicago were first documented as inflicted by Americans in Vietnam, where he was stationed. Likewise, the post–September 11 techniques are not a sharp break from tortures documented in detention centers of the U.S. Immigration and Naturalization Service or boot camps for juveniles in the 1990s.

We may think the war will end, and we'll be safe, but that is not the way it works. There is no sharp line between domestic and international policing. What happens out there comes back here.

The Supply of Torture Techniques

We may think a torturer's choice of technique comes from his abnormal psychology, but social scientific studies of torturers show that they are mainly normal people, not sadists.[6] They are usually chosen because they are loyal, patriotic, and obedient and can keep a secret. Organizations that torture don't like sadists because they don't obey the rules; they seek pleasure in what they do.

Torture is a craft, like tailoring or massage. One can go to bad tailors who make one-size-fits-all clothing or find those who custom tailor, and one can get bad massages or find specialized styles of massage. And so, too, with torture. One can get the one-size-fits-all or the individualized approach. Like masseurs and tailors, torturers have styles. They are creatures of habit, and they induct people into their group by saying "This is how we do it here." They combine tortures in predictable ways, and each style has a history.

Twelve years ago, I began the difficult project of mapping the spread of torture technology around the globe over the course of the last two hundred years. I mapped each technique as it changed over the decades, noting who used it, when, how it spread, and its effects. To be sure, this is unpleasant work, to think of how a leg clamp works or learn that the Gestapo used it first in interrogations in the 1940s or that it spread in a broad arc from northern France through Belgium and Holland to Norway and Denmark, but nowhere else in Gestapo Europe. It is nasty work, but the truth is that scholars know more about how hybrid corn spreads in Iowa than about how torture techniques change.

And this work yielded a surprising conclusion. With some exceptions, very few modern techniques originated with the Nazis, the Stalinists, or the Inquisition. The pattern is weird and unexpected. What has driven torture technology turns out to be something that no one considers as having anything to do with torture, namely, international monitoring and democracy.

To make this clear, let me distinguish simply between two types of techniques: those that leave marks and those that do not. Over the last two centuries, the more scarring techniques have been disappearing. No one uses leg clamps today. At the same time, clean techniques are spreading. There are two main clean styles, what I call "French Modern" and "Anglo Saxon Modern." French Modern is the classic combination of electricity and water, a procedure that leaves few marks. It appeared in French colonies in 1931, the Nazis picked it up from the Vichy police, and it is now common around the world. Anglo-Saxon Modern is older, a combination of sleep deprivation, exhaustion exercises, and forced standing. These come from old British and French military punishments, U.S. prison practice, and the global slave trade. Most techniques discussed in newspaper articles on Iraq and Afghanistan are part of this tradition.

Now these are painful techniques. Sleep deprivation doesn't deprive people of their naps. It reduces their ability to tolerate musculoskeletal pain. It causes deep aches first in the legs and then in the upper body. Animal tests suggest that when beings are deprived of sleep, they are also more sensitive to pain caused by heat, electricity, and punches. That is why torturers often prefer sleep deprivation as a supplement to other painful techniques. Clean torture isn't then a psychological tool just because it leaves no marks.

Mapping how clean techniques appear leads to a surprising conclusion: whenever we watch, torturers become sneaky. Whenever there's a free press, church groups, and politicians to watch the police, the interrogators literally pull their punches. Electrotorture was relatively unknown for most of the twentieth century except in the United States and in Vietnam, practiced by the French. It didn't really start spreading among police forces until the 1960s. And then the contagion effect is huge, with the numbers doubling every decade. It started in Latin America, the Middle East, and Asia, moved into Africa in the 1980s, and then reached Southern and Eastern Europe in the 1990s.

Clean techniques are valuable because allegations of torture are simply less credible when there is nothing to show for it. In the absence of visible wounds or photographs of actual torture, who are you going to believe? Clean torture breaks down the victim's ability to communicate with the wider community. Stealthy tortures are calculated to subvert this relationship, and that's why they become more common as human rights monitoring spreads.

And, frankly, people judge more by what they see than by what they hear. Would Americans have been so outraged by Abu Ghraib without the pictures? The army charged the first defendants in January 2004, Reuters had a story on it in February 2004, and the first trials began in March 2004, but it wasn't till the end of April 2004 that there was a crisis, that is, when CBS broke the story with photographs.

Does It Work?

In the foreseeable future, most American wars will be asymmetrical wars against insurgencies. This will create a demand for intelligence, and for some this will mean "Let's torture!" It is likely they will use clean techniques or outsource interrogations to private groups, thus reducing visibility and culpability. Others will follow the United States' lead. This will constitute a very serious challenge to human rights organizations. It also raises the question: How does one get good intelligence in war? On this point, I think we can all agree that we want good counterterrorism policy. The question is whether "good torture," if you want to call it that, is good counterterrorism policy.

The bottom line is that good torture is not good counterterrorism policy. To quote a Japanese Fascist military policeman, torture is the "clumsiest" method of interrogation and makes a "fool" of anyone who is prepared to use it. This is from an interrogation manual Allied troops found in Burma in 1943.[7]

As to the question of whether or not physically coercive techniques work, it doesn't matter what one calls these techniques: torture, not-torture, tough stuff, harsh methods, or enhanced interrogation. For this question, the only thing that matters is, do they work to get true information and capture one's enemies?

Here's where everyone goes into storytelling, ticking time bombs, and what not. And I have a story, too. A World War II veteran came to me and said, "In France, we caught this German soldier, and we put a knife to his throat and said, 'Where are the other soldiers?'" And I asked, "Did you get good info?" "Yeah," he said, "sorta." I said, "I am very happy for you. I really am. Because if you had bad info, you would be dead."

The problem is that everyone who knows torture doesn't work is dead. Those for whom it worked are walking around saying, "It worked for me!" This is what we call, in social science, a "biased sample." So testimonies are no good, only statistical cases, and there are some good cases of armies using torture to get information.

And here's the bottom line: In all these cases, soldiers tried to interrogate in the most professional and scientific way they could. And the best results they got were when they approached eight thousand to twenty thousand or more individuals and tortured most of them. And in these best-case scenarios, it turned out they tortured twenty to seventy-eight innocents for each bad guy they got.

So for every accurate piece of information, one has to torture innocents in the thousands, even if one is professional about it. The ticking-time-bomb case, with just one terrorist, is an old bait-and-switch technique. "Good torture" is always wholesale business, not a retail business. Good "not-torture," whatever the United States' apologists want to call their practices, is also wholesale, not retail.

So you tell me: Does torture work? Let me give you the opinion of the professional Gestapo. In 1942, the Czech resistance assassinated Reinhard Heydrich, Reichsprotector of Czechoslovakia. Hitler wanted results, and he didn't care how. The Nazis captured the assassins, but to get the three of them, they arrested, tortured, and killed 7,545 people, including annihilating two villages. They also captured about one hundred resistance members they weren't looking for. These are pretty typical results, comparable to all other known cases, like the Battle of Algiers and Vietnam.

In the middle of all this, Heinz von Pannwitz arrived. He was a career policeman and head of the Gestapo's antisabotage unit in Prague. Don't be stupid, he said. Depend on public cooperation, built up rapport, put up a reward. They received more than a thousand tips. And what broke the case was when Karel Curda, a member of the Czech resistance, betrayed the entire operation. Curda wasn't tortured, lived well, and collected a huge reward, and he was executed for treason after the war.

The professional Gestapo repeatedly decimated the resistance through public cooperation and informers: in France, Denmark, Poland, Norway, Russia, Austria, Czechoslovakia, and even in the camps. The Gestapo turned to torture when it lost seasoned pros like Pannwitz during the war. After that, it had young men with whips, and why learn good policing when you've got a whip?

Huge government-funded studies, including those by the U.S. government, proved Pannwitz right. Without public cooperation, the chances of solving a crime falls to 10 percent. If the professional Gestapo concluded that public cooperation was the best antiterrorist method, why would anyone argue differently?

Public cooperation works even when time is short. In London, on July 21, 2005, seven men boarded buses with ticking bombs, and the British police captured all of them and the ticking bombs in a week. The big break came within twenty-four hours, when the parents of Mukhtar Said Ibrahim turned in their son after they recognized him in a security video. Would these loyal British Muslims have turned him in if the British tortured? The answer is no. Good torture isn't just the source of bad intelligence; it destroys the only thing that really works, public cooperation. Good rapport weakens even the strongest bond we know, the connection between parents and child, even when time is short.

So we know what works—public cooperation and professional interviews. Matthew Alexander used these techniques in Iraq and captured Zarqawi. And using these techniques, the British managed to catch all 290 Nazi spies out of approximately 42,000 individuals crossing over from Europe without torturing *any* of them. Again, if that's true for torture, why is that also not true of not-torture? And if what makes torture moral is that it saves innocent lives, then the truth has to be that torture is immoral because it takes far more innocent lives than it has ever saved.

Actually some not-torture we use is even worse than torture. For instance, consider sleep deprivation. American interrogators used it all the time. Professionals with the Spanish Inquisition wouldn't go near it. They knew sleep deprivation has hypnotic effects. It is ideal for generating visions of pacts with the devil, and people will remember shooting

Kennedy from behind the grassy knoll if asked about it repeatedly. That's why Scottish witch-hunters liked it. But one can imagine Catholic inquisitors rolling their eyes when they heard about those amateur Protestant witch-hunters across the English Channel. They knew this not-torture was unreliable.

Good torture creates bad intelligence and sweeps up thousands of innocents. It also destroys our soldiers and undermines organizational discipline, the famous "slippery slopes," creating increasingly ineffective security services, much like the Gestapo in its final days. Limited time to gain information aggravates all these effects. Things get worse, not better. In short, torture works best when it is needed least, during peacetime nonemergency situations, and the few cases apologists often showcase are just these.

The Gestapo knew this. The Japanese Kempeitai knew this. Even the Spanish Inquisitors sometimes knew this. If these ruthless forces are to be our models, why should we be stupider than all of them? The answer is that we should not and we don't have to be. Good counterterrorism policy depends on winning public support and building up human intelligence.

Preventing Torture

There are concrete steps one can take to fight torture. Whenever governments apply them, they end organized torture in their societies. So how does one prevent torture?

Popular accounts present torturers as sadists, and in that case, one should prevent "bad apples" from getting into any system. But, empirically, torturers are rarely sadists; rather, normal people become torturers when simple situational factors are present. And that means changing situations in order to inhibit violent behavior. The conditions required are well known: clear lines of authority, clear rules, clear punishment for rule violators, regular medical monitoring at exit and entry points, and remand before judicial authority within forty-eight hours. Additionally, rotating guards regularly disrupts torture subcultures, that is, guards who through long association collude in brutality.

Abu Ghraib exemplifies how things go wrong when these rules aren't present. When authority is divided or distant, when rules are ambiguous, when rule violators are not punished, and when monitoring is absent—in short, when organizations are internally chaotic—violence, including torture, ensues. This applies to both policing and military contexts, including troop conduct in civil wars.[8]

Preventing torture, then, is not hard and requires no special democratic functions. Consolidated authoritarian states can do this just as well and have done so. Democracies aren't the only states with courts and laws.

Democracy to Prevent Torture

Fighting against torture might bring about more democracy, but the reverse is not necessarily true. More democracy is neither a necessary nor a sufficient condition for preventing torture.

Simple peace and economic growth are strongly associated with greater government respect for human rights.[9] For example, Amnesty International didn't record any torture in Soviet Hungary and Czechoslovakia in the last two decades of Communist government.[10] These authoritarian states lived in relative peace, were prosperous compared to other Communist states, and were engaged in détente with the West. Authoritarian rulers like good policing, too, and they, too, can learn that torture is not suited for sound government, as they understand it. But when states are at war or in economic trouble, governments are not likely to respect human rights, whether they are in authoritarian North Korea or democratic Sri Lanka. Indeed, human rights are most threatened when states transition from one socioeconomic condition to another, producing the "more murder in the middle" condition.[11]

Of course, democratization can lead to greater respect for human rights. And countries with sound democratic procedures are likely to have publics who are more opposed to torture. But this is also true of countries that aren't democracies but are prosperous, have higher per capita income, and have low incidences of state violence. Again, endorsement of torture depends on how wealthy people are and whether or not they live in relative peace, not merely whether or not they are enlightened democrats.

In conditions of relative peace and economic prosperity, even publics in nondemocratic states tend to oppose torture, and as they do, government officials stop using it.[12] As public opinion changes, even unelected public officials respond and adapt to this demand—a situation social scientists dub "dynamic representation."[13] When it comes to torture, dynamic representation seems to obtain under authoritarian as well as democratic states, although the mechanisms behind it are at the moment unclear.

People sometimes think that a state's ideology explains why it does or does not torture. If it possesses a Communist or national security ideology, it favors torture, and if it has a genuinely democratic ethos, it prevents torture. This hypothesis is false. Ideology explains neither the frequency nor the density of torture.[14]

So more democracy is not necessarily going to prevent torture. It is also not *sufficient* to prevent torture. This may be unsurprising to those who subscribe to the "fearful public" explanation of torture in democracies. On this account, a fearful or vengeful public drives democracies to approve government torture, and when the majority favors torture, elected officials implement torture. The more frequent the terrorist attacks and ticking bombs, the more pro-torture the public, and the more governments torture. Torture won't stop. It's no surprise, then, that democratic systems aren't enough to prevent torture; when everyone is scared, people and politicians approve outrageous things.

But this can't be the explanation for why modern democratic procedures aren't sufficient to prevent torture. There is little empirical evidence to support "fearful public" accounts, and the fact that journalists and pundits keep repeating it reveals more about them than about the world they live in (discussed in the section "Pundits and Social Forgetfulness").

For the moment, these two points may be adequate. First, there is no link between terrorism and growing public approval of torture, as "fearful public" accounts postulate. A survey of thirty-one countries found pro-torture majorities are rare everywhere, even among countries experiencing frequent terrorist attacks.[15] Nor is there any obvious link between terrorist attacks and a government's decision to torture. States experiencing terrorist attacks are slightly more likely to engage in extrajudicial killings and disappearances than are states that do not experience terrorism, but they are no more likely to engage in torture than are states that have no experience with terrorism.[16] This should not be surprising. As noted earlier, officials turn to torture for many reasons, not just national security crises. These other circumstances include permissive judicial systems as well as local arrangements between police and property owners, both of which can be powerful motivations for torture in times of peace.

So to understand why more democracy is not sufficient to prevent torture, one has to set aside the "fearful public" theory and start with the known facts. One is that modern states torture *despite* widespread public disapproval of torture. This is true even of democracies. The Bush administration tortured despite unchanging anti-torture majorities among the American public between 2001 and 2008.[17] Dynamic representation seems to break down in conditions of war and economic downturn. Public officials, whether elected or unelected, become unresponsive to public demand *not* to torture. This seems to be true whatever the motivation for torture happens to be.

In times of peace and prosperity, democratic institutions are slightly better than other kinds of institutions at preventing torture, but those who have looked at this phenomenon closely know it is a very mixed picture.[18] On the one hand, states that have popular suffrage and a free press have an edge in preventing torture. On the other hand, a state is *less* likely to terminate its use of torture when its political system includes a lot of veto points. The more democratic veto points there are — a basic feature of most checks-and-balances systems — the more likely it is that efforts to stop torture bog down and states continue using torture.

There is similar evidence from other quarters. For example, we know that human rights interventions succeed when three conditions are present: national leaders perceive no security threat, human rights organizations have broad popular support, and economic elites aren't threatened by the actions of these organizations.[19] This is true whether states are democratic or authoritarian. When these conditions aren't present, organizations can't prevent abuses.

Let us suppose for the moment, however, that all the conditions for successful human rights action on torture are present. Let us suppose, in other words, that human rights organizations are wildly popular and political and economic leaders are receptive to their demands. What exactly should these organizations do to prevent future torture? In these situations, many people want truth commissions and investigations. People focus on past harm, and politicians can't discount the demand to have the "whole story" told. And it is hard to underestimate the value of procedures that force governments to disclose information about torture, such as requests under the Freedom of Information Act, as they reinforce fundamental civic rights.

However, if one aims to prevent future torture and not merely to learn about the past, then the bottom line has to be this: Nothing predicts future torture as much as past impunity. That means we need well-timed trials, not truth commissions or investigations. Standard torture prevention practice implies this: clear authority, clear rules, and swift punishment for rule violators. Other data also imply that trials prevent abuses. For example, the most likely predictor of a coup anywhere is a successful coup in the past six years.[20] Officers reason, "If they could get away with it, why not us?" A successful coup seriously erodes a country's political culture, but where coups fail and retribution follows, officers are more hesitant.

Obama and Political Forgetfulness

Government in principle requires sound security policy, and that means preventing torture and trying torturers. But trials must be timely to be effective, and that is not likely in the United States at this time. Although it is a consolidated democracy with institutionalized liberal norms, the United States is experiencing one of the worst economic downturns in a generation and is engaged in war abroad. Its national leaders perceive persistent security threats, and its economic elites feel deeply threatened. Until recently, the only bright spot in the area of torture prevention was that public opinion opposed torture, but for reasons I will discuss, policy makers did not understand this and assumed the public supported torture. And so even public opinion did not translate into policy initiatives.

Based on this information alone, we would conclude, then, that conditions for trying torturers and preventing torture are not auspicious. And that is the case when one looks at the Obama administration's policies, which are mainly the following: close Guantánamo, give responsibility for interrogation to the FBI, and put the really bad CIA guys on trial. The administration will not try or investigate those who authorized torture, and it has urged judges to dismiss civil suits against some, such as John Yoo.

With Guantánamo, the issue has always been what to do with the prisoners, particularly the Yemenis. No one knows where to put them. As for trials, the administration has said that it will try those who do not fit within the directives of the Bush administration memos. This leaves alive the precedent of legal torture, along with the myth that torture can somehow be legally regulated. As for interrogation, the Obama administration is now talking about making interrogation a science, authorizing research projects to identify liars using technology such as functional Magnetic Resonance Imaging. This does not simply undervalue a professional interrogation corps, suggesting, as it does, that machines can do a better job; it is also dangerous. Interrogation is not a science and cannot be one. And once the white lab coats are brought back into interrogation rooms, the path leads back toward the CIA's chamber of horrors of the 1950s.

Critics have already latched onto some problems with these policies, but I want to briefly mention what we are likely to forget, for this is the age of forgetfulness.

For example, the Obama administration has not urged Congress to change the definition of torture in the Military Commissions Act of 2006 so that it agrees with international law. The Military Commissions Act of 2009, introduced after Obama took office, still defines torture in terms of major organ failure or major bodily injury, which excludes most acts captured by international law. Obama states that military interrogation will now conform to Army Field Manual 35-42, but few remember that the Bush administration hastily changed it. The new manual allows extreme solitary confinement. It does not explicitly prohibit stress positions, such as forced standing, or close confinement, or environmental manipulation, including extreme sounds (although it disallows hypothermia and "heat injury," i.e., burning). And it allows interrogators to exhaust prisoners by depriving them of sleep. While the manual explicitly urges humane treatment of prisoners, it undermines this injunction in the specifics.[21] And Obama's task force recommended no changes to the manual in August 2009.

Other laws and policies failed, too, and again one sees no efforts to remedy these. The previous administration hounded whistle-blowers who revealed torture, including at Abu Ghraib, and many still live in fear.[22] Without good, enforceable whistle-blower laws, one can't even catch corruption, much less torture, in the military. No one is discussing revamping U.S. Army human rights training or investigating how badly army lawyers botched many torture allegations.[23] And soldiers are coming home and experiencing atrocity-related trauma.[24] They are a danger to themselves, their families and communities, and the universities where they go to get further education, yet funding for treatment of atrocity-related trauma is inadequate.

Torture had a deprofessionalization effect on U.S. intelligence agencies. Many anti-torture professionals retired, while many other people joined to be tomorrow's Jack Bauers, using torture's shortcuts. Some architects of the torture policy took positions in private security firms after the elections. This Washington-based torture subculture will be a potent source of demand when the next terrorist attack happens on American soil.

Politicians want to be reelected. Bureaucrats don't want to change. Peer pressure and party competition create resistance to policies that would break torture subcultures apart. No one wants to be a fool in a time of war. And so forgetting becomes convenient. One doesn't need to believe in a conspiratorial national torture state to explain these outcomes.

Pundits and Social Forgetfulness

We are not just forgetting political facts. We are also propounding torture stories about the Bush years, stories that ignore inconvenient social facts. For one example, among many, it is now routine to say that Americans were always supportive of torture during the Bush years, but a public majority favoring torture is a very recent, post-Obama phenomenon.

My colleague, Paul Gronke, and I just completed the first comprehensive record of public opinion surveys that ask respondents about using torture on suspected terrorists in order to gain information or save lives.[25] This record consists of thirty-two polls taken over the last nine years. As the data make clear, not once during this nine-year period was there a majority that favored torturing terrorists. Approximately 55 percent of the public expressed opposition to torture during this period, even during the three years preceding the Abu Ghraib scandal. In all but two surveys, opposition to torture exceeded support for torture. The mean over the nine-year period is 55 percent opposed to and 40.8 percent in favor of the use of torture. Opposition to torture remained stable and consistent during the entire Bush presidency. Even soldiers serving in Iraq opposed using torture.

A pro-torture majority did not emerge until June 2009, six months after Obama's inauguration, and after former vice president Cheney took to the public stage to vigorously defend coercive techniques. Torture likely has become a partisan symbol, distinguishing Republicans from Democrats, signifying hawkishness on national security, the same way that supporting the death penalty signals that one is tough on crime.

Defenders of the torture policy badly misjudged public opinion on torture during the Bush years. But why? A recent survey we commissioned reveals a psychological process of misperception called "false consensus," whereby an individual mistakenly believes that his or her viewpoint represents the public majority.[26] False consensus has a long history in social psychological research, but our survey is unique in that it examines for the first time how false consensus may have shaped the public debate on torture.[27]

Our survey shows that nearly two-thirds of Americans overestimated the level of national support for torture, but more important, these misperceptions are not evenly distributed across the population. The stronger an individual's support for torture, the larger the gap in his or her perception. Those who believe that torture is often justified—a mere 15 percent of the public—think that more than 33 percent of the public agrees with them. Another 30 percent say that torture can "sometimes" be justified but that 62 percent of Americans do as well and think that another 8 percent "often" approve of torture. The people who had the most accurate perception of public attitudes turned out to be the people nobody believed or supported throughout the Bush administration—the 29 percent who were most opposed to torture

Those who supported torture got it wrong for the most human of reasons—they believed that their view represented the public majority and overestimated how many people agreed with them. And the journalists believed them. For example, Mark Danner wrote in the *New York Review of Books* in April 2009, "Polls tend to show that a majority of Americans are willing to support torture only when they are assured that it will 'thwart a terrorist attack.'"[28] Polls did not show this trend at all, and the swing toward torture happened two months *after* Danner made this incorrect assertion, yet journalists commonly repeated this kind of story in articles and blogs from the left and the right as well as in European papers for years.[29] Danner was not alone. Since so many journalists deeply opposed torture, what explains this?

Sometimes people misjudge the public norm but also disagree with it. Still, they go along, because no one wants to be called a fool. This is known as pluralistic ignorance.[30] And sometimes people habitually pass off one activity or situation as another because they are invested in particular ways of thinking about themselves and others. To proceed otherwise would be unthinkable or, at least, deeply disconcerting. For life to go on as usual, we must proceed in *this way*. These convenient truths are socially maintained. We recruit others into sharing convenient truths and thus misrepresenting the world along with us. Forging convenient truths (*mesconnaissance*) differs, then, from false consensus and pluralistic ignorance in which individuals judge what *others* think incorrectly and act accordingly.[31]

So it may be that journalists misrepresented public opinion because they didn't want to be judged fools by others. Castigating a pro-torture American public seemed plausible, given how deeply the pro-torture camp believed it. And the story had to be filed quickly, so who had time for research? Or journalists may be invested in the story. Repeating the story reaffirms their self-images as hardy muckrakers, enlightened citizens, or morally pure activists. In the early Bush years, few journalists reported on torture, but everyone needed to be at the front of the parade after Abu Ghraib. Castigating the American public distracts attention from their own failings. It's unlikely we'll know for sure which of these explanations is correct, or even if both are true. What is certain is that journalists got it wrong, and this does require an explanation.

The Coming Torture Crisis

Torture will persist in the United States. It will persist as soldiers bring it back and use it when they become private security personnel and police officers in neighborhoods near you. It will thrive on ambition, custom, rumor, selective memory, poverty, and media publicity. It will live off the violence in stockyards, schools, barracks, and homes. These are less sensational sources of evil but far greater dangers to life and limb today than the national torture state or an ignorant fearful public.

And when torture does return, it will invigorate more torture talk. Some critics will want to educate the ignorant pro-torture masses with truth commissions. Others will paint the origin of modern torture in acts of hidden conspiracy beyond our reach. Both would be as anti-democratic and disempowering as they are misleading. Others will argue that no one did anything wrong and put the issue behind them. Everyone will seize on torture and chatter about it in a manner that allows lives to go on as before. This is as true of radicals in Wisconsin as conservatives in Texas. Most nations have a torture culture; this happens to be the one *we want.*

All this talk will serve to draw our attention away from how the very ordinary products and habits of our lives contribute to the continuing practice of torture in modern democracies, and how it is within our power, indeed, has always been within our power, to bring more justice to the lives of others, if we were willing to do so. Unfortunately, more often than not, we prefer believing our convenient stories than confronting the heavy burden of human responsibility.

NOTES

1   Matthew Alexander, "Torture's Loopholes," *New York Times,* January 21, 2010, section A.

2   Matthew Alexander, *How to Break a Terrorist* (New York: Free Press, 2008).

3   Michael Desch, "The More Things Change, the More They Stay the Same: The Liberal Tradition and Obama's Counterterrorism Policy," *PS Symposium: "Torture and the War on Terror,"* ed. Jim Piazza and Jim Walsh (July 2010): 425–29.

4   The following sections summarize research in Darius Rejali, *Torture and Democracy* (Princeton, N.J.: Princeton University Press, 2007).

5   Ibid., 36–39.

6   See Martha Huggins, Mika Haritos-Fatouros, and Philip Zimbardo, *Violence Workers* (Berkeley: University of California Press, 2002); and Mika Haritos Fatouros, *The Psychological Origins of Institutionalized Torture* (London: Routledge, 2003).

7   The full manual is available in Raymond Toliver, *The Interrogator* (Fallbrook, Calif.: Aero Publishers, 1978), 360–65.

8   Macartan Humphreys and Jeremy M. Weinstein, "Handling and Manhandling Civilians in Civil War," *American Political Science Review* 100, no. 3 (2006): 429–47.

9   Emilie Hafner-Burton and James Ron, "Seeing Double: Human Rights Impact through Qualitative and Quantitative Eyes," *World Politics* 61, no. 2 (April 2009): 370–73.

10   See Rejali, *Torture and Democracy,* 322–24.

11   Helen Fein, "More Murder in the Middle: Life-Integrity Violations

and Democracy in the World, 1987," *Human Rights Quarterly* 17, no. 1 (1995): 170–91; and Conway Henderson, "Conditions Affecting the Use of Political Repression," *Journal of Conflict Resolution* 35, no. 1 (1991): 120–42.

12   Peter Miller, "Torture and Social Modernization," paper presented at the 2010 Western Political Science Association 2010 annual meeting. Paper is forthcoming under the title "Torture Approval in Comparative Perspective," *Human Rights Review*, December 2011.

13   James A. Stimson, Michael B. MacKuen, and Robert S. Erikson, "Dynamic Representation," *American Political Science Review* 39, no. 3 (September 1995): 543–65. There is little evidence that it works in the opposite way, that is, that public opinion changes as state policy changes (ibid., 559).

14   Rejali, *Torture and Democracy*, 414–22.

15   Miller, "Torture and Social Modernization."

16   James A. Piazza and James Igoe Walsh, "Physical Integrity Rights and Terrorism," *PS Symposium: "Torture and the War on Terror,"* 411; and Emilie Hafner-Burton and Jacob N. Shapiro, "Tortured Relations," *PS Symposium: "Torture and the War on Terror,"* ed. Piazza and Walsh, 415.

17   Paul Gronke and Darius Rejali, "U.S. Public Opinion on Torture, 2001–2009," *PS Symposium: "Torture and the War on Terror,"* ed. Piazza and Walsh, 437–44.

18   Courtenay Ryals Conrad and Will H. Moore, "What Stops the Torture?" *American Journal of Political Science* 54, no. 2 (April 2010): 459–76; and Will H. Moore, "Incarceration, Interrogation and Counterterror: Do (Liberal) Democratic Institutions Constrain Leviathan?" *PS Symposium: "Torture and the War on Terror,"* ed. Piazza and Walsh, 421–24.

19   Hafner-Burton and Ron, "Seeing Double," 370–73.

20   John B. Londregan and Keith T. Poole, "Poverty, the Coup Trap, and the Seizure of Executive Power," *World Politics* 42, no. 2 (January 1990): 151–83.

21   Alexander, "Torture's Loopholes."

22   For recent examples of this problem, see Jesselyn Radack, "When Whistle-Blowers Suffer," *Los Angeles Times*, April 27, 2010, http://www.latimes.com/news/opinion/la-oe-radack-20100427,0,754088.story; and Mark Benjamin, "Navy Supervisor Doctored Whistleblower's Records," Salon, February 1, 2010, http://www.salon.com/news/feature/2010/01/31/camp_lejeune.

23   Joshua E. S. Phillips, *None of Us Were Like This Before: American Soldiers and Torture* (New York: Verso, 2010), 110–29.

24   See, for example, Phillips, *None of Us Were Like This Before*; and Mark Benjamin's series in Salon on soldier suicides (e.g., "Soldier Suicides

Rocket," Salon, March 19, 2009, http://www.salon.com/news/feature/2009/03/19/army_suicides/index.html).

25 Gronke and Rejali, "U.S. Public Opinion on Torture, 2001–2009," 439.

26 Ibid., 437–38.

27 Lee Ross, D. Greene, and P. House, "The False Consensus Phenomenon: An Attributional Bias in Self-Perception and Social Perception Processes," *Journal of Experimental Social Psychology* 13, no. 3 (1977): 279–301.

28 Mark Danner, "US Torture: Voices from the Black Sites," *New York Review of Books* 56, no. 6 (April 9, 2009): 76.

29 See, for example, Justine Sharrock, "Am I a Torturer?" *Mother Jones*, March/April 2008, 42; Brothers Judd, Review of *Torture and Democracy*, BrothersJudd, March 4, 2008, http://brothersjudd.com/index.cfm/fuseaction/reviews.detail/book_id/1642/Torture%20and%20.htm; Alex Koppelman, "Obama Reframes the Torture Debate," Salon, April 29, 2009, http://www.salon.com/politics/war_room/2009/04/29/obama_torture/index.html; and "L'essor inquiétant du «supplice propre» en démocratie" Libération, December 16, 2008, http://www.liberation.fr/sciences/0101305811-l-essor-inquietant-du-supplice-propre-en-democratie.

30 David Krech and Richard S. Crutchfield, *Theory and Problems of Social Psychology* (New York: McGraw-Hill, 1948), 388–89.

31 Pierre Bourdieu, *Outline of a Theory of Practice*, trans. Richard Nice (Cambridge: Cambridge University Press, 1989), 21–22, 195–96; and Pierre Bourdieu and Loïs Wacquant, *An Invitation to Reflexive Sociology* (Chicago: University of Chicago Press, 1992), 167–68.

2

NOW THAT WE'VE TORTURED

Image, Guilt, Consequence

Mark Danner

Let me begin with what today has been a key word: amnesia. It is
a striking word, and it makes a provocative point. When it comes
to torture as practiced by the United States during the war on
terror, there is certainly amnesia and an ongoing quest on the part of
some to encourage and cultivate it.

But alongside that quest to forget and bury the recent past, there has
also come in recent days a flurry of news about torture, much of it center-
ing around certain vital questions of public policy that, as we speak, are
being fired in the hot furnace of debate in Washington. When I boarded
the plane to fly out here last night,* I opened up the *New York Times*— the
New York Times I hold in my hand—and here on its front page found in
this article, headlined "U.S. Will Give Qaeda Suspect a Civilian Trial," the
news about Mr. Ali Saleh Kahlah al-Marri, who has long been held in a
U.S. Navy brig in Charleston, South Carolina. Mr. Al-Marri was arrested

---

* Editors' note: Mark Danner delivered his talk at Whitman College on February 28, 2009.

in Peoria, Illinois, that famously typical American city, on December 12, 2001, and, without ever passing before a judge or seeing a lawyer, was held incommunicado and in solitary confinement for nearly six years under direct order of the president of the United States.[1]

If you turn to the inside pages of this same edition of the newspaper of record, you find not only a photograph of Mr. Al-Marri, with his long beard and kaffiyeh, but another article, headlined "Senate Panel to Pursue Investigation of CIA," in which we learn that the Senate Select Committee on Intelligence is undertaking an investigation that will review the CIA's detention and interrogation programs. This article mentions the demand by Senator Patrick Leahy, Democrat of Vermont and chairman of the Judiciary Committee, that a truth and reconciliation commission, or simply a truth commission, be appointed to investigate the alleged crimes of the George W. Bush administration. Senator Leahy's proposal is matched by that of his counterpart in the House, Representative John Conyers, Democrat of Michigan, and the demands of various other prominent human rights groups to establish a blue-ribbon, independent commission, perhaps modeled on the 9/11 Commission, to investigate these issues.

I think it important to emphasize here, since we are discussing "amnesia" about torture, that these demands have been prominently reported in the press, as indeed has much of the recent discussion of torture. This was not always the case. Indeed, I have heard more use of the term "waterboarding" in the broadcast press during the past two months than I have during the past five years. The word is all over the television news and discussion programs—despite the fact that, so far as we know, there has been no waterboarding under United States authority since 2003, almost six years ago. So it seems to me that one could argue, and support the argument with a good deal of evidence, that there is more discussion about torture right now, on television, in the newspapers, among those serving on prominent committees of Congress, than there has been during the half dozen years since that practice was first disclosed in the national press.

Decisions about this country's policies on interrogation and related matters are now being debated at the highest levels, both publicly and in the three interagency task forces that President Barack Obama established by executive order on his second full day in office in one of his first official acts. One of those orders directed that Guantánamo be closed within a year, and the associated review of the status of its individual detainees has already begun. Another directed that the United States intelligence services, and indeed all agencies of the U.S. government, limit themselves in any interrogation to those techniques set out in the army's field manual on interrogation, which, as rewritten and published in 2006, explicitly forbids many of the techniques, including waterboarding, walling, use of prolonged nudity, and so on, that have been so controversial during the last seven years. While the matter is not quite as clear-cut as that summary may suggest—the field manual contains important loopholes that must be closed, including a troubling appendix listing various exceptions—this executive order is nonetheless very significant indeed.

As we gather here, then, on the last day of February 2009, we find ourselves at an interesting moment at which torture—which has been looming before Americans since the spring of 2004, when torture rose, as it were, out of the gray newsprint and assumed for a time what might be called a "televisual shape" in the form of Hooded Man and Leashed Man and the naked human pyramids and the other horrible, indelible images from Abu Ghraib and then just as quickly sank back into the newsprint—torture has begun to assume prominence as a true issue of public policy. We seem actually to be having a real public discussion about it. I think that that singular fact deserves mention here. And however much I respect my colleagues on this panel here today, and feel the honor of having been included in such a distinguished group, I do think that there is a certain danger in saying about torture, in effect: Well, you know, we've done it, we've done it a lot, we're still doing it, we're going to keep doing it, and, having done it, we're going to forget about it.

This may indeed prove to be quite true—perhaps, alas, it is likely—but it does seem worth saying that if you want to judge by the evidence that is actually before us at this moment, that evidence points largely in the contrary direction. One must acknowledge, of course, what my colleagues on this stage know very well: that we have had a great number of investigations since 2004, more than a dozen or so, depending on how you count. You can find the texts of many of the major early ones in my book *Torture and Truth*,[2] which was published way back in October 2004. And indeed I would encourage anyone who is interested in torture to read those documents, because regardless of how similar this instance of torture may be to others, regardless of what may be a certain consistency in the history, what is indisputably distinct about what has happened over the past seven years is that there is available a full official record produced by the very government in which the policies were devised, the legal opinions rendered, and the decisions made. What is different, in other words, is that much of that official record of the very government that made torture the official policy of the United States of America is publicly available to us almost in, as it were, real time.

Whatever you want to say about what the U.S. military did during the war in the Philippines at the beginning of the twentieth century, or what influence American training and advice and military aid had over what governments did in South and Central America during the late 1970s—dark histories many of us here know very well—I don't believe a similar public record exists from those periods in which people said: "You know, it is imperative in this situation that we use 'extreme interrogation,' or torture. Here are the techniques we have to use. I, as secretary of defense; I, as counsel to the president; I, as the responsible Department of Justice attorney, will now determine that we as a government are going to do these things, and write down in black and white what our official rationale for them is." And though one of the functions of a truth commission, if ever one is convened, would be to complete that documentary record, the fact is that we already have a fairly clear understanding of the narrative, beginning in the days immediately after the attacks of September 11, 2001, that shows how these matters were debated, how the decisions were made, who resisted them and how those (alas, very few) people were circumvented—a documentary record that clearly shows, for example, what decisions were specifically made by the secretary of defense, what boxes he checked that said: You can do this, you can't do that.

So I'm making an appeal—and in doing so, I confess, feeling very "journalistic" before this impressive academic audience—that we *start with the facts*. Not least because the facts are interesting. The facts are rich. And they tell a story of public officials, very few, if any, of whom, I would argue, can be described as *evil*—no matter what you may think of former vice president Dick Cheney, who, in part by his incessant and highly public advocacy, has become the poster boy for the entire issue—and most of whom were in government to try to do the right thing. And these people sat down in their air-conditioned offices and conference rooms and decided to do these things to these people, and in doing so, some of them put their names on documents. I know some of these people slightly. One of them, the now infamous John Yoo—who is my colleague on the Berkeley faculty, and I have publicly debated him on that campus—was certainly in no way the evil sadist of the caricatures; I believe Professor Yoo was doing what he sincerely thought was right. Of course, that doesn't mean what he did *was* right—on the contrary. But I believe one of our obligations, if we truly want to understand these matters, is to ask why: Why did they make these decisions? Why did they do what they did?

We have talked about a lot of emotions today, but one of the emotions that hasn't been mentioned is fear. Nobody has said anything about fear. Fear. I think that you can't talk about Jack Bauer and his popularity—because the television program, *24*, of which he is the hero is immensely popular—without talking about fear. Why is that show so popular? Or, to put it more bluntly, why do Americans like to sit and watch Jack Bauer torture people? Why does this spectacle, communally witnessed—and I agree with my colleagues that this is a social phenomenon—serve in some way to comfort people as well as to entertain them? Because this uncomfortable question gets us, it seems to me, rather closer to the heart of the matter. We have all been traipsing around talking about this issue for years, exposing and denouncing torture in one way or another, but with the singular exception of the Abu Ghraib images, television hasn't been much interested in it—except to make money off of it by broadcasting dramatizations like *24*. This should point us, however hesitantly, toward a significant— *the* significant—political reality of torture: that in general, and however doggedly parts of the intellectual elite denounce it, when it comes to torture, for many if not for most politicians, the raw political calculus cuts the other way.

What do I mean by that? That most politicians, when they think about torture, think: "Why in heaven's name would I want to make a public issue of denouncing *that?* Such a stance is apt to hurt me, for it will be described as 'coddling terrorists'—and at least some number of my constituents, and maybe even most of them, will agree with that description." I'm not speculating here but drawing on the stark legislative history. The Detainee Treatment Act of 2005 and the Military Commissions Act of 2006 were approved by Congress long after the images of Abu Ghraib and much of the history of the Bush Administration's decision to use torture had become public. Indeed, Republicans introduced the Military Commissions Act—a bill that granted to the president the power to decide what was and was not torture and sheltered those who had used these techniques from prosecution under the War Crimes Act of 1996—in the fall of 2006 in significant part because a very tough midterm election was looming and the Republicans calculated that they could maneuver Democrats into a position of opposing it. And indeed Democrats could have filibustered it, stopped it from becoming law, but they declined to do that—not least because they calculated, no doubt correctly, that to do so would have been to walk into a political trap. Opposing this law that prevented prosecutions of those who had tortured might have damaged their chances in the midterm elections.

Among the minority in Congress who did oppose it was a young senator elected the previous year from Illinois, who, when announcing his opposition to the bill, stood up in the chamber and made this blunt—almost shockingly blunt—declaration: "I realize that soon we will adjourn for the fall, and the campaigning will begin in earnest and there will be thirty-second attack ads and negative mail pieces and we will be criticized as caring more about the rights of terrorists than the protection of Americans, and I know that the vote before us was specifically designed and timed to add more fuel to that fire."[3]

That was Senator Barack Obama, before he voted against the Military Commissions Act of 2006, which is now the law of the land. The political analysis he offered has not been disputed; indeed, he seems to have taken it as obvious that voting against this law would leave one open to "thirty-second attack ads" and all the rest, placing one on the side of the terrorists. The premise here is that when the matter is presented in this crude political form, a substantial part of the country approves of these "extreme interrogation techniques"—or at the very least does not think their use should be foreclosed. Depending on what is in the news and various other political factors, it may be a growing or shrinking part of the country, but sometimes, perhaps, it is a majority—especially if what we mean by "approves" comes down to agreeing with this: Our government should maintain the possibility of using these techniques if its leaders deem them necessary. And politicians know this.

Why? Why do Americans watch Jack Bauer and cheer him on? I spoke a moment ago of fear. Fear is the most lucrative political emotion. In the wake of a frightening terrorist attack, many people find comfort in the idea or the image of untrammeled government power. That is, when people have been killed as they sit down to do their work—as they sit in their offices at the World Trade Center trading stocks or selling insurance over the telephone or preparing for the luncheon service at Windows on the World—and when this death comes wholly without warning out of the sky and kills three thousand people, it tends to leave a society fairly, well, terrorized. After such an event, it isn't surprising that many find comfort in the thought that their government has within it highly intelligent, highly able people who are willing to do *absolutely anything* to protect them. I call this "the *Dirty Harry* Effect." *Dirty Harry*, of course, is that famous movie starring Clint Eastwood and set, not coincidentally, in liberal San Francisco at the end, also not coincidentally, of the liberal 1960s, in which Eastwood plays a tough police detective, Harry Callahan, who, in desperately struggling to protect his city from a serial killer, is willing to do just about anything, including torturing the suspect to find out where one of his victims can be found. To put it another way, Callahan is willing to cut like a chainsaw through all that liberal red tape—including laws against torture—which, in restricting what the police can do (so the presumption is), helps keep killers on the loose. Dirty Harry slices through all that in order to protect citizens from killers and criminals. The appeal here, whether we are talking about Harry Callahan or Jack Bauer, is obvious: it is reassuring to think there are strong and determined people out there who are willing to cut through all those frustrating obstacles and *protect us.* The difference is, in 1971 Harry Callahan was a rebel cop, fighting against the system from within. Three decades later, Jack Bauer works directly for the president of the United States.

We are at an interesting moment, when the issue of torture threatens to move from being something we knew about—indeed, have known about for years—but didn't really discuss, at least not as a serious public policy issue, to something we begin to confront. Thus the title of my talk: "Now That We've Tortured: Image, Guilt, Consequence." I've talked a bit about the consequences and touched on the images. I think it essential as well to offer some images in the words of the people who have actually been subjected to these techniques. We heard a bit earlier about the absence of "survivor accounts" and how this has led the press to focus on these journalistic stunts—or, better, media stunts—in which journalists volunteer to be waterboarded, and so on. One should point out that as we meet here today we do not possess reliable first-person accounts of waterboarding, for example, though I think it is likely that we will have them at some point.[4] Right now you cannot interview the three people known to have been waterboarded; they remain at Guantánamo. And though we do have Khalid Sheik Mohammad's deposition, or the equivalent of it, he was not permitted by the tribunal to say anything specific about abuse, enhanced interrogation, torture—whatever you'd prefer to call it.

If we have not yet had reliable accounts from the so-called high-value detainees, we do indeed have a considerable number of accounts from other prisoners taken in the war on terror who have experienced "enhanced interrogation techniques." The following account, drawn from a deposition taken by officers of the Criminal Investigation Division (CID) of the U.S. Army, is that of a man known as Detainee 7, who tells of what happened to him at Abu Ghraib prison in the fall of 2003. Detainee 7 had been arrested at a roadblock in Iraq in October 2003. I was actually reporting in Iraq then, and I remember vividly the tension and anxiety and insanity of that moment: the insurgency was growing rapidly, the U.S. military knew little about it and was desperate for intelligence to combat it, and because of this, the Americans were conducting neighborhood sweeps and arresting a great many Iraqi men and sending them off to Abu Ghraib for interrogation. Abu Ghraib quickly became immensely overcrowded, had at that time certainly well over ten thousand detainees—a vast number of people, most of whom shouldn't have been there—and they were being slowly worked through the system by a handful of highly overworked interrogators, and also by military policemen, who were not supposed to be involved in interrogation but at the direction of a desperate Defense Department had become involved, with the catastrophic results that we have all seen depicted in lurid colors in the Abu Ghraib photographs.

It was around this time, in the fall of 2003, that the man who came to be known as Detainee 7 was stopped at a roadblock, found to have a Republican Guard ID card in his pocket, and was arrested and shipped off to Abu Ghraib. Following are excerpts from his account, given to the CID officers of the U.S. Army, of what happened to him when he got there:

> The first day they put me in a dark room and started hitting me in the head
> and stomach and legs. They made me raise my hands and sit on my knees.
> I was like that for four hours. Then the interrogator came and he was looking
> at me while they were beating me. I stayed in the room for five days, naked,
> with no clothes. They put handcuffs on my hands and they cuffed me high
> for seven or eight hours.[5]

"Cuffed high" is a familiar position for interrogations of this kind. The idea is to pull the arms behind the back and then up, thus putting great stress on the shoulders, which, in extreme versions, can be dislocated. It's fiercely painful and also quite familiar: the French cuffed prisoners this way when trying to suppress the Algerian rebellion during the late 1950s and early 1960s. Officers of some Latin American regimes, including Brazil and Argentina, favored this treatment—sometimes suspending prisoners with their hands cuffed behind their backs—during their "dirty wars" in the 1960s and 1970s. The prolonged high cuffing brings not only pain but physical damage, as Detainee 7 describes:

> That caused a rupture to my right hand. I had a cut that was bleeding and
> had pus coming from it. They kept me this way on 24, 25 and 26 October.
> In the following days they put a bag over my head. The whole time I was
> without clothes, without anything to sleep on.

This placing of a bag over the head, or hooding, is a simple means of producing sensory deprivation and the anxiety that accompanies it: this heavy black cloth placed over your head and face means you can't see and also that you can't hear very well. Your face and head grow hot and sweaty; you have trouble breathing. It is claustrophobic and causes great anxiety, for the detainee has no idea when, if ever, the hood will be removed.

So thus far in Detainee 7's interrogation, to use the professional jargon, we see the use of "stress positions," combined with "adjustment of clothing to induce stress"—the prolonged forced nudity—and sensory deprivation.

> One day in November they started a different type of punishment where
> American police came into my room and put the bag over my head, cuffed

my hands, took me out of the room into the hallway. He started beating me—him and five other American police. I could see their feet only from beneath the bag.

The hood greatly increases the effectiveness of beatings: the detainee doesn't know when the blows are coming; he can't cringe, can't protect his face or any other sensitive parts of his body. This vulnerability makes beatings more unpredictable and thus more terrifying.

A couple of those police were female, I knew because I heard their voices and I saw two of the police before they put the bag over my head. One of them was wearing glasses; I couldn't read his name. He put tape over his name. Some of the things they did were make me sit down like a dog holding the string from the bag and they would make me bark like a dog. They were laughing at me.

Shame—the use of shame. You see this in Abu Ghraib and at Guantánamo: this focus on sensory deprivation together with shaming the prisoner. Female interrogators were often used to magnify this effect, for they were thought to be more effective in shaming devout Muslim men, who now found themselves naked and vulnerable and impotent before the women. Shame shortens the road to humiliation.

One of the police was telling me to crawl in Arabic, so I crawled on my stomach and the police were spitting on me while I was crawling and hitting me. The police were hitting me in my kidneys, then they hit me in my right ear, it started bleeding and I lost consciousness. A few days before they hit me on my ear, the American police, the guy who wears glasses, he put red woman's underwear over my head. And then he tied me to the window that is in the cell with my hands behind my back until I lost consciousness. And also when I was in Room #1 they told me to lay down on my stomach and they were jumping from the bed onto my back and my legs. And the other two were spitting on me and calling me names, and they held my hands and legs. After the guy with the glasses got tired, two of the American soldiers brought me to the ground and tied my hands to the door while laying down on my stomach. One of the police was pissing on me and laughing at me. . . . And the soldier

and his friend told me in a loud voice to lie down, so I did that. And then the
policeman was opening my legs, with a bag over my head. . . .

So here Detainee 7, naked but for the hood over his head, is forced to
lie on his stomach on the floor, prone. He can't see what is happening to
him, doesn't know what this military policeman intends to do.

> He sat down between my legs on his knees, and I was looking at him from
> underneath the bag. And they wanted to do me—I saw him, he was opening
> his pants, so I started screaming loudly and the other police started hitting
> me with his feet on my neck and he put his feet on my head so I couldn't
> scream. And then they put the loud speaker in the room and he was yelling
> into the microphone.

This is called, in the Department of Defense documents, "use of noise
to induce stress." Sometimes, as here, it is done with amplified voices;
sometimes, as at Guantánamo, the same music is played over and over
again at very high volume.

There is not time to read all of Detainee 7's account—these are
excerpts—but here is a final word from him, recounting events from a
couple days later:

> They took me to the room and they signaled me to get on to the floor. And
> one of the police he put a part of his stick that he always carries inside my
> ass and I felt it going inside me about 2 centimeters, approximately. And I
> started screaming, and he pulled it out and he washed it with water inside
> the room. And then two American girls that were there when they were beat-
> ing me, they were hitting me with a ball made of sponge on my dick. And
> when I was tied up in my room, one of the girls, with blonde hair, she is
> white, she was playing with my dick. . . . And they were taking pictures of me
> during all these instances.

We know, of course, about these photographs, and indeed this deposition became public only in the late spring of 2004, after the first of the
Abu Ghraib photos had been aired by CBS News' *Sixty Minutes II* and
published in the *New Yorker* along with Seymour Hersh's pathbreaking
report. Though government officials, from President Bush on down,

assured Americans that these actions were the perverted improvisations of a few low-level troops, in fact many people—including people at this table today—will recognize in Detainee 7's account familiar techniques and common themes. I've pointed to a few of them. While the abuses just described by Detainee 7 were not committed by professional interrogators—these were military police who didn't have any real training in what they were doing—these MPs claimed to be, and in my view clearly were, trying to follow loose guidelines that had been given to them by superior officers, some of whom almost certainly were professional interrogators.

Let me read you another account, this one very short, that is drawn from an e-mail sent by an FBI counterterrorism official at Guantánamo in August 2004, four months after the Abu Ghraib photographs had been made public:

> On a couple occasions I entered a room to find a detainee chained hand and foot in the fetal position on the floor, with no chair, food, or water. Most times they had urinated or defecated on themselves. They had been left there for eighteen to twenty-four hours or more. When I asked MPs what was going on, I was told that interrogators from the day prior had ordered this treatment and the detainee was not to be moved. On another occasion, the detainee was almost unconscious on the floor with a pile of hair next to him. He had apparently literally pulled his own hair out throughout the night.[6]

We see here the stress positions, the nudity, the "adjustment of temperature to induce stress," and so on. We also see the collaboration between the interrogators and the military police, new for the military, in which the former tell the latter, essentially, "Do such and such to 'soften this guy up.'"

We have many accounts from FBI officials—most, like this one, declassified thanks to the efforts of the American Civil Liberties Union—about what was going on at Guantánamo. Most of these e-mails were sent during the months after the Abu Ghraib photographs became public, and it is fair to say that in many of these cases, a familiar bureaucratic motivation is at work, the one commonly known as "CYA": cover your ass.

It is not cynical to point this out, for it is important to remember that the torture story is in part a bureaucratic story. We have many of the documents we do have for bureaucratic reasons. The famous "torture memos" written by lawyers in the Department of Justice, for example, exist certainly in large part because officials in the intelligence community wanted a so-called golden shield that would protect them when the press and the public learned about these techniques—at a moment, presumably, when sympathy for their use would be less universal than it might have been in the months after 9/11. "You want me to do this stuff to prisoners, I want an ironclad legal opinion from the Department of Justice approving them." That's in effect what the CIA officials said, and as a consequence, we have these torture memos—which is to say, the people who were doing this *anticipated this very moment.* No doubt many of the senior people remembered vividly those post-Watergate months during the mid-1970s when the Church Committee and the Pike Committee were investigating CIA "misdeeds" of the 1950s and 1960s, those distant times when the agency had perpetrated assassinations, coups d'état, and other dirty tricks of the early Cold War. In their hearings and in their final reports, the committees exposed those activities to an elite and a public that, post-Vietnam, had become much less sympathetic to the heretofore unquestioned claims of national security; careers were ruined, people went to jail. And so when the Bush administration made certain requests after 9/11, when they demanded that CIA officers undertake certain legally questionable activities, those high up in the agency with long memories said—I am speculating here—"Hold on just a moment. When this happens again, when a few years down the road the next commission gets around to doing its investigative work on what happened in the wake of the 9/11 attacks, we are not going to be the ones left without the get-out-of-jail-free card." Or, to use another metaphor, "When the music stops this time, I am not going to be the only one standing without a chair."

Speaking of the CIA, let us move for just a moment from the techniques used by military interrogators and policemen at Abu Ghraib and Guantánamo to those used by CIA officers on "high-value detainees" at the so-called black sites, the secret interrogation centers established in various countries around the world, including Pakistan, Afghanistan, Thailand, Morocco, Poland, and Lithuania, among others. I'd like to read one other document, this one from 2005, which sets out what I am going to call "the six techniques." As my colleagues will know, this is an allusion to the famous Five Techniques, which British intelligence employed on Irish Republican Army prisoners during the early 1970s in Northern Ireland. These six techniques—first described to the public by Brian Ross of ABC News, together with his colleague Richard Esposito—were allegedly those used, almost always in combination, by CIA officers in secretly interrogating those who are deemed to be the most valuable prisoners.[7] Here is Ross's and Esposito's list:

1) The Attention Grab: The interrogator forcefully grabs the shirt front of the prisoner and shakes him.

This technique—favored for years by the Israeli domestic intelligence agency, the Shin Beit—is really not grabbing but very forceful shaking: back and forth, hard. The only risk is that if it is not done right, it may break the detainee's neck and kill him, which is, needless to say, a very considerable downside.

2) Attention Slap: An open-handed slap aimed at causing pain and triggering fear.

3) The Belly Slap: A hard open-handed slap to the stomach. The aim is to cause pain, but not internal injury. Doctors consulted advised against using a punch, which could cause lasting internal damage.

4) Long Time Standing: This technique is described as among the most effective. Prisoners are forced to stand, handcuffed and with their feet shackled to an eye bolt in the floor for more than 40 hours. Exhaustion and sleep deprivation are effective in yielding confessions.

This fourth technique, long-time standing—the Soviets called it *stoika*—is simple and, indeed, among the most effective, as we know from a great deal of research, much of it commissioned by the CIA when it was investigating Soviet interrogation techniques during the 1950s and 1960s. When a person stands immobile for more than a couple hours, his legs begin to swell, eventually blisters form, the skin actually breaks, and finally the renal system begins to shut down. This is terribly, excruciatingly painful. At the same time, the technique sounds relatively harmless and inoffensive. Donald Rumsfeld, then secretary of defense, when asked to approve long-time standing for up to four hours in late 2002, famously scrawled at the bottom of one of these documents: "However, I stand for

8–10 hours a day. Why is standing limited to 4 hours? D.R."[8] Secretary Rumsfeld, of course, preferred to work at a standing desk—though it perhaps should go without saying, even if apparently it doesn't, that standing at your desk, drinking coffee, signing papers, pausing for a meeting or two, talking to your aides and assistants, and so on, is not quite the same thing as being chained to an eyebolt in the floor, naked and immobile in a very cold room, for hour after hour. For long-time standing is often combined with "adjustment of temperature to induce stress," the fifth of the six techniques.

5) The Cold Cell: The prisoner is left to stand naked in a cell kept near 50 degrees. Throughout the time in the cell the prisoner is doused with cold water.

A variation of this technique was used in Iraq. The Special Forces guys, for example, reportedly used this in Mosul and elsewhere in northern Iraq. They would chain up prisoners on the ground outside, naked in the cold, and repeatedly douse them with cold water, and they would place a thermometer in the prisoner's rectum to give them constant body temperature readings so they would avoid inducing hypothermia and accidentally killing their prisoners, which, again, is always a risk.

6) Water Boarding: The prisoner is bound to an inclined board, feet raised, and head slightly below the feet. Cellophane is wrapped over the prisoner's face and water is poured over him. Unavoidably, the gag reflex kicks in and a terrifying fear of drowning leads to almost instant pleas to bring the treatment to a halt.

This is the most famous of the six techniques. Though Americans have contributed a few innovations—the cellophane, for example—the technique, which in its essence is nothing more than interrupted drowning, goes back a long way—centuries, in fact, to at least the Spanish Inquisition. More recently, the French used it extensively in fighting the National Liberation Front, or FLN, in Algeria during the 1950s and 1960s; the Argentines used it in their dirty war during the 1970s, calling it *el submarino*. So far as we know, American interrogators have used waterboarding on three prisoners, then held at the black sites and now at Guantánamo.

Those three were among the fourteen high-value detainees whose transfer from the black sites was announced by President Bush during his remarkable speech of September 6, 2006, in which the president of the United States, standing in the East Room of the White House, defended quite explicitly the U.S. government's use of "enhanced interrogation techniques." Though the speech had an obvious immediate political purpose—introducing the Military Commissions Act in the run-up to the 2006 midterm elections, as discussed earlier—I believe this is one of the most important speeches President Bush ever gave. It will be remembered. It is, for many reasons, historic.

The documents I have quoted are not new. They have been public for years. Detainee 7's deposition dates from spring 2004, the FBI officer's e-mail from August 2004, and Ross's and Esposito's piece from November 2005. Americans have known about torture for a very long time. For half a dozen years now, people have been writing about it, reporters have been publishing prominent pieces about it—including, as early as December 2002, on the front page of the *Washington Post.* So for years now, we have been talking about torture, writing about torture. One thing about torture we can say with confidence: We have learned to live with it.

The question before us now is whether we will do anything about it. We have elected a new president, a Democrat, who has been outspoken in his opposition to torture. What will our political leaders now do, if indeed they do anything?

One answer we can give already is that they will go on producing reports. As I said, we already have a good many of these, but it should be acknowledged that their quality has been improving dramatically. The Senate Armed Services Committee, for example, recently released an executive summary of its report on the development and application of these extreme interrogation techniques that was authoritative, comprehensive, provocative—and absolutely devastating. Americans can find this very easily online.[9] The Senate Intelligence Committee, as I mentioned, is said to be hard at work on another such report, and we can expect that this will add essential details to an already vivid and thorough record.

Then there is the Senate Judiciary Committee, whose chairman, Senator Leahy, has proposed establishing a kind of truth commission to investigate these matters. As we meet today, Senator Leahy's proposal is not given much chance of success. It is, to put it mildly, controversial. One memorable response was that of Senator Arlen Specter, Republican of Pennsylvania, who declared, on hearing it, "This is not Latin America!"

One can't help laughing a bit at this, but of course the laughter is of the mirthless sort. It masks the obvious question: What does this mean—that this is not Latin America? And if this is not Latin America, what is the difference exactly? One obvious difference is that of magnitude. On the one hand, American officials did not kidnap thousands of people, torture and murder them, and bury them in secret graves. On the other hand, Americans did torture a great many people—we can't say precisely how many, but it certainly seems to have been in the hundreds—and this record has been public for some time. Argentines, while their dirty war was being fought, knew people were being disappeared, but this wasn't broadly acknowledged, not to mention reported, in the nation's press. We as North Americans are, it seems to me, distinguished by having been able to read in the press about much of what was happening as it was happening, which is indeed a remarkable thing—not least because it means that when we look at these proposals to establish a truth commission, or even to undertake prosecutions, we find ourselves having to cope as well with the question of how implicated the entire society, including the public, actually is. Can we truly prosecute "to the full extent of the law" those who not only acted under legal cover—that is, who acted with documents in hand, as it were, that said "authoritatively" that what they were doing was legal—but acted with the documented knowledge of many officials at the highest reaches of the government and, increasingly as the years went on, with the growing knowledge of the public?

Many concerned about these issues attack the very idea of establishing a truth commission because the phrase "truth commission" implies to some that people will be invited to testify—people, perhaps, like former vice president Cheney or David Addington, his chief of staff—in exchange, presumably, for some kind of immunity. As many in this room know well, this is how the South Africans managed their Truth and Reconciliation Commission. In that case, broadly speaking, testimony—truthful testimony—brought with it amnesty for crimes that may have been committed.

Now there are practical problems here, fairly obvious ones. The first is that the Military Commissions Act of 2006, as I mentioned earlier, tries explicitly to shield those who have committed these acts from prosecution under the War Crimes Act of 1996—and if you can't credibly threaten to prosecute people, how will you persuade them to testify in exchange for immunity from prosecution? Those difficulties aside, however, many in the human rights community, in particular, find any proffer of immunity in exchange for testimony to be an egregious idea, because it would allow these people to avoid prosecution. I am sympathetic to this sentiment, but I do find myself compelled to observe that this argument also very quickly brings in its wake another question: What kind of guilt do these people bear—and to what extent do we share in it?

We've had an emphasis here today on "the social phenomenon of torture," and I couldn't agree more that it's a social phenomenon. Sometimes it's more social than others. We have had in the United States an example of torture as a truly social phenomenon, for not only has it been reported on fairly extensively but the society has known about it, and countenanced it, for years. Given this, can we as a society sit in judgment of and then prosecute Dick Cheney? Can we say: "How could you have done this? We are appalled by these illegal actions, and now, years after learning of them, we are going to put you in jail as punishment."

I hasten to add that I am not trying to imply, by asking this rhetorical question, that we can't investigate people, including former high officials, and prosecute them and put them in jail—not at all. Of course we can do it. I am saying: If we were to do that, what exactly would we be doing? Imagine for a moment Dick Cheney, sitting in the dock, looking out at the court and at the country and saying, in that steely way of his, "You used me when you needed me. When you wanted me to calm your nerves—when I was the guy who was kicking ass and taking names and torturing people. But now, now your nerves are calm. There have been no further attacks. So now you're going to punish me—and in so doing, you're lying to yourselves, because you're doing no more than trying to punish your own worst instincts. However satisfying it might be to your own sense of decorum, this supposed act of law is a sham, for in its essence, it has nothing to do with justice." Now, however far we are today from such a moment—and we are very, very far—my question to this distinguished panel and this very patient audience is: If Dick Cheney said those words or others like them, would he be wrong? And if so, why?

So I turn now from these aggressive provocations to my point of departure, which was my objection to the somewhat static idea that "societies torture": that they did torture, they do torture, and they will continue to torture. Despite our distance from my little Dick Cheney thought experiment—and we are, as I say, very far indeed, if it ever happens—it seems to me that one thing to be hoped for from this interesting moment is a bit of societal education, which might begin with a communal effort to investigate and state clearly, in a communally acceptable and communally agreed-on way, what exactly happened. Here: *this* is the truth—the truth set out in a way that we as a society can agree on. You can argue all you want about the implications of these things and what should be done about them, but here are the indisputable facts. Here is what was done and who ordered it, and when. This is what the Senate Select Committee on Watergate did during the early 1970s.

When it comes to torture, we have much of this story already, as I have said. But what we certainly don't have is the story of the use of these techniques, told by people who have access to *all* the documents, of whatever classification—a story that then leads to a reliable judgment of their effectiveness and a persuasive verdict on whether or not they really were essential to saving thousands or even millions of lives, as the former vice president and other officials have repeatedly, though generally quite unconvincingly, insisted.

Now I absolutely agree that torture does enormous political damage to a society and that the use of it by the United States has done incalculable harm to the country's cause in fighting what is largely a political war—an international counterinsurgency war for hearts and minds. I believe that the use of these techniques was not only illegal and morally wrong but that it constituted a terrible, terrible mistake, which did much damage to the country. But, as I have pointed out, it is impossible to understand where we are on this issue if we don't acknowledge that many Americans—a substantial minority and perhaps on a given day, and depending on how the question is posed, a majority—do not agree with this. Many believe that these techniques are effective and necessary. They believe in Jack Bauer; they like to think that he is out there, struggling, with his superhuman vigilance and power and ruthlessness, to keep us safe. In this as in virtually all other things, our political leaders tend to play the role not of leaders but of followers. They understand this sentiment, the fear that leads to the need to project toughness and ruthlessness and the willingness to "do whatever is necessary to keep us safe," and many of them—and no doubt more every day, as the issue gains salience under a

Democratic administration—will attempt to profit politically from that. We already see this happening, in the increasingly aggressive comments of the former vice president.

We need to acknowledge this political reality—not give in to it, but acknowledge it. It seems to me that if we are going to escape our current impasse on torture, if we are going to cleanse our society of it, we need a credible, nonpartisan or anyway bipartisan commission, led by people of unquestioned integrity, experience, and trustworthiness, who not only can investigate fully and deeply, with all necessary security clearances, what was done, but who can say this clearly, persuasively, and vividly: that torture is not only illegal and wrong but that, on balance, torture profoundly damaged the country, not just its reputation but its cause in the war on terror. You might ask: Well, what if such a high-level, deeply respected, and authoritative commission reaches a very different conclusion? My answer would be that everything I have learned over these past half dozen years or more tells me that this is most unlikely, if not inconceivable, but that if it did happen, we would have to deal with that as a society as well. For at the end of the day, we all have an interest in its conclusions and how it reaches them because we are all, to some degree, implicated in this issue. We all bear, I believe, our own bit of guilt, for our society, about whose moral distinction we so like to boast, did this. If we are going to redeem ourselves, this dark story must be probed, constructed, presented, and communally sanctioned, and the crimes expiated—expiated in a way that is just and not vengeful. Only then can we as Americans, as an American community, begin to make our way back to a relative—relative—state of grace.

NOTES

1   See David Johnston and Neil A. Lewis, "U.S. Will Give Qaeda Suspect a Civilian Trial," *New York Times*, February 26, 2009.

2   Mark Danner, *Torture and Truth: America, Abu Ghraib, and the War on Terror* (New York: New York Review of Books, 2004).

3   See "Statement on Military Commission Legislation: Remarks by Senator Barack Obama," September 28, 2006, quoted in Mark Danner, "US Torture: Voices from the Black Sites," *New York Review of Books* 56, no. 6

(April 9, 2009), and in Mark Danner, *Stripping Bare the Body: Politics Violence War* (New York: Nation Books, 2009), 517.

4   We now do have such accounts, by way of the Red Cross report. See Mark Danner, "Voices from the Black Sites," *New York Review of Books* 56, no. 6 (April 9, 2009), reprinted in Danner, *Stripping Bare the Body*.

5   These and the excerpts that follow are drawn from "Translation of Sworn Statement Provided by [Name Blacked Out] Detainee #[Number Blacked Out], 1430/21JAN04," in Danner, *Torture and Truth*, 247–48. Originally posted on the Web site of the *Washington Post* in 2004 and reprinted in Mark Danner, "The Logic of Torture," *New York Review*, June 24, 2004.

6   See "Email from [REDACTED] to [REDACTED]," August 2, 2004. Quoted in Mark Danner, "We Are All Torturers Now," *New York Times*, January 6, 2005, section A, late edition, and in Danner, *Stripping Bare the Body*, 417.

7   See Richard Esposito and Brian Ross, "CIA's Harsh Interrogation Techniques Described," *ABC News*, November 18, 2005.

8   See "General Counsel of the Department of Defense Action Memo," November 22, 2002, in Danner, *Torture and Truth*, 182.

9   See Senate Armed Services Committee, "Inquiry into the Treatment of Detainees in U.S. Custody," November 20, 2008, http://armed-services. senate.gov/Publications/Detainee%20Report%20Final_April%20 22%202009.pdf (accessed June 23, 2010).

3

"WE ARE ALL TORTURERS NOW"

Accountability after Abu Ghraib

Timothy V. Kaufman-Osborn

"We are all torturers now." So reads the title of an op-ed written by Mark Danner and published in the *New York Times* in January 2005. The gist of Danner's argument, which followed revelations of the abuse meted out by U.S. security personnel at the Abu Ghraib prison complex, is as follows: "By using torture, the country relinquishes the very ideological advantage—the promotion of democracy, freedom and human rights—that the president has so persistently claimed is America's most powerful weapon in defeating Islamic extremism. . . . By using torture we Americans transform ourselves into the very caricature our enemies have sought to make of us." But how exactly, we might wonder, are "all" Americans implicated, and what sort of accountability is at stake when persons participating in the United States military campaign in Iraq commit atrocities, quoting Danner, "in their name"?[1]

Danner's response to these questions, implicit in the op-ed's title, presupposes a specific conception of democracy and, more particularly, of the constitution of popular sovereignty in a democratic political order. If, however, this representation is anachronistic, as I believe it is, then derivative claims regarding the locus of collective accountability for torture will prove flawed as well. Accordingly, my aim in this essay is, first, is to indicate why an appreciation of certain features of the contemporary U.S. security state should cause us to pause before endorsing the allegation that "we are all torturers now" and, second, more speculatively than conclusively, to suggest how we might begin to rearticulate the question of political accountability after Abu Ghraib.

Liberal Legalism and Accountability

In this essay, I am not concerned with recent discussions about how the term "torture" is to be defined. Nor am I concerned with recent arguments condemning this practice, no matter how defined. Nor, for that matter, am I concerned with the specific events that transpired at Abu Ghraib, no matter how characterized and no matter how abhorrent. Instead, I am interested in judgments of accountability regarding what happened there, emanating from the political right as well as the left, within the United States.

Such judgments have ranged from the particular to the general, depending at least in part on whether the social contractarian premises presupposed by conventional liberal legal discourse are or are not expressly called into play. Most narrowly, one finds members of the current administration. President George W. Bush, for example, effectively settled the question of accountability by characterizing what took place at Abu Ghraib as the "disgraceful conduct by a few American troops who dishonored our country and disregarded our values."[2] This characterization was echoed by the official investigative reports issued in the wake of Abu Ghraib, all of which explained these events in terms of the pathological and/or immoral conduct of a handful of rogue soldiers. To cite but one of many possible examples, according to the "psychological assessment" appended to the report commissioned by Lieutenant General Ricardo Sanchez, the incidents at the Baghdad prison complex were the work of a small number of "immoral men and women" who engaged in "sadistic and psychopathic behavior."[3]

These characterizations, as well as the judgments of accountability that derive from them, are unsurprising but also quite inadequate. They are unsurprising insofar as they presuppose the methodological individual-

TIMOTHY V. KAUFMAN-OSBORN

ism that informs most liberal legalism, which, as a rule, defines punishable wrongdoing as the deliberately willed acts of identifiable perpetrators. This is what one would anticipate in a political order in which holistic affirmations of group liability are often countered by the claim that a collectivity is nothing more than an aggregate of the individuals composing it, and that therefore culpability can be assigned only to those persons immediately and proximately implicated in a specific misdeed. (To see the point, think of neoconservative critiques of arguments avowing collective white guilt for structural racism as well as of affirmative action programs aimed at alleviating such racism.) Leaving aside the question of whether "psychopaths" can be deemed fully competent and so liable for their conduct, these characterizations effectively dictate the appropriate response to what those at Abu Ghraib are alleged to have done. Construed as criminal suspects, the accused are to be charged, tried, and, if found guilty, punished for violations of specific provisions of the Uniform Code of Military Justice.

The inadequacies of this way of resolving the issue of accountability are multiple. For present purposes, it suffices to note that this construction makes it far too easy to assign the role of patsy to Charles Graner, Lynndie England, and their ilk and that in turn diverts attention from the larger chain of command in which they were severable links.[4] The disingenuousness of this resolution, I suspect, at least partly explains why in 2005 the American Civil Liberties Union and Human Rights First filed four suits on behalf of eight and, later, nine plaintiffs who allegedly were tortured and subjected to cruel, inhuman, and degrading forms of treatment by U.S. military personnel at Abu Ghraib and elsewhere in Iraq as well as in Afghanistan. These suits, which were consolidated in 2006, named as defendants Janis Karpinski, commander of the U.S. Army unit responsible for detention facilities in Iraq from June 2003 to May 2004; Thomas Pappas, commander of the army unit responsible for intelligence-gathering operations, including those conducted at Abu Ghraib; Ricardo Sanchez, commander of the U.S.-led military coalition from June 2003 to July 2004; and, finally, Donald Rumsfeld, then the highest-ranking civilian in the U.S. Department of Defense.

In *Ali et al. v. Rumsfeld*, the American Civil Liberties Union and Human Rights First contended that the defendants had violated the Fifth and Eighth Amendments to the U.S. Constitution, the Geneva Conventions, and the United Nations Convention against Torture and Other Cruel, Inhuman or Degrading Treatment or Punishment insofar as they "1) formulated or implemented policies and practices that caused the torture and other cruel, inhuman or degrading treatment of plaintiffs; and 2) had effective command and control of U.S. military personnel in Iraq and/or Afghanistan and knew and had reason to know of torture and abuse by their subordinates and failed to promptly and effectively prohibit, prevent, and punish unlawful conduct."[5] As the legal foundation for these charges, the complaint invoked the doctrine of command responsibility, which specifies the conditions under which officers and/or officials may be deemed liable for the acts of subordinates.

Seeking to expand the scope of accountability beyond those proximately and personally responsible for the harms inflicted at Abu Ghraib, this suit posed a host of potential conundrums for the law, including but not limited to the question of the appropriate remedy should the defendants be found legally liable.[6] These questions were never given a full hearing because, in March 2007, a federal judge dismissed the case, chiefly on the ground that government officers, when acting within the scope of their official duties, are either largely or entirely immune from lawsuits.[7] This outcome, which surprised only the naive, is not of primary concern to me in this context. What is of concern is the way in which the doctrine of command responsibility opens up the possibility of moving beyond the confines of a strict construction of legal liability, that is, one that limits culpability to Graner, England, and others foolish enough to pose for the camera while inside the walls of Abu Ghraib.

Once the possibility of such expansion is admitted, especially in a political order predicated on the subordination of military to civilian authority, there is no reason in principle why application of the doctrine of command responsibility should stop with Donald Rumsfeld. Consider, in this regard, a 2005 article written by former congresswoman Elizabeth Holtzman and published in the *Nation*, in which Holtzman calls for creation of a congressional commission to

> see who, including those at the highest level of our government, directed the inhuman treatment or torture of detainees. . . . If the inquiry finds that the President or Secretary of Defense (or other high-level government officials) directed or knowingly condoned the inhuman treatment or torture of U.S.

detainees, then a special prosecutor should be appointed, with guarantees of full independence, to determine whether there is any criminal liability under the War Crimes Act (and the U.S. anti-torture statute) or any other applicable criminal statutes.

However, recognizing that neither Congress nor the U.S. attorney general was likely to take such steps, Holtzman directed her final appeal to the American public at large:

Those in the public who care deeply about the rule of law and governmental accountability must keep the issue alive. Failure to investigate wrongdoing in high places and tolerating misconduct or criminality can have only the most corroding impact on our democracy and the rule of law that sustains us.[8]

The editors of the *Nation* indicated in a July 2004 editorial just how this issue might best be "kept alive." Following a denunciation of the so-called torture memos, that is, the legal counsel offered to the Bush administration regarding the tactics that could be employed in interrogating suspected terrorists, the editors declared: "It seems that the Administration's attitude is that all the Constitution's clauses but one — the Commander in Chief clause — are irrelevant. That view is perilously close to totalitarianism, and calls for more than a special prosecutor. Voters must remove those responsible for this assault on democracy."[9] On this account, acts of torture, like unfettered exercises of executive prerogative, are incompatible with the principles of democracy, presumably because neither respects the rule of law. In a democracy, which rests on the principle of popular sovereignty, citizens must hold their leaders accountable for such violations of the rule of law by removing them from office, whether via conventional electoral methods or, more dramatically, via impeachment proceedings.

From this place, only a few short steps are necessary in order to arrive at the conclusion that all Americans are in some nontrivial sense liable and so accountable for what happened at Abu Ghraib. As the *Nation*'s 2004 editorial intimates, whether narrowly or more broadly construed, liberal legalism is situated on the terrain defined by social contract theory and its commitment to popular sovereignty. That terrain, which is presupposed by the headline of Danner's 2005 op-ed, includes the following familiar premises: The unity of the people in a liberal political order is imagined to arise from a quasi-juridical contract. Via that contract, persons bind themselves to one another and, in so doing, constitute themselves as a popular sovereign. Government, whose paradigmatic mode of action is the law and whose privileged representative is the legislature, is created in order to do the bidding of this sovereign; its authority, as specified in and limited by that foundational contract, is a function of the sovereign's authorization. As such, all participants in this contract are final authors of the deeds of those who act in their name, whether elected representatives, executive officials, or simply soldiers. "Our" implication in their deeds, in other words, is in the mode of indirect but ultimately responsible authorization. Consequently, it falls to all of us, as express or tacit signatories to the social contract, to acknowledge our collective wrongdoing when misdeeds are committed in our name and so to seek legal or political redress, either by bringing the offenders into a court of law and/or by removing them from their positions.

In at least one respect, this way of resolving the question of accountability may prove as problematic as that advanced by the president. Although not a logically necessary consequence, by ascribing responsibility for such conduct to its ultimate authors, namely, to "all" Americans, the thrust of Danner's op-ed may distract attention from the specific culpability of those in the chain of military command as well as the civilian officers to whom its officers ultimately report. It is something akin to this worry that prompted Hannah Arendt, in a brief essay written in the midst of the American civil rights movement, to draw a sharp distinction between affirmations of responsibility and judgments of guilt. Specifically, Arendt rejected the contention that collective accountability for the evils of racism on the part of white liberals should be framed in the language of guilt. While never expressly endorsing the methodological individualism that informs liberal legalism, Arendt nonetheless insisted that "there is no such thing as being or feeling guilty for things that happened without oneself actively participating in them."

> I do not know how many precedents there are in history for such misplaced feelings, but I do know that in postwar Germany, where similar problems arose with respect to what had been done by the Hitler regime to Jews, the cry "We are all guilty" that at first hearing sounded so very noble and

tempting has actually only served to exculpate to a considerable degree those who actually were guilty. Where all are guilty, nobody is. Guilt, unlike responsibility, always singles out; it is strictly personal. It refers to an act, not to intentions or potentialities. It is only in a metaphorical sense that we can say we *feel* guilty for the sins of our fathers or our people or mankind, in short, for deeds we have not done, although the course of events may well make us pay for them.[10]

Guilt, Arendt argues, can serve as either a moral or a legal category; in both instances, though, its referent is a specific person and what that person has done. This category, Arendt would no doubt assert, is appropriate when we assign culpability and then punish persons who directly participated in the atrocities of Abu Ghraib, and it is perhaps appropriate when we seek to identify those in the chain of command who either authorized these atrocities, or, knowing of them, did little or nothing to bring them to a halt. Affirmations of collective guilt, by way of contrast, are predicated on little more than "phony sentimentality in which all real issues are obscured."[11] While such sentimentality may elicit the cheap gratification that accompanies politically correct hand-wringing, it is a sorry substitute for the work of careful thinking about collective accountability (or "responsibility," to use Arendt's term) for what happened at Abu Ghraib.

Prerogative Power Unbound

As the preceding discussion indicates, when the question of account-ability for Abu Ghraib in particular and torture more generally has been posed in recent debates within the United States, the terms of that exchange have been predictable, if not hackneyed. On the one hand, there are those who, for reasons of political expediency, seek to sever the chain of mutual political implication and so confine accountability to those most immediately involved. On the other hand, there are those who seek to reconnect the links of this chain, whether in an effort to hold accountable officials in Washington, D.C., or, sometimes, all citizens of the United States. None, however, step beyond the terrain defined by a social contractarian conception of liberal political order, and none ask about the adequacy of this characterization to the regime in which we now find ourselves.

If the question of specifically collective accountability for wrongdoing, like that committed at Abu Ghraib, is to be more adequately formulated, transformation of the United States into what Iris Young labeled a "security state" must be appreciated.[12] To understand that transformation requires an excursus into the history of liberalism's efforts to ensure the accountability of political power, especially as exercised by executive agencies. In large measure, whatever success this effort has enjoyed has turned on its capacity to erect and then effectively patrol specific borders between this and that. Although others might be cited, in this section, I am particularly concerned, first, with the spatial boundary between domestic and foreign and, second, with the temporal boundary between routine and emergency. Working in tandem, these distinctions have helped sustain the claim that when executive agencies find it necessary to act at odds with liberalism's commitment to the rule of law, and so beyond the structure of accountability inherent in law's articulation of popular will, the harm done to democracy can be minimized by confining such damage to the realm of the external and episodic. If these walls have now been breached, perhaps irreparably, then neither affirmations of collective accountability for torture and other misdeeds committed by those who are said to act in our name nor calls to employ conventional liberal mechanisms (e.g., lawsuits and elections) to rein in executive power retain much plausibility.

The historical tale related here has been told with far more nuance and detail by others. Even in bare-bones fashion, though, this tale bears repeating in a post–September 11 context, if only because its specific content will invariably be informed by the present's distinct imperatives. In saying this, I do not mean to endorse the contention, advanced by persons whose political views are as different as those of George W. Bush and Anthony Lewis, that 9/11 and its aftermath ushered in a fundamentally new order.[13] Although I will indicate what I believe is in fact distinctive about the political present in the next section, I also want to claim that the constitution of the security state has tangled roots in American history. And I want to claim that reflection on the question of accountability will remain compromised as long as we accept the foreshortened historical perspective implicit in the statement that everything changed after 9/11, especially since that statement echoes and reinforces the pinched temporal perspective inherent in liberal legal efforts to assign blame for evils like those perpetrated at Abu Ghraib.

TIMOTHY V. KAUFMAN-OSBORN

Erosion of the border between domestic and foreign can be introduced by recalling the implications of the aggrandizement of executive power for the traditional doctrine of separation of powers. Among other things, the separation of powers is intended to constrain power by creating a system of checks and balances among the principal branches of government: "Ambition must be made to counteract ambition," as James Madison wrote in Federalist 51. In principle, this system enables the national legislature, acting in the name of the people, to check executive unilateralism and so safeguard the rule of law from arbitrary power, and, in principle, this system enables the federal courts, acting in the name of the people's will, as that will is expressed in the higher law that is the U.S. Constitution, to rein in an unbalanced executive.

On the domestic front, one can find reason to express misgivings about the efficacy of this structure of countervailing powers even in the earliest years of the republic; think, for example, of Alexander Hamilton's aggressive promotion of a national bank as well as the federal government's assumption of debts incurred by the several states. That said, the expansion of executive power was relatively constrained until at least the Progressive era, when it gained momentum, first, as a result of efforts to regulate the U.S. domestic economy (e.g., through establishment of regulatory agencies such as the Interstate Commerce Commission) and, second, as a result of efforts to mobilize the economy in support of the U.S. military campaign in World War I. Far more rapid acceleration occurred in conjunction with the New Deal's creation, following passage of sweeping Congressional authorizations, of various social welfare programs, including, for example, the National Labor Relations Act, the Agricultural Adjustment Act, and the National Industrial Recovery Act. Each of these programs dramatically expanded the scope of executive power in the form of administrative agencies whose officials are formally subject to legislative oversight but, for the most part, operate in its absence. The cumulative effect of the New Deal's programmatic and institutional innovations, to quote Sheldon Wolin, was to tie a vast number of Americans "into the system of state power, a system based on bureaucratic, military, and corporate institutions and operated by elites equally at home in any one of the components."[14] These ties were twisted still more tightly, argues Wolin, during the Reagan administration (and, I would add, the second Bush administration), not simply through enormous increases in military expenditures and adoption of more comprehensive efforts to rationalize the national economy, but also, to cite a very small selection of possible examples, through "the strengthening of agencies of law enforcement; the relative indifference to the rights of the accused; the steady development of surveillance techniques, especially those relying on centralized data collections; federal drug-testing programs; and tightened security procedures for federal employees."[15]

Significant expansion of executive power in the realm of foreign affairs can also be traced to the late nineteenth and early twentieth centuries, especially in conjunction with the early forays of the United States into colonialism (e.g., in the Philippines). That said, the high-water mark of this expansion is most plausibly located in the aftermath of World War II as the United States sought to secure its global supremacy during the Cold War. This expansion was effectively institutionalized in 1947 when Congress adopted the National Security Act, which, among other things, resulted in unification of the command structure of the military under the Joint Chiefs of Staff and creation of two new entities, the National Security Council and the Central Intelligence Agency, each of which report directly to the president.

Since passage of the National Security Act, augmentation of executive power in the realm of foreign affairs has continued apace, as illustrated by the conduct of the Vietnam War during the Johnson and Nixon administrations, the Iran-Contra scandal during the Reagan administration, and, last but certainly not least, the Bush administration's undeclared war in Iraq. Granted, especially following the Vietnam debacle, Congress sought to rein in the executive's near monopolization of this domain, for example, via the War Powers Resolution (1973) and the Foreign Intelligence Surveillance Act (1978), but, to quote Kim Scheppele, these efforts have proved

quite ineffectual. Not only has the president asked permission of the Congress before committing the country to military engagements or foreign policy obligations only as a matter of courtesy rather than as a matter of law (and then only sometimes), but Congress has typically not attempted to enforce any of its powers under the 1970s-era legislation. . . . The balance of powers struck during the Cold War, with a bulked-up executive, a wizened Congress, their disputes only partly subject to refereeing by courts, remains largely intact.[16]

The aggrandizement of executive power at home and abroad has over time corroded the very distinction between domestic and foreign, and that in turn has vitiated a key premise undergirding liberalism's affirmation of power's accountability. Vitiation of the border between domestic and foreign is signified by familiarization of the phrase "national security," which, as Daniel Yergin notes, had not been part of common parlance before World War II. Its employment

postulates the interrelatedness of so many different political, economic, and military factors that developments halfway around the globe are seen to have automatic and direct impact on America's core interests. Virtually every development in the world is perceived to be potentially crucial. An adverse turn of events anywhere endangers the United States. Problems in foreign relations are viewed as urgent and immediate threats. Thus, desirable foreign policy goals are translated into issues of national survival, and the range of threats becomes limitless. The doctrine is characterized by expansiveness, a tendency to push the subjective boundaries of security outward to more and more areas, to encompass more and more geography and more and more problems. It demands that the country assume a posture of military preparedness; the nation must be on permanent alert.[17]

Among other consequences, chronic invocation of the imperatives of national security has encouraged the cult of secrecy that shields large swaths of executive conduct from scrutiny. Consider, for example, the Truman administration's announcement in 1951 of its authority to classify information bearing on national security, which made it more difficult for Congress, let alone ordinary citizens, to know what actions were being taken by the executive branch and hence to hold it accountable for those deeds. Still more important, appeals to national security have had the effect of turning inward exercises of power once more typically confined to foreign affairs. In this regard, consider executive initiation of various programs of internal surveillance during the Cold War, which effectively confused the domestic law enforcement responsibilities of the FBI and the foreign intelligence responsibilities assigned to the CIA. (In this sense, the Bush administration's decision to authorize the National Security Agency to eavesdrop on citizen and noncitizen alike in order to search for evidence of terrorist-related activity without the court-approved warrants ordinarily required for domestic spying continues by more sophisticated technological means the accomplishment of executive ambitions long in the making.)

What we see here is not simply the aggrandizement of executive power in the name of national security but, to turn to the second concern of this section, the executive's growing reliance on the doctrine of emergency to justify such expansion. As already noted, liberal political theory has always been haunted by the specter of unaccountable power, especially when exercised by an executive in response to situations that appear to demand action absent or even violative of legal authorization. A key response to this anxiety, argues Jules Lobel, has been to divide executive action into two distinct spheres: "normal constitutional conduct, inhabited by law, universal rules, and reasoned discourse; and a realm where universal rules are inadequate to meet the particular emergency situation and where law must be replaced by discretion and politics."[18] Here, once again, the building of a wall and the subsequent policing of the boundary it marks are central to sustaining the tenability of the distinction said to demarcate liberal political orders from those in which power, because unbounded, cannot be held to account.[19]

This distinction was elaborated by John Locke in his account of prerogative power, and that account was well-known to the framers of the U.S. Constitution. It suggests that under nonexceptional circumstances, executive power will respect the separation of powers, civil liberties, and the rule of law. However, under conditions of political emergency, which are most likely to arise in the context of international relations (which Locke distinguishes as the domain of the "federative power," although he effectively folds this domain into the executive branch), such respect will be supplanted by forms of extraconstitutional executive discretion, even, as Locke states, "without the prescription of law, and sometimes even against it."[20] As a rule, Locke believed that a desire for collective security will induce people to acquiesce in the executive's possession and exercise of prerogative power, and that acquiescence, understood as a form of tacit consent, suffices to render this power legitimate. At the same time, though, Locke insisted that a people is forever authorized to initiate a revolution aimed at restoring violated or purloined rights. Admittedly, given his contention that persons are more disposed to endure than to remedy governmental abuse,[21] this insistence may ring hollow.

That Locke does not in fact find it empty is largely an expression of his belief in the meaningfulness of the distinction between ordinary and extraordinary. The extraordinary form of power labeled prerogative, on Locke's account, does not fundamentally compromise or imperil the rule of law, and the commitment to popular sovereignty it expresses, because its exercise can be distinguished from everyday political life and confined to truly exceptional circumstances.

In the context of U.S. history, it was Thomas Jefferson who offered the most vigorous expression of Locke's insistence on the ultimate accountability of executive rule when exercised in the mode of prerogative power. In 1803, for example, Jefferson acknowledged that the Louisiana Purchase was extraconstitutional and, strictly speaking, illegal insofar as it was completed absent a "previous and special sanction by law."[22] However, and going beyond Locke's contention that popular acquiescence in the legitimacy of prerogative power should be presupposed unless it meets with express rejection, Jefferson insisted that each specific exercise of such power must secure express ex post facto legislative ratification. In the absence of such ratification, executive agents are subject to legal sanctions for violating the dictates of the law, no matter how noble their motivations might have been.

Arguably, the most significant challenge to the Jeffersonian understanding can be found in Abraham Lincoln's suspension of habeas corpus in 1861 (although one's understanding of that act depends in large measure on whether or not one thinks that in doing so Lincoln affirmed a doctrine of inherent constitutional powers, including emergency powers, which would then imply that actions taken in the name of necessity are constitutional and so do not require ex post facto ratification).[23] Less ambiguous harbingers of the growing irrelevance of liberalism's distinction between the everyday and the emergency can be located in the late nineteenth and early twentieth centuries. Consider, for example, Theodore Roosevelt's statement that, in responding to national crises, the president has the "legal right to do whatever the needs of the people demand, unless the Constitution or the laws explicitly forbid him to do it."[24] Still more pointedly, consider Franklin Roosevelt's claim that the economic crisis of the Great Depression created an emergency akin to that posed by an invading foreign power and that the powers granted by the Constitution may expand in order to deal with such a crisis. The

Supreme Court effectively granted this view its imprimatur, first, in 1934, when it applied the emergency powers doctrine to a situation outside the context of war[25] and, second, in 1936, when it stated that, in matters relating to national security, the president enjoys exclusive powers that extend beyond the specific affirmative grants found in the Constitution but are nonetheless inherent within it.[26]

These precedents notwithstanding, Scheppele is surely correct when she suggests that it was the Cold War era that initiated "an indefinite future of crises and a perpetual alteration of both separation of powers and individual rights. In short, the Cold War ushered in an era of 'permanent emergency' in which the constitutional sacrifices to be made were not clearly temporary or reversible."[27] Indeed, from the Great Depression through the Cold War, Congress passed no less than 470 statutes granting the executive discretionary authority to wield one power or another, ordinarily exercised by the legislature, in response to specific states of "national emergency." Many of these statutes, remaining in effect long after dissipation of the circumstances that initially prompted their passage, were subsequently trotted out by the executive for very different purposes (as when the Feed and Forage Act of 1861 was invoked as authorization for the allocation of funds to invade Cambodia in 1971). Congress imposed a nominal measure of restraint in 1976 when, in response to abuses of executive power, including the Watergate scandal, it passed the National Emergencies Act, terminating all existing states of emergency and requiring, among other restrictions, that the president report to Congress on emergency orders and expenditures. An additional layer of largely symbolic restraint was imposed the following year when Congress passed the International Emergency Economic Powers Act of 1977, which included an affirmation of Congress's authority to suspend any declared emergency by concurrent resolution but, at the same time, formally authorized the president to declare such emergencies in response to "any unusual and extraordinary threat, which has its source in whole or substantial part outside the United States, to the national security, foreign policy, or economy of the United States."[28] Reviewing presidential invocation of these statutes in order to impose trade, travel, and technology restrictions, adopt wage and salary controls, detain immigrants and refugees, deploy military personnel alongside civilian law enforcement officials engaged in the so-called war on drugs, and so forth, Lobel concludes that the success of congressional efforts to restrain executive emergency authority has proved "dismal. These statutes lie in shambles, wrecked by presidential defiance, congressional acquiescence and judicial undermining."[29]

To summarize, since the New Deal and, still more emphatically, the Cold War (but well before 9/11), the principal borders erected by liberalism in order to protect against unaccountable power, especially unchecked power exercised by the national executive, have eroded, if not collapsed outright. Also, and perhaps best illustrated by official establishment of the National Security Agency in 1954, disintegration of the spatial distinction between domestic and foreign as well as the temporal distinction between the ordinary and the emergency has generated not a political vacuum but a complex of recalcitrant bureaucratic institutions, whether as a result of broad delegations of power from Congress and/or sweeping executive reorganizations. The net result is the constitution of a security state that bears only passing resemblance to the liberal political order imagined by social contract theory.

How 9/11 Matters

A standard response of the political right to the developments traced in the previous section is to defend the accumulation of executive power in the name of national security; as a rule, though, this comes at the cost of jettisoning the commitment to accountability that is crucial to liberalism's tale of how power is transmuted into authority. A standard response of the left is to contest the aggrandizement of executive power by calling on liberalism's traditional mechanisms of accountability in the name of popular sovereignty; as a rule, though, this comes at the cost of failing to see that the border projects that once distinguished liberalism from other regime types are now incapacitated and, more likely than not, cannot be reconstructed.

Naming the regime we now inhabit is difficult. This regime, Wendy Brown explains,

is not fascism or totalitarian [the *Nation*'s claims to the contrary notwith-standing] as we have known them historically nor are these appellations likely to be most helpful in identifying or criticizing it. Rather, this is a political condition in which the substance of many of the significant features of constitutional and representative democracy have been gutted, jettisoned, or end-run, even as they continue to be promulgated ideologically, serving as a foil and shield for their undoing and for the doing of death elsewhere.[30]

As noted above, adopting Iris Young's terminology, I call this regime the "security state," and, in this section, I indicate the second Bush administration's participation in the constitution of that state.

The second Bush administration was heir, as well as an innovative contributor, to the developments tracked in the preceding section. The complicated relationship between past and present is perhaps best illustrated by this administration's recasting of the rule of law, which is itself one of the key means by which liberalism, historically, has aimed to erect a barrier against arbitrary power and so ensure power's accountability. Corresponding to the evaporation of the distinction between war and peace, exemplified by Vice President Richard B. Cheney's assertion that the struggle to defeat terror "may never end,"[31] we now witness dissolution of the distinction between ordinary legal rules and counterterrorism measures. In consequence, a not insignificant portion of the "ordinary" legal order has been refashioned to fit the exigencies of emergency.

In this section, I first cite several elements of the second Bush administration's policy and doctrine with respect to the realm labeled "foreign affairs" and then turn to the equally suspect realm labeled "domestic" affairs. In the former, the administration has sometimes sought to expand executive prerogative in the name of emergency but to do so under the cover provided by legislative authorization. Arguably, this is what transpired when the president sought and secured from Congress approval to use "all necessary and appropriate force" against those implicated in the 9/11 attacks and, later, to "defend the national security of the United States against the continuing threat posed by Iraq"[32] (although these resolutions may also and perhaps better be read as abdications of Congress's constitutional responsibility to determine whether and when the United States will go to war).

Alternatively, when the Bush administration found it politically expedient to secure authorization for executive prerogative in the form of standing law (as opposed to ad hoc authorizations), more often than not it sought to evade any significant restrictions on, and hence accountability for, the exercise of that power. Perhaps the most obvious example is the USA PATRIOT Act, which, among other things, expands the executive's authority to search, seize, and detain persons, thereby reducing the judiciary's authority to review and limit such actions; allows for greater sharing of information between intelligence and law enforcement agencies, thereby blurring the line between civilian and military rule; and expands the jurisdiction of the Foreign Intelligence Surveillance Act, thereby permitting the FBI to obtain secret warrants for intelligence gathering without observing the restrictions that apply to searches granted for ordinary law enforcement purposes. Four years after 9/11, following adoption of minor cosmetic modifications, both houses of Congress voted to extend indefinitely the provisions of the PATRIOT Act that were scheduled to expire, and in doing so, went a long way toward normalizing the exceptional. Such normalization expands its scope in yet another way, as the Justice Department employs the powers granted in the PATRIOT Act to prosecute criminal investigations that have little or no connection to terrorism, including cases dealing with white-collar crime, child pornography, and drug trafficking.

Importantly, the Bush administration made clear that it considered congressional authorization, whether in the form of resolutions or standing laws, a useful but not a necessary ingredient of the exercise of its power. This is perhaps best illustrated by the debates, immediately following 9/11, about how to deal with former members of the Taliban regime, members of Al Qaeda, and, more generally, those suspected of involvement in terrorism. Whereas some argued that these persons should be handled in accordance with a military model derived from the conventions of war, others argued that they should be handled in accordance with established judicial tribunals employing domestic criminal law. As Ruti Teitel notes, the Bush administration opted for neither of these two possibilities:

> The position that emerged is that the military appeared not to be accountable to the ordinary domestic legal regime, but neither was it subject to a general application of an international humanitarian realm. Whereas in ordinary times the military would have been fully subject to a juridical regime, what became apparent was the attempt to use September 11 as an occasion for an "extended" emergency and a state of exception regard-

ing the law. More and more, the administration called for law that was "exceptional." The claim was that because the United States was in an exceptional position, whatever related law was exceptional, and determining instances of departure, or exception, from law would be fully up to the administration.[33]

In order to see how, after 9/11, the traditional opposition between the rule of law and the rule of the exceptional became not a problematic dilemma within liberalism but a distinction without much of a difference, recall (1) the executive order of November 13, 2001, creating military tribunals whose procedures are bound neither by U.S. criminal law nor by the rules appropriate to the conduct of military courts martial, (2) invention of the category of "enemy combatant" in order to elude restrictions on the treatment to which prisoners of war are otherwise subject under the Geneva Conventions, and (3) the choice to define Guantánamo Bay as a site of detention, which, although entirely under the control of the U.S. government, is nonetheless deemed outside the boundaries of the United States and so exempt from the jurisdiction of its courts and hence any habeas petitions that might be filed therein.

These examples illustrate the second Bush administration's most pointed (but by no means unique or unprecedented) contribution to the constitution of the security state. All of these measures were taken in the name of an emergency in order to escape the forms of accountability imposed by conventional legal processes. Yet, at the same time, all were justified by the Bush administration through reference to the Constitution's grant of power to the president in his capacity as head of the executive branch and/or as commander in chief of the armed forces. Specifically, so the argument goes, because Article II does not expressly indicate what powers are granted to the executive branch, unless expressly forbidden by the Constitution, the executive's inherent powers exist without limit.[34] A grant of unlimited power can also be found in Article II's commander-in-chief clause, which authorizes the executive to initiate military action absent congressional authorization whenever there is a perceived threat to the nation's security.[35] Together, these positions add up to what Benjamin Wittes calls a creed of "Article II fundamentalism" whose essential tenet reduces to "the same basic position: Trust us."[36]

Granted, on rare occasions, the Supreme Court rebuked the president for overreaching, as it did in *Rasul v. Bush*, 124 S.Ct 2686 (2004), and, later, in *Hamdan v. Rumsfeld*, 126 S. Ct. 2749 (2006). And, on rare occasions, Congress reconfigured specific displays of executive prerogative, as when it passed the Military Commissions Act of 2006, which ignored most of the substantive constitutional concerns registered in *Hamdan* but furnished a veneer of legality to the tribunals created in late 2001. However, when located within the broader historical context elaborated in the previous section, and when considered in light of the Bush administration's contention, advanced in various signing statements, that it considers itself free to ignore challenges to its exceedingly broad reading of Article II, one would be hard pressed to represent the actions of the Court and Congress as a restoration of meaningful judicial oversight or a significant legislative contestation of rule by executive fiat.

Much the same blurring of the line between the rule of law and rule by executive discretion can be found on the field once designated as "domestic." Perhaps the most profound manifestation but also one of the most significant causes of this conflation is that consummate act of faux border fortification: establishment of the Department of Homeland Security. As Amy Kaplan has suggested, the founding of this bureaucratic behemoth, which merged twenty-two federal agencies into one, signifies disintegration of the very borders it is said to reinforce:

> The homeland is not like the home front for which war is a metaphor; homeland security depends on a radical insecurity where the home itself is the battleground. If every facet of civilian life is subject to terrorist attack, if a commercial airliner can be turned into a deadly bomb, then every facet of domestic life . . . must be both protected and mobilized against these threats. Homeland security calls for vast new intrusions of government, military, and intelligence forces not just to secure the homeland from external threats but also to become an integral part of the workings of home, which is in a continual state of emergency.[37]

On the domestic front, perhaps the most unsettling manifestation of the logic of homeland security is the post-9/11 detention on U.S. soil of foreign nationals and citizens alike, sometimes without charge, without a hearing, without access to a lawyer, and without judicial review. This practice becomes still more unsettling when one considers the parallels between it and the practice of extraordinary rendition, whereby foreign nationals, declared outside the protection of federal and international law, have been secretly seized and then removed to the prisons of governments not known for their observance of the niceties of due process. Much like the "ghost detainees" subject to extraordinary rendition, the very fact that those seized within the United States have themselves often been designated as "detainees," as opposed to "criminal suspects," has the effect of rendering them unclassifiable according to the conventional categories of law (although, once again, their detention is represented as a constitutional and so lawful expression of executive prerogative).

While the indefinite and incommunicado incarceration of suspected terrorists is perhaps an extreme symptom of the logic of homeland security, it is worth recalling that the treatment now often meted out to undocumented and/or illegal aliens residing within the territorial boundaries of the United States is not entirely dissimilar. The war on terror, note Christopher Eisgruber and Lawrence Sager, has "made hash" of the boundaries between domestic law and the international arena by "blend[ing] criminal law enforcement with immigration policy, foreign intelligence operations, and military force."[38] When immigration authorities are designated as administrative agents of the national security apparatus, when they are officially tasked with "eliminating vulnerabilities in the nation's border, and with economic, transportation and infrastructure security,"[39] when they are granted broad discretionary power to conduct proceedings in secret and to deport persons with minimal if any judicial oversight, it should come as no surprise that noncitizens as well are routinely denied the protections that liberalism traditionally afforded those charged with criminal offenses. In sum, within the borders of the United States (to the extent that this distinction retains any sense), we witness the creation of a vast army of unelected administrative agents whose discretionary rule, for the most part, is accountable to neither legislature nor court, complementing the hollowing out of congressional and judicial authority with respect to matters beyond the country's borders. (And if one were so inclined, one could readily extend this analysis to the status of welfare recipients as well.)

These examples suggest not the formation of an utterly lawless regime but, rather, within an order that continues to understand itself in terms of the categories provided by liberal contractarianism, the more insidious creation, multiplication, and institutionalization of what David Dyzenhaus calls "grey holes." Such holes are "spaces in which there are some legal constraints on executive action . . . but the constraints are so insubstantial that they pretty well permit government to do as it pleases."[40] As such, they are more harmful to the rule of law than are outright dictatorial usurpations, first, because the provision of limited procedural protections masks the absence of any real constraint on executive power and, second, because location of the authority to create such spaces within the Constitution implies that, in the last analysis, they bear ex ante authorization by the people. When created, in other words, they may receive but do not require ratification, whether by Congress or by those whom its members are said to represent. What this means in effect is that the second Bush administration dispensed with Jefferson's stipulation that extraconstitutional executive acts (or, rather, acts that Jefferson deemed to be outside those constitutionally permitted) require ex post facto ratification and with Locke's contention that, however unlikely, at least in principle, specific exercises of extralegal prerogative power (or, rather, acts that Locke deemed to be outside those legally permitted) are properly subject to revolutionary rejection. What one finds in the second Bush administration, then, is a denial of both models of accountability combined with an aggressive commitment to the constitution of a security state that is liberal only in name. As it extends its reach, perfection of that state renders the prospect of popular repudiation of prerogative power ever more chimerical, and, indeed, such perfection renders recognition of the problematic character of the exercise of such power ever less likely.

Disavowing Accountability under the Security State

The security state is not readily understood in terms of liberalism's commitment to the rule of law or in terms of the social contractarianism that represents such rule as an articulation of popular sovereignty. In its ideal typical form, this is a state in which formal governmental institutions are dominated by the imperatives of executive prerogative justified in the name of national security and in which the domain of law is ever more completely colonized by the imperatives of emergency decree and administrative discretion. To share in the exercise of political power within this regime is, in large measure, to partake in the spectacle of state power in its more brutal forms, as when Americans were invited to become vicarious participants in the "shock and awe" aerial bombardment campaign that toppled the regime of Saddam Hussein or, alternatively, as Donald Pease has suggested, when the current administration "encouraged the formation of a society of captivated spectators who agreed to the abridgement of their civil liberties in exchange for the spectacle" of detainees "disappearing into the maze of an unaccountable juridical system,"[41] whether at Guantánamo, within the United States, or inside secret CIA prisons in Eastern Europe.

The authority of the security state mimics that of its liberal counterpart insofar as it is predicated on a kind of tacit consent on the part of the governed. Specifically, as Iris Young argues, the security state is based on a "bargain." The content of this bargain, though, is unlike that offered by classical liberalism as the formal ground of governmental authority and, so, accountability. In a nutshell, that content reduces to the following: "obey our commands and support our security actions, and we will ensure your protection."[42] This bargain differs from that imagined by Locke (although it is not altogether unlike that imagined by Thomas Hobbes) to the extent that it is rooted not in a collective obligation grounded in a rational act of mutual promise making but, rather, in the interlocking passions of fear and desire. Such fear is not entirely without foundation, but, to a considerable degree, it is a passion manufactured by mass media that profit from obsessive speculation regarding possible future attacks, no matter how statistically slight their concrete probability, and by politicians whose election and reelection are contingent on fear's chronic cultivation: "Public leaders invoke fear," explains Young, "then they promise to keep those living under them safe. Because we are afraid, and our fears are stirred by what we see on television or read in the newspaper, we are grateful to the leaders and officers who say that they will shoulder the risk in order to protect us."[43] Such fear is also bound up with the incitement of desire, for, anxiously, sometimes desperately, we seek the reassurance offered via this bargain. As such, this "contract" positions those who "agree" to its terms as those who need something they do not currently have but which others have promised to provide in return for acquiescence.

The bargain at the heart of the security state also differs from its traditional counterpart insofar as it dispenses with the two features, equality and freedom, that Locke stipulates as indispensable preconditions of participation in the social contract. Democratic equality, argues Young, is not a matter of equal power per se but of equal right and responsibility to participate in making the political judgments that shape the exercise of collective power; absent that premise, it makes little sense to render those entrusted with positions of governmental power accountable to those in whose name it is exerted. "Institutions of due process, public procedure and record, organized opposition and criticism, and public review both enact and recognize such equal citizenship."[44] Granted, the fear engendered by terrorism is peculiarly egalitarian in the sense that few consider themselves entirely immune to its random threats. That said, approbation of the ruled within the security state takes the form of gratitude on the part of those who have been positioned as more or less helpless dependents, as something akin to women and/or children under the care of a (male) protector, and, if that is so, the contract of the security state cannot be imagined as a bargain among those who are equal, let alone among those who are in a position to reclaim their equality should they one day conclude that this deal is not all it is cracked up to be.

Nor can this deal be imagined as a bargain among those who are free. Hobbes notwithstanding, it cannot be said that those who elect to enter into this bargain because they fear violent death, or because they feel perpetually vulnerable to unseen dangers, are free. Or, more precisely, they cannot be said to be free in the sense required by liberal theory if this theory is to sustain the claim that entry into the contract generates political obligation because the participants are "free," where this term means something akin to "capable of autonomous choice." A fearful, infantilized subject, one who renders obedience in order to ensure protection from an executive masquerading as a father, is no more capable of meaningful consent than is a child. The language appropriate to such a relationship is closer to that of domination and subordination. Granted, this is not a form of subordination, which, like torture, eliminates all agency and possibility for meaningful consent by reducing what was once a human being to a body in pain, but neither is it a form of rule that is reasonably understood in terms of popular sovereignty and collective accountability for governmental conduct.

Nor, finally, is it apparent in what sense the regime created by this bargain is democratic, for its perpetuation can tolerate little dissent from the rule of those who promise security. Here, Young's analogy of a woman who participates in the "logic of masculinist protection" is instructive:

> In return for male protection, the woman concedes critical distance from decision-making autonomy. When the household lives under a threat, there cannot be divided wills and arguments about who will do what, or what is the best course of action. The head of the household should decide what measures are necessary for the security of the people and property, and he gives the orders that they must follow if they and their relations are to remain safe. . . . Feminine subordination, in this logic, does not constitute submission to a violent and overbearing bully. The feminine woman, rather, on this construction, adores her protector and happily defers to his judgment in return for the promise of security that he offers.[45]

Because it threatens the raison d'être of the state, dissent must be deemed a dangerous anachronism, the practice of which imperils everyone. This understanding, as noted earlier, warrants unauthorized surveillance of domestic groups that question governmental policy; indefinite detention of immigrants, documented and undocumented; and vitiation of those branches of government that seek to contest or oversee the prerogatives, punishments, and preemptive strikes of a militarized executive claiming to safeguard its charges from diabolical aggressors who lurk everywhere. Internal division, in short, is equated with weakness; civic participation, except in certain highly ritualized modes, with a threat to order; and citizenship with endorsement, or at least passive acceptance, of the suspension of civil liberties required by a perpetual state of normalized emergency.

If this characterization of the security state is apt, what are its implications for the question of accountability, for example, for the atrocities committed at Abu Ghraib? As noted at this chapter's outset, efforts to limit culpability to those most immediately implicated, whether that be U.S. military personnel on the ground or, more broadly, their superiors in the Pentagon and/or the White House, are predicated on an attenuated form of methodological individualism that aids and abets the antipolitical bent of much liberal legalism. As also noted, critics of the Bush administration (e.g., Danner) have sometimes sought to move beyond such parochial implications by ascribing accountability to all Americans. Although this move is appealing, both because it counters the mendacity of the second Bush administration and because it reanimates the satisfying liberal confessionals that became so fashionable in the late 1960s and 1970s, under present circumstances, this temptation is to be resisted.

Appeals of the sort made by Danner foster and prop up a mythological conception of popular sovereignty and so occlude the regime change we now confront. Within the context of the contemporary security state, when it is said that torture is committed "in our name," it is no longer clear in what sense "we" may be said to be authors of that abuse. Indeed, I would argue that such invocations of collective identity may be read as performative utterances that help call into being and constitute the foundational entity, which they then claim to designate. In other words, when such invocations are advanced, the sovereign people is fictitiously called into being by an ever more groundless appeal that constitutes "us" as the collective author of abuse perpetrated by agents and agencies of executive power. This mode of address involves little more than a reification of and transfer to "the people" of the characteristics said to define the sovereign and neatly bounded individual presupposed by the liberal legal order, which, in turn, furnishes the conceptual foundation for determinations of liability within the context of criminal law. Once "the people" have been invested with comparable autonomy and determinate boundaries as a result of such invocation, they can then be held similarly liable for acts of torture committed in their name. Methodological individualism, however, is a bad premise for thinking about specifically political accountability, whether ascribed to particular legal subjects or to those subjects who, considered as a collectivity, are seen as a popular sovereign.

Especially when such invocations are joined to calls to hold Rumsfeld and his ilk legally liable for the deeds of those they ultimately command, whether via conventional modalities of political accountability such as elections or less conventional forms such as impeachment proceedings, this mode of address facilitates an understanding of the sovereign people as a body whose freely given consent is articulated in the form of law duly enacted by its elected representatives acting within the confines of limited government. That, of course, cloaks the transformations noted in the previous two sections and, in particular, the displacement of such law, on the one hand, by the discretionary rule of the petty sovereigns that now administer homeland security policy and, on the other hand, by the proliferation of gray holes that enables circumvention of all but the most modest forms of oversight exercised by representative institutions and the courts. In short, such invocations of collective accountability help manufacture the sort of popular sovereign, the "we," that is required in order to sustain the apparent legitimacy of a regime that now bears little resemblance to that imagined by classical social contract theory, and this in turn cannot help but play into the hands of those interested in masking the machinations of executive prerogative.

This "we," moreover, is composed of persons who, in order to acknowledge their shared accountability, must regard themselves as specifically public beings—that is, they must define themselves as citizens who set aside their "private" selves so that they may acknowledge that what they possess in common (i.e., their mutual culpability) is of greater salience to their identities than those dimensions (e.g., race, class, gender, and life prospects more generally) that divide them from one another. Such invocations, in other words, facilitate the constitution of the nation-state as a homogeneous unity, and that superimposed identity glosses over the fact that some of "us" are immigrants whose access to legal protections is tenuous at best, while others can readily afford the benefits that accompany full citizenship; some draw material benefit from the constitution of the security state, while others are asked to endure the indignities and sacrifices necessary to its perpetuation; and some, by virtue of surname alone, are perpetual suspects, while those more fortunate are unlikely to be detained at the border or listed on the federal government's no-fly list.

Correlatively, uncritical deployment of the term "we" constructs the political community as a self-contained unit, which in turn facilitates the illusion of national unity that is crucial to mobilization of popular support for the "war on terror." The sine qua non of the security state's success, Young argues, is maintenance of unity within the body politic: "We affirm our oneness with our fellow citizens and together affirm our single will behind the will of the leaders who have vowed to protect us."[46] Claims that reinforce the construction of 9/11 as an attack upon a state and its people (rather than, say, as a crime against humanity) call into being an even more politically pernicious "them," and, in order to perfect this rhetorical binary, the second Bush administration required no additional assistance. Such claims, moreover, foster the sort of collective identity that, in pitting one state against another, invites (but does not necessitate) military responses in the name of national security. Therefore, however unwittingly, when the left affirms collective accountability for Abu Ghraib and like crimes, it proves complicitous in perpetuating the very regime it seeks to criticize.

From Liberal Guilt to Complicitous Accountability

If what happened at Abu Ghraib is ultimately a manifestation of unaccountable prerogative power, and if invocations of "our" collective accountability for the abuses committed there rest on a tissue of illusions, and if uncritical affirmation of these illusions helps prop up the regime that made these atrocities possible in the first place, then, surely, it is tempting to wash our hands of the whole business. But this, too, is a temptation to be resisted. A wholesale renunciation of accountability is even more unpolitical than is its confinement to those deemed legally liable or, alternatively, its ascription to an undifferentiated "we" bounded by the confines of the nation-state. In this brief conclusion, therefore, I urge that "we" do indeed repudiate "our" responsibility for Abu Ghraib, as that claim is framed in the terms of social contract theory, but that we do so in the name of democratic principles that are not and perhaps cannot be realized within the present regime. Or, to put this differently, I propose that we ask how such principles might be affirmed in opposition to the contemporary security state and, more particularly, its aggrandizement of modalities of power, which, ungrounded and unrestrained, can tender no credible claim to legitimacy.

In suggesting this course, I do not mean to urge categorical abandonment of the mechanisms of liberal legal accountability, although this, too, is tempting. Yet I do mean to remind us that because deployment of these mechanisms comes at a steep price, careful strategic calculations are in order before they are enlisted in any particular instance. As noted earlier, these mechanisms lend themselves to scapegoating of the most easily targeted; they share the pinched historical orientation of liberal legalism and so do little to illuminate what might be done to reduce the likelihood of such abuses in the future; they encourage belief in the myth of power's accountability; and, finally, they are of limited efficacy when, as a rule, Congress is cowed into acquiescence by, and the federal courts are pawns of, an executive whose rule is ever more predicated on assertions of secrecy and privilege.

Most important, though, reliance on these mechanisms fails to capture the kernel of truth implicit in the title of Danner's op-ed. Specifically, they fail to grasp the sense in which even if Graner, Rumsfeld, and their like were to be found guilty and then punished, no matter how satisfying that might be, the rest of "us" would not thereby be entirely absolved. To see why that is so, the conventional mechanisms of liberal legal liability need to be supplemented by a specifically political understanding of accountability, and if that understanding is not to bolster the regime it seeks to contest, it must cut itself loose from key premises of the social contractarianism implicit in Danner's remarks. In order to hint at the contours of such an understanding, in this context, I will confine myself to two of the departures it requires.

First, this understanding cannot be predicated on the autonomous agents that classical social contract theory imagines as denizens of the state of nature, nor can it be predicated on the conception of consent that derives from that hypothetical, which, in turn, sustains an anachronistic understanding of popular sovereignty. If we are to facilitate these presuppositional shifts, I suggest that, borrowing a phrase from Christopher Kutz, we adopt the terminology of "complicitous accountability."[47] This phrase is not to be confused with the liberal legal doctrine of complicity, which holds that an individual can be held culpable for another's crime if he or she intentionally encourages or aids the second in the commission of that crime and, in consequence, can be charged with "derivative" or "accomplice" liability. True, the idea of complicitous accountability bears connotations of abetment and even collusion in wrongdoing, but it is not meant to imply that the intent of the complier is identical to either that of the wrongdoers in question (e.g., Graner) or that of those officials who arguably authorized its performance (e.g., Rumsfeld). Nor is it intended to imply that the accountability of those who engaged in such deeds, or those who authorized them, is coextensive with those who have but a modest capacity to reshape the existing regime.

Instead, and appropriating a central notion advanced by much feminist theory, complicitous accountability is predicated on a relational understanding of conduct, one that reminds us that human action is always implicated with as well as conditioned by the actions of others. This understanding invokes the etymology of this term (*com* = with + *plico* = to fold), which suggests that actions are invariably enfolded together, spatially and temporally, in ways that are beyond anyone's full comprehension and control. Accountability predicated on an acknowledgment of complicity is not assumed as a result of voluntary choice or deliberate endorsement. Instead, as a consequence of joint enmeshment in complex and historically specific constellations of power relations, such co-implication is for the most part a fruit of habitual submission to the current order of things. In the security state, as Young reminds us, that submission is often rooted in fear and, more specifically, a desire to be shielded from harm. No matter how understandable, though, such acquiescence reproduces the current order of things, and so it is not entirely without reason that we sometimes feel ashamed by the conduct of those who have acted "in our name." Yet that shame will prove of little moment unless it advances from the personal to the political and, more specifically, unless it gives rise to shared outrage at institutions and exercises of unaccountable power that implicate everyday conduct in profoundly antidemocratic policies and practices.

This brings me to the second point of departure from social contractarianism. A key element of the transition from personal to political involves recognizing that just as the notion of complicitous accountability calls into question the sovereign individual presupposed by liberal legalism, so, too, does it call into question the sovereign state that is its counterpart. Complicitous accountability's subjects, qua states, are constituted by a web of global, national, and regional interactions such that, almost invariably, actions in any single one will have consequences for others and vice versa. Because it acknowledges the confusion of the boundaries (e.g., between domestic and foreign) that once made liberalism a reasonably serviceable doctrine, the category of complicitous accountability renders problematic any effort to confine responsibility within the borders of the nation-state. As such, this category contests Danner's claim that Graner and his cohorts, or Rumsfeld and his cronies, acted in the name of some foundational community and, more particularly, in the name of a neatly circumscribed citizenry in its capacity as popular sovereign. True, these boundaries are neither irrelevant nor altogether porous, as reflection on the mammoth military resources that can be deployed by the

U.S. government reminds us, nor can they be considered exhaustive of any determination of complicitous accountability. If, as Young suggests, "responsibility in relation to injustice . . . derives not from living under a common constitution, but rather from participation in the diverse institutional processes that produce structural injustice,"[48] there is no good reason to assume that the borders of accountability will map neatly onto those specified on political maps. By the same token, and as indicated by the participation of private contractors in the interrogation of prisoners at Abu Ghraib, the construction of for-profit corporate prisons in the United States, and, more generally, the decentering (but not the decentralization) of political power, there is no good reason to assume that the borders of accountability will map neatly onto liberalism's traditional divide between state and civil society.[49]

There is nothing inherently or necessarily democratic about this understanding of complicitous accountability. At most, I can claim that it evades certain of the antipolitical pitfalls of an understanding based in social contractarianism, as I have just suggested, and that it opens up avenues of inquiry effectively foreclosed by liberal legalism. For example, the liberal doctrine of criminal complicity is defined primarily by a backward temporal orientation insofar as its aim is to assign blame, comprehended as guilt, for already accomplished deeds and then assign appropriate punishments. By way of contrast, the notion of complicitous accountability is more ambiguous in its temporal orientation. It involves an acknowledgment of participation in the relations of power that sometimes generate atrocities like those committed at Abu Ghraib, but it also involves an appreciation of the reach of those relations into an uncertain future for which we cannot help but bear some measure of responsibility.

In addition, whereas the liberal legal doctrine of accountability, when extended to a people, performatively participates in reifying a false universal, the notion of complicitous accountability reminds us that implication in power is never symmetrical. Or, rather, co-implication in the processes that generate injustices, structural as well as particular, is never distributed equally but varies in terms of position, privilege, and power, and so the opportunity and capacity to reshape relational entanglements. This recognition offers absolution to no one, but it does remind us that judgments of accountability can never be made apart from inquiry into the institutionalized inequalities that define the contemporary security state and the political economy in which it is thoroughly invested.

Finally, the notion of complicitous accountability reminds us that for inhabitants of the contemporary security state, at present, perhaps the best bet is to refuse the seductive but politically ineffectual temptations of liberal guilt (but without denying "our" inescapable implication in evil); to reveal the mythological character of claims of accountability, when formulated in the discourse of liberal contractarianism; and to do so in the aspirational name of democratic norms that at present appear real only in the breach; and, when openings avail themselves, to affirm a shared responsibility to refashion the relations of power, which, although differentially constituting everyone as a subject, leave no one innocent.

NOTES

1   Mark Danner, "We Are All Torturers Now," *New York Times*, January 6, 2005, section A, late edition. See, in much the same vein, Frank Rich, "The 'Good Germans' Among Us," *New York Times*, October 14, 2007, section 4, late edition, in which Rich condemns what he calls "Gestapo tactics" employed by U.S. forces in Iraq and writes: "But we must also examine our own responsibility for the hideous acts committed in our name." For a scholarly argument that presupposes much the same understanding of collective accountability, see Sanford Levinson, "Contemplating Torture," in *Torture* (New York: Oxford University Press, 2004), 23–43, as well as the concluding section of this chapter, "From Liberal Guilt to Complicitous Accountability."

2   George W. Bush, "President Outlines Steps to Help Iraq Achieve Democracy and Freedom," October 24, 2004, http://www.whitehouse.gov/news/releases/2004/05/20040524-10.html (accessed October 3, 2007).

3   "Article 15-6 Investigation of the 800th Military Police Brigade," in *The Torture Papers: The Road to Abu Ghraib*, ed. Karen J. Greenberg and Joshua L. Dratel (New York: Cambridge University Press, 2005), 448–49.

4   As of March 2006, ten enlisted soldiers and noncommissioned officers had been prosecuted and convicted in the Abu Ghraib affair. Their punishments, for offenses including dereliction of duty, maltreating prisoners, assault, battery, indecent acts, and conspiracy, ranged from demotion to imprisonment for ten years. See Eric Schmitt, "Iraq Abuse Trial Is Again

Limited to Lower Ranks," *New York Times*, March 23, 2006, section A, late edition. In addition, as of August 2007, the only commanding officer who had stood trial on charges related to the Abu Ghraib scandal was acquitted of all charges except that of disobeying an order to refrain from discussing his case. See Paul von Zielbauer, "Army Colonel Is Acquitted in Abu Ghraib Abuse Case," *New York Times*, August 29, 2007, section A, late edition.

5   The consolidated and amended complaint filed by the American Civil Liberties Union and Human Rights First is available at http://www.aclu. org/images/general/asset_upload_file600_23378.pdf (accessed October 2, 2007).

6   Citing *Bivens v. Six Unknown Named Agents of Federal Bureau of Narcotics*, 403 U.S. 388 (1971), *Ali* argued that the plaintiffs were entitled to compensatory damages for the harms they had suffered.

7   *In re: Iraq and Afghanistan Detainees Litigation*, 479 F. Supp. 2d 85 (2007).

8   Elizabeth Holtzman, "Torture and Accountability," *Nation* 281, no. 3 (July 18, 2005): 20, 24.

9   "Torture and Democracy," *Nation* 279, no. 1 (July 5, 2004): 4.

10   Hannah Arendt, "Collective Responsibility," in *Responsibility and Judgment*, ed. Jerome Kohn (New York: Schocken Books, 2003), 147.

11   Ibid., 148.

12   Iris Marion Young, "The Logic of Masculinist Protection: Reflections on the Current Security State," *Signs* 29, no. 3 (Autumn 2003): 1–25.

13   George W. Bush, "President Bush's Address on Terrorism before a Joint Meeting of Congress," *New York Times*, September 21, 2001, section B, late edition; and Anthony Lewis, "A Different World," *New York Times*, September 12, 2001, section A, late edition.

14   Sheldon Wolin, "Collective Identity and Constitutional Power," in *The Presence of the Past* (Baltimore, Md.: Johns Hopkins University Press, 1989), 22.

15   Ibid., 24.

16   Kim Scheppele, "Law in a Time of Emergency: States of Exception and the Temptation of 9/11," *University of Pennsylvania Journal of Constitutional Law* 6 (May 2004): 1020, 1022.

17   Daniel Yergin, *Shattered Peace: The Origins of the Cold War and the National Security State* (Boston: Houghton Mifflin, 1977), 198, quoted in Scheppele, "Law in a Time of Emergency," 1016–17.

18   Jules Lobel, "Emergency Powers and the Decline of Liberalism," *Yale Law Journal* 98 (May 1989): 1390.

19   For an indication of the enormous body of literature on this question, see the bibliography in Oren Gross and Fionnuala Ní Aoláin, *Law in Times of Crisis* (Cambridge: Cambridge University Press, 2006). See also chapters 1–3 for an account of the principal models that have been offered in

response to the dilemma posed by unconstrained executive authority in times of emergency.

20   John Locke, *Two Treatises on Government,* ed. Peter Laslett (New York: Cambridge University Press, 1965), 375. For a discussion of whether Locke's doctrine of prerogative power is or is not intended to sanction extraconstitutional exercises of power (when the term "constitution" references a form of higher law that is popularly authorized even though it is more encompassing than formally enacted law), see Gross and Aoláin, *Law in Times of Crisis,* 122–23. For present purposes, I accept their claim that, on balance, Locke suggests "that the prerogative power ought to be recognized for what it is, namely an extra-constitutional and extra-legal power" (122).

21   Locke, *Two Treatises on Government,* 380.

22   Thomas Jefferson, quoted in Lobel, "Emergency Powers," 1393.

23   See Gross and Aoláin, *Law in Times of Crisis,* 48–50, 128–29, for an elaboration of the controversy regarding how best to understand Lincoln's suspension of habeas corpus.

24   Theodore Roosevelt, quoted in Lobel, "Emergency Powers," 1399.

25   *Home Building & Loan Assn. v. Blaisdell,* 290 U.S. 398 (1934).

26   *United States v. Curtiss-Wright Export Corp.,* 299 U.S. 304 (1936).

27   Scheppele, "Law in a Time of Emergency," 1015.

28   International Emergency Economic Powers Act, Pub. L. No. 95-223, 201-8, 91 Stat. 1625, 1626-29 (1977) (codified as amended at 50 U.S.C. 1621 [1994], 1701-7).

29   Lobel, "Emergency Powers," 1414.

30   Wendy Brown, "Neo-liberalism and the End of Liberal Democracy," *Theory & Event* 7, no. 1 (2003).

31   Bob Woodward, "Cheney Says War against Terror 'May Never End,'" *Washington Post,* October 21, 2001, section A, final edition.

32   See "Authorization for Use of Military Force," Public Law 107-40 (September 18, 2001), and "Joint Resolution to Authorize the Use of United States Armed Forces against Iraq," Public Law 107-243 (October 10, 2002).

33   Ruti Teitel, "Empire's Law: Foreign Relations by Presidential Fiat," in *September 11 in History,* ed. Mary Dudziak (Durham, N.C.: Duke University Press, 2003), 197.

34   See, for example, the president's military order of November 13, 2001, "Detention, Treatment, and Trial of Certain Non-citizens in the War against Terrorism," in *Torture and Truth: America, Abu Ghraib, and the War on Terror,* ed. Mark Danner (New York: New York Review of Books, 2004), 78–82.

35   See, for example, the 2002 advisory memo issued by Assistant Attorney General Jay Bybee, in the Office of Legal Counsel, which includes the

following claim: "Congress lacks authority under Article I to set the terms and conditions under which the President may exercise his authority as Commander-in-Chief to control the conduct of operations during a war." Jay Bybee, "Re: Standards of Conduct for Interrogation under 18 U.S.C. §§ 2340-2340A (August 1, 2002)," in *The Torture Papers*, ed. Greenberg and Dratel, 203.

36 Benjamin Wittes, "Checks, Balances, and Wartime Detainees," *Policy Review* 130 (April and May 2005): 14.

37 Amy Kaplan, "Homeland Insecurities: Transformations of Language and Space," in *September 11 in History*, ed. Dudziak, 64.

38 Christopher Eisgruber and Lawrence Sager, "Civil Liberties in the Dragons' Domain: Negotiating the Blurred Boundary between Domestic Law and Foreign Affairs after 9/11," in *September 11 in History*, ed. Dudziak, 163.

39 "ICE Operations," U.S. Customs and Immigration Enforcement, http://www.ice.gov/about/operations.htm (accessed October 31, 2007).

40 David Dyzenhaus, "Schmitt v. Dicey: Are States of Emergency Inside or Outside the Legal Order?" *Cardozo Law Review* 27 (March 2006): 2005–39. Because these holes are gray rather than black, I believe it is too simple to claim, as does Judith Butler in "Indefinite Detention," *Precarious Life: Powers of Mourning and Violence* (London: Verso, 2004), that we now live in a regime governed by "a form of power that is fundamentally lawless, and whose lawlessness can be found in the way in which law itself is fabricated or suspended at the will of a designated subject" (95).

41 Donald Pease, "The Global Homeland State: Bush's Biopolitical Statement," *Boundary* 2 30, no. 3 (2003): 17.

42 Young, "The Logic of Masculinist Protection," 3.

43 Ibid., 13.

44 Ibid., 16.

45 Ibid., 5.

46 Ibid., 9.

47 Christopher Kurtz, *Complicity: Ethics and Law for a Collective Age* (Cambridge: Cambridge University Press, 2000), 11.

48 Iris Marion Young, "Responsibility, Social Connection, and Global Labor Justice," in *Global Challenges* (Cambridge: Polity Press, 2007), 175–76.

49 With this claim, however obliquely, I mean to signify my recognition that mechanisms of "disciplinary" and "bio-political" power, to cite two of Foucault's central categories, now blur liberalism's border between public and private. More generally, the situation of the security state on the more comprehensive field Foucault calls "governmentality" enormously complicates the questions of accountability posed in this essay.

4

DYING IS NOT PERMITTED

Sovereignty, Biopower, and Force-Feeding at Guantánamo Bay

Lauren Wilcox

n the U.S. naval base at Guantánamo Bay, Cuba, prisoners captured in Afghanistan and around the world are held in indefinite detention without a juridical decision as to their guilt or innocence. Since the time the detention center opened in July 2002, 775 prisoners have been brought to Guantánamo Bay, and around 175 remain in January 2011. They have been subjected to techniques that the George W. Bush administration referred to as "enhanced interrogation techniques" but that fit the legal definition of torture. As a protest against their treatment and detention, as many as 200 prisoners have undertaken hunger strikes. One hunger striker, Binyam Mohamed, said to his lawyer, "I do not plan to stop until I die or we are respected."[1] In response, military officials have opted to force-feed these prisoners by inserting tubes into their stomachs through their nasal passages while restraining them. Defending this practice, military physician John Edmonson asserted, "I will not allow them to do harm to themselves."[2]

Hunger strikes have occurred at Guantánamo from the time the detention center opened. In June 2005, hunger strikes reached a peak, when between 130 to 200 out of approximately 500 prisoners at Guantánamo Bay began hunger strikes. The *New York Times* has reported that at least 12 prisoners have been subjected to force-feeding, while lawyers say the prisoners have reported 40 or more.[3] In January 2009, the *Times* of London reported that 44 out of the 248 inmates were refusing food (though visiting lawyers reported that more than 70 were on hunger strikes).[4] These strikes take place in the context of practices that are widely considered to constitute torture, such as sleep deprivation, humiliation, and the use of stress positions. While the Bush administration consistently denied that these abuses were in fact "torture," a senior official admitted that torture was indeed practiced at Guantánamo Bay in January 2009.[5] Six high-ranking members of the Bush administration are now under indictment in Spain for torture of detainees,[6] and the Obama administration is currently weighing what, if any, accountability there will be for torture as well as how best to close the Guantánamo Bay facility while still preserving its functions of gathering information on terrorist activities and preventing dangerous persons from entering the United States.

The simultaneous torture and force-feeding of hunger-striking prisoners points to the exercise of two distinct logics of power: sovereign power and biopower. By being tortured, the prisoners are objects of the sovereign's ability to act directly on their bodies or, in Michel Foucault's terms, to "take life or let live." However, the deaths of the detainees pose a limit for the exercise of sovereign power—simply put, they cannot be killed. Rather, the health of prisoners is closely monitored by medical professionals, and hunger-striking prisoners are force-fed in order to prevent their deaths, evidence of what Foucault calls the exercise of "biopower"—a technology of power that can, in Foucault's terms, "let die" and "make live" through the management of biological life and populations.[7] This entwinement of military and medical discourses forces the prisoners to live as a particular type of subject. In other words, through the conjunction of torture and force-feeding, the prisoners' bodies are made into not only "useful bodies" for providing intelligence but "dependent bodies" that are not autonomous agents but recipients of care that must be efficiently managed.

In the context of the war on terror, torture has been assessed in terms of its usefulness in providing citizens with short-term as well as long-term protection.[8] Torture is also justified by the crimes and identities of the

terrorists—they are the "worst of the worst."[9] These two logics are contradictory, because the security rationale for torturing prisoners does not
require the prisoner to be guilty of any crimes, only to have knowledge
that could be used to save lives. In academic as well as policy debates,
the hypothetical ticking-time-bomb scenario has structured the ethical
question of torture in the war on terror; assuming that the guilty captive
has the necessary knowledge, this scenario asks whether torture should
be authorized in order to prevent the deaths of dozens or hundreds
of civilians (people who are presumed innocent, just as the captive is
presumed guilty). The ticking-time-bomb scenario also assumes that the
torture will work, that causing the captive bodily pain will yield "actionable intelligence." The body of the prisoner is thus produced as a site of
information to be gleaned in the most efficient way possible as well as a
site for the exercise of sovereign power, the power to punish. But while
the bodies of prisoners may be subject to violence for the extraction of
information, they are also objects of care for the preservation of their
useful lives.

Forcing hunger-striking prisoners to live does more than breach the
state's moral obligation not to torture: torture and force-feeding serve
to enact U.S. sovereign power while displacing vulnerability onto the
individual subjectivity of the prisoners. Held in a legal and territorial
gap and subject to torture for an indefinite period of time, the prisoners'
existence is defined by an array of technologies that refuse them even the
choice to die in order to end their endless imprisonment. The exercise
of torture at Guantánamo Bay and elsewhere by U.S. officials is not an
instance of sovereign power exercised on a juridical subject, as portrayed
in Foucault's *Discipline and Punish*, but is rather a moment in the exercise
of sovereign power though biopolitics on subjects produced not as liberal
subjects of consent, nor economic subjects of rationality, but as a quasi-
population of dependents who must be managed. In these cases, violence
is best understood as *expressive*: the violence serves to create and reinforce
subjectivities and relations of power between the U.S. military and the
prisoners through the exercise of sovereign power on the bodies of prisoners. These uses of violence are expressive precisely because they enact
and express U.S. sovereignty while undoing the individual subjectivity of
prisoners who are held indefinitely. The use of torture and force-feeding
expresses the troubled, uneasy relationship of sovereign power and bio-

power and highlights the sociality of violence as effecting the production of "worlds" or the possibilities of existence as a human subject.

In developing this argument, I first discuss the motivations for the use of torture in terms of Foucault's categories of sovereign power, discipline, and biopower in order to articulate the paradox of applying violence through torture while maintaining the health of prisoners, including force-feeding hunger strikers. I then demonstrate how the exercise of sovereign power through torture meets with anxieties over injuring and killing the human body. In the final section, I discuss how anxieties that constitute the paradox of sovereign power and biopower are manifested in the force-feeding of hunger-striking prisoners, an exercise of power that transforms prisoners from dangerous "enemy combatants" to a biopolitical subjectivity as recipients of care.

Torture as Sovereignty, Discipline, and Biopower

Why has the United States resorted to torture in its war on terror? Torture is something that liberal political communities are supposed to have left behind in their premodern pasts, rejected as an abuse of state power against vulnerable people. For Foucault, torture exemplifies sovereign power in the classical period. Torture was used ritually to extract confessions and punish criminals. If sovereign power is the power to "take life or let live,"[10] then the sovereign uses torture to punish in self-defense, and as such, the tortured body represents an enemy of the sovereign rather than a citizen. Torture marked the body directly and thus performatively established the power of the sovereign.

But in the war on terror, torture and indefinite detention in Guantánamo Bay take place not as part of a juridical discourse of truth and guilt but rather as a means for gathering ostensibly life-saving information and to quarantine dangerous subjects apart from the U.S. population. While the use of torture in the detention camps at Guantánamo Bay at first glance appears to resemble the tactics of disciplinary power, torture in this context is more consistent with the exercise of sovereign power through biopolitics. The bodies of the prisoners at Guantánamo Bay, though subject to torture, cannot legitimately be killed.[11] Torture demonstrates a contradiction in the exercise of biopower and sovereign power: while sovereign power names the power to "take life or let live," and biopower names the power to "make live and let die,"[12] the simultaneous exercise of torture and force-feeding at Guantánamo Bay indicates the exercise of power that not only injures the body but refuses to kill or allow the death of the tortured body. In order to explain the contradictions of sovereign power and biopower in the exercise of torture at Guantánamo Bay, I first argue that discipline, while seemingly apparent in the prison setting, is not the primary logic of power operating. Rather, the logic of torture is biopolitical, meant to protect one population at the expense of a "risky" population. However, this explanation, too, is insufficient to account for the operation of Guantánamo Bay. Torture in this case is a practice of sovereign power, exercised through biopolitical techniques.

Insofar as Guantánamo Bay is a detention camp, with daily life managed and controlled, it would seem to exemplify disciplinary power—a mode of power in which people are not dominated directly, as in sovereign power, but are turned into docile subjects, their bodies micromanaged so that they will be useful and compliant. Unlike biopower, which works on populations, disciplinary power is centered on molding individuals. Several key techniques of disciplinary power described by Foucault are used at Guantánamo Bay, from the division of space into cells, the control of activities by timetables, and the organization of men by categories and ranks.[13] Prisoners are kept to a precise schedule of eating, drinking, washing, and saying prayers, with these activities denied to prisoners who engage in "bad behavior." These details of the regulation of prisoners' movements and activities in order to compel cooperation with interrogators are contained in a 263-page document on standard operating procedures at Guantánamo Bay.[14] The prisoners are subject to the documentation of every deviation from what is considered acceptable behavior in order to produce specific knowledge about each detainee so as to better manage all of them. Minute details about a prisoner's behavior are noticed and reported, an example of how disciplinary power "allows nothing to escape,"[15] in its quest to create docile subjects.

Sovereign power and disciplinary power produce the subject the sovereign purports to regulate, rather than reflecting a preexisting subject. Through torture, the body of the prisoner is made to signify the guilt of the prisoner. Likewise, through force-feeding, the body of the hunger striker becomes intelligible as the social type "terrorist." The nominal purpose of torture at Guantánamo is to produce a docile, productive subject who will give information to interrogators. The "stress and duress" torture techniques, such as solitary confinement for days and lowering the temperature in cells, are specific disciplinary technologies used to make prisoners submissive and useful to interrogators.[16]

However, the fact that Guantánamo Bay is to be kept out of the public eye suggests that something other than disciplinary power is at work. Both sovereign power and disciplinary power are meant to be visible: the former through spectacles that make the power of the sovereign present to the citizenry and the latter through the creation of a morality tale about a dangerous person being reformed and becoming an obedient person. The ambiguous legal place that the prisoners of Guantánamo Bay occupy points to difficulties in considering them as strictly objects of disciplinary power. Peremptorily declared guilty by the United States, they have not been convicted and also are not subject to rehabilitation. Unlike a prisoner who breaks a social contract, the "terrorist" is a decidedly foreign subject, as evidenced by the difficulty in assigning the label "terrorist" to domestic perpetrators of political violence.[17] Even though international law is clear that everyone must have some status under the law (a disarmed person is either a prisoner of war or a civilian), the United States has claimed the special, extralegal status of "enemy combatants" for prisoners at Guantánamo Bay. Many prisoners at Guantánamo have been held for more than seven years without charge or trial. The Bush administration has denied that even Common Article 3 of the Geneva Conventions applies to al Qaeda detainees because the conflict between the United States and al Qaeda is neither between states nor a domestic civil war.[18] Even though, in 2010, the U.S. Supreme Court ruled in the 2006 case of *Hamdan v. Rumsfeld* that the prisoners at Guantánamo Bay must be given fair trials, by 2011, trials have yet to occur for all but one of the detainees.[19] As the prisoners are not domestic subjects, the intended audience for detention and torture seems obscure. However, there is a way in which torture and indefinite detention play to a U.S. domestic audience—Americans are made to feel safe not only from terrorists but from the techniques of biopower. The torture of Guantánamo Bay prisoners, who are bodies of information, is consistent with the instrumental logic of biopower and the management of populations.

While the lack of juridical guilt and the indefinite detention of the prisoners at Guantánamo Bay indicate that disciplinary power is not the

only, or even primary, technique of power, these very characteristics sig-
nal that techniques of biopower are being exercised. Biopolitics is a moral
discourse that moves away from the political realm of rights and obligations of and to individuals and toward a model of familial care in which
the main justification of sovereign power is to provide for the health
and welfare of its people. Biopower concerns itself with risk and chance
events that affect populations, such as diseases, famines, and the seemingly random violence of terrorist attacks. As the prisoners are detained
on the basis of their assumed dangerousness to the United States if they
were to be released, what they present is not an established danger but
a risk of future danger. They are presumed to have the capacity to commit random, violent acts: in other words, the risk is that they will carry
out violence that is itself constituted by chance and uncertainty in the
form of a terrorist attack. The Justice Department has declared that the
United States may detain prisoners not only if they are known or suspected of being agents of al Qaeda or affiliated organizations but also if
they are deemed to "constitute a clear and continuing threat to the USA
or its allies."[20] Thus, aside from any evidence of involvement in a terrorist
organization or the planning of terrorist acts, a person may be detained
indefinitely on the declaration that he or she is dangerous to the United
States. These subjects of biopower are not necessarily the villains and
enemies of society who break the law out of malice; rather, they are aberrations, whose threat to society is more diffuse and amorphous.[21] They
are not necessarily immoral subjects; they are amoral, as they cannot be
rehabilitated into obedient domestic subjects.

Techniques of security are intended to minimize risk, and, to this
end, torture has been deployed as a means of quickly obtaining information intended to prevent terrorist attacks. Thus the use of torture is
made consistent with the exercise of biopower. Yet torture is known to
be ineffective as a tool for information gathering. In the United States,
interrogation experts have long recognized that the victims of torture
frequently provide inaccurate information, as tortured people often say
whatever they believe their torturers want to hear.[22] There is evidence that
official documents cautioning against the utility of torture, even if it were
deemed to be legal, were suppressed.[23] Prisoners at Guantánamo Bay have
made false confessions under torture, and those false confessions have
provided the basis for ongoing torture of the original prisoner as well

as others.[24] More recently, the capture of failed airplane bomber Umar Farouk Abdulmutallab in late December 2009 led to renewed calls for torture to be used to gather information from terrorist suspects, despite Abdulmutallab's willingness to cooperate with authorities.[25] Given that interrogational torture is known to be ineffective at obtaining useful, accurate information, the question still remains of why torture is used.

Carried out behind closed doors, modern torture is an invisible spectacle in which the emphasis is on an exchange of pain and information; however, the experience of the body being tortured does not fit with this logic. Torture relies on a calculation of pain, such that the precise amount can be applied that will make the target "break," a logic of information based on biopolitical concepts of rationality and utility. This logic does not match the realities of the experience of torture. Humans vary greatly in their ability to endure pain. Pain is also not a singular, measurable experience but can take the form of many sensations, which may counterbalance one another.[26] As the experience of pain is subjective, it is difficult to quantify or control. The experience of psychological torture is even more difficult to predict. The subjective experience of pain suggests that the infliction of torture is not entirely consistent with an exercise of biopower, as it is not ordered or structured.

Biopolitics is also insufficient to explain the practices of torture at Guantánamo Bay because the prisoners are not being killed. In fact, the preservation of the lives of the prisoners despite their torture is at the core of the tension between biopower and sovereign power in the treatment of the prisoners at Guantánamo Bay. Foucault writes that the sovereign must make a distinction between who must live and who must die as a necessary component of the practice of sovereign power in biopolitical regimes.[27] By this logic, in order to protect the lives of the domestic population, the source of risk must be killed. In the contemporary torture regime at Guantánamo Bay, however, sovereign power is exercised on "undesirables" in such a way that the object is not their deaths but their production as a particularly risky subject. Torture prevents its victims from having the kind of lives that biopolitics promotes in its positive form of furthering the health and longevity of the population. In the practice of torture, "the violence can unfold as something irresistible, even unlimitable, except that the death of the vulnerable one . . . always does constitute a limit."[28] Biopower, in this sense, has not led to the intentional deaths of the prisoners but, rather, has imposed a limit on the extreme use of sovereign power — the power to kill. Bodies are tortured, but they are not allowed to die. Death operates as a limit on the torturer as well as on the agency of the prisoner. The prisoner cannot be killed because he must be made to speak. This limit suggests a different interpretation of the role of sovereign power and biopower than the interpretation of those who suggest that sovereign power produces a subject who can be killed.

Torture as an Anxious Practice of Sovereign Power

As the prisoners at Guantánamo Bay have been declared enemy combatants who have no standing in international law, what then prevents the United States from killing them outright, as they might have done if they encountered these "terrorists" in a battle? Despite the insistence on the prisoners' lack of legal status, the prisoners' lives are officially protected. They may be tortured, but they must be kept alive. Judging by its willingness to use violence, but its unwillingness to take lives or let the prisoners take their own lives, the United States appears troubled by the exercise of sovereign power.

In ancient Greece, torture could be used to release the truth from a slave's body but not a citizen's. Slaves (and women and barbarians) were bodies, pure materiality, while citizens had reason.[29] But the distinction between slave and free is unstable, not "given by nature." Judicial torture served to maintain the distinction, as only the bodies of women and slaves were thought to be able to release truth through bodily pain. Torture served as a way of marking these social hierarchies. While the context and meaning of torture have changed, the use of torture to produce and sustain hierarchies of political subjectivities remains. Torture serves a similar function in the context of Guantánamo and the war on terror: it produces its own rationale by using pain to unmake the subjectivity of the prisoner while making present the power of the sovereign.

By the infliction of pain, torture produces hierarchical relations through its demonstration of the torturers' strength in an act of sovereign power. Elaine Scarry's *The Body in Pain* describes how torture can destroy the victim's subjectivity. Undergoing intense pain and unceasing questioning, the victim is reduced to the space of the "natural body" incapable of speech, of entering the symbolic realm of language. Scarry's thesis is that torture reduces the body to a world of pain. The extreme pain of torture is inexpressible in language, and thus the subject's world is unmade because the pain has no referent in the outside world. The victim's lack of language destroys his or her subjectivity. Scarry writes:

> It is the intense pain that destroys a person's self and world, a destruc-
> tion experienced spatially as either the contraction of the universe down to
> the immediate vicinity of the body or as the body swelling to fill the entire
> universe. Intense pain is also language-destroying; as the content of one's
> world disintegrates, so the content of one's language disintegrates; as
> the self disintegrates, so that which would express and project the self is
> robbed of its source and its subject.[30]

Scarry presents a model of torture in which there are two distinct subjects: a torturer and a prisoner. The torturer comes to be identified with voice and world, while the prisoner experiences only pain and the body.[31] The torturer speaks with the voice of the sovereign, and the victim, deprived of subjectivity, is made to speak as the sovereign wishes, making present the existence of the sovereign. The sovereign is made present in the body of the tortured, not by the death of the prisoner, but by the unmaking of the world of the prisoner.

Scarry's analysis of torture shows the extent of sovereign power in the twenty-first century. While her work has been criticized for its separa-tion of language and body,[32] it powerfully demonstrates precisely how language and bodies are mutually entailed. Torture demonstrates sover-eign power's ability to reduce bodies to materiality. In torture, the victim is made to "speak the name of the sovereign," in Paul Kahn's telling phrase.[33] Torture serves as the means not only of producing "truth" but also of making present the sovereign.

The tortured body is broken, but it must be kept alive so that it can provide information or labor. It must be able to speak or work. The imprisoned victim of torture is meant to provide information, his body made to speak, to subvert his own will to silence. As bodies reduced to pain, tortured prisoners are not liberal speaking subjects, able to make claims against the state. While torture is a bare display of sovereign power, it destroys the type of subject that would constitute that sovereignty. By disabling the prisoner's ability to speak, the United States prevents the speech act that underpins the consent of the ruled that characterizes liberalism; rather, the prisoners are forced to speak with the voice of the sovereign. Neither can the subjects of torture be "remade" as Scarry's exemplars are, because they are not being prepared for reintegration into society. The bare display of sovereign power destroys the very subjects of sovereign power. Scarry frames her discussion in terms of world-making and world-destroying. World-making and world-destroying can have multiple intended audiences, however. While the torture may be world-destroying for the tortured, it can be world-making for its intended audience in the United States and abroad in terms of its substantiation of U.S. sovereign power.

The torture of prisoners at Guantánamo Bay is an expression of sovereign power that is met with much anxiety in the United States. This anxiety is manifested in two modes of distancing the sovereign from torture: a geographic distancing and a political distancing. The special status, or lack of status, that the prisoners at Guantánamo Bay hold, as the United States declared, suggests that the United States could claim the sovereign right to kill as well as torture, as the prisoners are enemies outside the protections of any social contract. Yet the prisoners are maintained and sustained in camps. The prisoners must be held by the sovereign — witness the outcry from politicians over various proposals in 2009 to release Guantánamo Bay detainees in the states represented by these politicians. Likewise, there is great anxiety over the proposal for housing Guantánamo Bay prisoners in maximum-security prisons in the United States, despite the presence of other persons convicted of terrorism within these very facilities.[34] The prisoners, and their torture, must be kept at a distance from the sovereign. Anxiety over the status of prisoners who were captured in Afghanistan as suspected al Qaeda members who pose a threat to the United States has led to the quarantine of these prisoners within U.S. control but outside U.S. sovereign territory. Since 2002, the U.S. government has used Camp Delta at the Guantánamo Bay naval base to house prisoners captured in Afghanistan and elsewhere, citizens of countries such as the United Kingdom, Saudi Arabia, Yemen, Pakistan, Afghanistan, and Syria. Guantánamo Bay is not the only such site; others include Bagram Airfield in Afghanistan, numerous prisons in Iraq including Abu Ghraib, plus an unknown number of Central Intelligence

Agency black sites in a secret internment network that comprises facilities in Thailand, Afghanistan, Morocco, Poland, and Romania.[35]

Torture is also distanced from the sovereign by the use of euphemism and official denial. Referred to as "enhanced interrogations," torture is not outright accepted. President Bush has famously stated that "we do not torture," while administration spokespeople and supporters vehemently assert the necessity of conducting these "enhanced interrogations." The Obama administration, while denouncing torture and promising to close Guantánamo, has yet to do so, ostensibly pending acceptable alternative arrangements for the prisoners.

While torture violates liberal values prohibiting the illegitimate use of violence by states against citizens, it also appears necessary or at least useful in performing the presence of the sovereign. One key example of torture in reproducing sovereign power through the obliteration of subjectivity is the repeated waterboardings of several "high-value" prisoners. Khalid Sheikh Mohammed was waterboarded 183 times and Abu Zubaydah waterboarded at least 83 times according to declassified Bush administration documents.[36] The sheer number of waterboardings casts doubt on the official rationale of information gathering, as the likelihood that each successive waterboarding will make the subject more likely to share information he is holding back seems small, yet the rationale for the use of waterboarding remains that it will compel the prisoner to produce information. If the subject occasionally provides some information after waterboarding, the question then becomes at what point has he given all the information he has to give and how much of that information was false. This repeated performance of violence suggests an ongoing attempt at stabilizing sovereign power through the destruction of subjectivity. The medicalization of the torture techniques also shows unease with the practice of torture.

Taking humans as biological entities, the medical regime of truth about the bodies and psyches of prisoners and their reaction to harsh treatment plays out in the medicalization of debates about torture, with torture advocates citing the many safeguards in place to secure the life and health of the subjects of torture and medical professionals objecting to the violation of patients' rights as well as to the inherent harm of torture. Modern practices of torture, unlike the ones Foucault describes as examples of sovereign power in *Discipline and Punish*, are designed to avoid leaving permanent marks on the body. The body of the torture victim is an intermediary rather than the object of the torture. Instead of the bloody spectacles of flogging, amputation, limb stretching, and beating associated with torture in the classical era, contemporary torture practices are aimed at bloodlessness and invisibility.[37] The torture techniques used by the U.S. military and its proxies include waterboarding, sleep deprivation, exposure to heat and cold, electric shock, sensory deprivation, intimidation by dogs, insects, and humiliation by sexual abuse.[38] These tactics have been labeled "stealth technologies" because they are difficult to document.[39] The experiences of prisoners released from Guantánamo Bay and other detention sites suggest that different techniques were tried out in order to judge their efficacy at causing pain without seriously threatening the life of the subject.[40] Famously, the "Bybee memo" argued that to be considered torture, the pain inflicted had to be "equivalent in intensity to the pain accompanying serious physical injury, such as organ failure, impairment of bodily function, or even death."[41]

The torture program has created, and made use of, a body of knowledge about the human body and what it can endure without dying. The complicity and assistance of medical personnel are essential to the practice of torture. The discourse of the biological body, in its physical limitations, not only is essential to the practice of torture but is produced from the knowledge gained through torture. Medical professionals are on hand to ensure that such torture tactics are not taken so far as to permanently damage the bodies of the victims.[42] In fact, part of the Bush administration reasoning as to why these "enhanced interrogation techniques" do not constitute torture is that medical personnel are present to ensure the safety of the prisoners. Memos from the Justice Department to the CIA's Office of General Counsel, for example, provide numerous assurances that no detainee will be subjected to treatment that is "counterindicated" by psychological or physiological evaluations. The Justice Department claims, for example, that "OMS [the CIA's Office of Medical Services] closely monitors the detainee's condition to ensure that he does not, in fact, experience severe pain or suffering or sustain any significant or lasting harm."[43] This is not to say that prisoners subjected to torture techniques in truth do not experience "severe pain or suffering." Rather, this demonstrates the extent to which medical knowledge is integral to the practices of torture in not only producing effects on the prisoners

113

but also attempting to limit harmful effects so that the prisoners are kept alive. The purpose of medical supervision is made clear in the statement of a CIA official speaking of Abu Zubaydah, "He received the finest medical attention on the planet. We got him in very good health so we could start to torture him."[44]

Despite the protestations of the Justice Department, the attempt to conduct these "enhanced interrogations" in a perfectly controlled manner is based on the idea that health, life, and death are, in fact, controllable. As of 2006, at least nineteen prisoners have died of their treatment at the hands of U.S. soldiers and interrogators, though the deaths of many more may have been covered up.[45] More than one hundred prisoners have died in U.S. custody in Afghanistan and Iraq in the first three years of the war on terror, a number that is surely higher today, although the government has not released more recent information.[46] The claims that the techniques used by U.S. forces do not cause severe or lasting harm have also been shown to be false.[47] The dream of perfectly controllable violence, in which medical and legal safeguards prevent any lasting illness or harm despite increasing levels of deprivation, suffering, and violence, is a fantasy of sovereign power—the perfect gaze of the panopticon.[48]

Force-Feeding and the Transformation of Political Status

Widespread hunger strikes at Guantánamo Bay began over allegations of mistreatment of the Koran and became a mode of resistance to the indefinite detention and ill-treatment more broadly.[49] To the American people and the rest of the world, hunger strikes and the force-feeding of hunger strikers are part of the battle over the meaning of the violence committed against prisoners' bodies. U.S. officials defend the use of force-feeding, which medical ethicists claim is a violation of human rights, by insisting not only that the hunger strike is a tactic of war but that they are force-feeding prisoners for the prisoners' own well-being. These seemingly contradictory logics of health and war are, in fact, part of the same logic of sovereign power. Only representatives of the United States are allowed to inflict pain and violence on the bodies of detainees—the detainees themselves are forbidden the same right. The exercise of biopower on the bodies of the hunger strikers is a perverse form of biopower's power to "make live," as it is exercised directly on the bodies of the negative subjects of biopower, the dangerous bodies of "terrorists." Force-feeding has the effect of making the "terrorists" legible and forces a type of normative status onto them, as infantilized "dependents." This effort is aimed more at an American audience as well as a broader global audience, in terms of assuring people of the safety and efficacy of such techniques of biopower.

Even in an environment in which sovereign power is exercised to a remarkable degree over the lives and bodies of prisoners, the refusal to consume food and water constitutes an act of resistance by the hunger strikers. In the face of a power whose goal is to keep prisoners alive but indefinitely imprisoned, the hunger strikers attack their own bodies by refusing to live indefinitely in such conditions. Under conditions in which their worlds and subjectivities are being so destroyed, hunger strikes are the only way of enacting self-government. By harming their own bodies, they attempt to exercise power over meaning. In trying to martyr themselves, they deny the presence of the sovereign and assert their own sovereignty over their bodies. The hunger strikers' attempts to enact subjectivity comes at the cost of the very materiality of their bodies.

In June 2009, Mohammad Ahmed Abdullah Saleh al Hanashi, a Yemeni who had been detained for seven years, was reported to have committed suicide. Al Hanashi had been on a hunger strike, and at one point weighed eighty-seven pounds. He had been force-fed and was one of seven prisoners in a psychiatric ward, where all were kept under sedation.[50] His death was initially ruled a suicide by military officials, although there is some question as to how he could do this to himself while under twenty-four-hour surveillance.[51] After all, prisoners at Guantánamo Bay are not supposed to die—their deaths, whether intentional or accidental, are seen as a failure. Recent investigations have revealed that three Guantánamo Bay hunger strikers who were previously reported by the military to have committed suicide are likely to have been murdered. These deaths were covered up as suicides and, as such, were portrayed as acts of war committed by al Qaeda agents. Rear Admiral Harry Harris declared, "I believe this was not an act of desperation, but an act of asymmetrical warfare waged against us,"[52] even though all three men were scheduled to have been transferred due to lack of evidence that they were involved in terrorist activities.

The hunger striker is neither a juridical subject of sovereignty nor the liberal, rational subject of biopower but a dangerous subject who

115

is attempting to reconstruct a political subjectivity. Given that "terrorists" are not considered to act rationally, torture is somewhat paradoxical under the biopolitical rationale of seeking information through the infliction of pain and discomfort. To inflict pain upon a "terrorist" is to expect that person to act rationally to preserve his body from pain and injury and provide the information the interrogators seek. By courting death through hunger strikes, the prisoners at Guantánamo Bay refuse this attempt to normalize them. They resist sovereign power's rights over life and death as well as biopower's determination to ensure life.[53] The rational, liberal subject must single-mindedly strive for his self-interest. This also cannot meaningfully describe the hunger-striking prisoner, who suffers pain and harms his own body, eventually leading to his death if he is not force-fed.

The force-feeding of hunger strikers not only robs the prisoners of one possibility of enacting sovereignty over their own bodies but also has the effect of forcing normative status on them, not as moral subjects but as dependents of the state. They are made into legible subjects who, it might be said, never had it so good. The military reports that the detainees are fed very well and are gaining weight. Chief Petty Officer Colleen M. Schonhoff, who is in charge of preparing food for the detainees, stated, "I like to believe they're eating a lot better here than they were wherever they were before they got here. We take pretty good care of them."[54] Lindsay Graham, Republican of South Carolina, has stated that the Guantánamo Bay detainees receive better treatment than the Nazis did because the Supreme Court ruled that the prisoners were entitled to habeas corpus.[55] Senator Jim Bunning, Republican of Kentucky, was impressed to learn that the detainees "even have air-conditioning and semiprivate showers."[56] Michael D. Crapo, Republican senator from Idaho, reported that the military personnel at the camp "get more abuse from the detainees than they give to the detainees."[57] Democratic senators Richard Durbin of Illinois and Ron Wyden of Oregon have also given assurances regarding the treatment of the prisoners after a visit to Guantánamo Bay. By affirming the camp's relative comfort, despite the complaints of prisoners, these accounts reinscribe the prisoners as a quasi-population in need of management, even though they neither are domestic subjects nor are intended to be a permanent population.

The use of force-feeding to keep hunger-striking detainees alive indicates a transformation of the political status of the prisoners from enemy combatants, to terrorists, to a quasi-population. Force-feeding makes the prisoners into objects of medical knowledge, a prerequisite for making them into objects that can be managed as dependents of the sovereign state. They are transformed from illegible terrorists into threats that are being managed competently. The force-feeding is conducted by medical professionals who are screened before they are deployed to Guantánamo to make certain they don't have moral objections to force-feeding.[58] Around February 2006, the military began using restraint chairs to hold the prisoners while they were being force-fed. These chairs resemble dentist's chairs with restraints for the arms, legs, head, and torso. The military says they are necessary for the safety of the prisoners as well as to prevent them from throwing up after the feeding. Journalists have reported on the use of unnecessarily large nasal tubes that cause extreme pain and bleeding when forcibly inserted.[59] Overfeeding, which causes cramps, nausea, and diarrhea, is also frequently accompanied by prolonged restraint in these chairs, ostensibly to ensure absorption of the nutrients and prevent self-induced vomiting.

Outside the terms of any social contract, the "terrorists" are transformed into subjects of a minimal exchange in which information is traded for the sustainment of life. This exchange is far from the liberal ideals of equal and autonomous subjects contracting with one another. By force-feeding the hunger-striking prisoners, the United States makes its sovereign power present over the bodies and lives of prisoners. In a fully biopolitical regime, not permitting the deaths of prisoners is central to the logic of sovereign power. Force-feeding is justified in biopolitical terms of preserving the lives of the prisoners and produces the prisoners as a quasi-population to be managed by doctors and administrators. A Pentagon spokesperson has responded to charges of ill-treatment in force-feeding by saying that Defense Department officials "believe that preservation of life through lawful, clinically appropriate means is a responsible and prudent measure for the safety and well-being of detainees."[60] In a facetious dismissal of accusations of abuse, one report asserted that hunger strikers were said to be given a choice of colors for their feeding tubes and lozenges to soothe their sore throats.[61] Hunger-striking prisoners are force-fed if they have refused sixty-three consecutive meals or have not eaten for twenty-one days, or if they drop below 85 percent of their healthy body weight. A doctor's approval is also needed, in the latter case.[62] Dr. William Winkenwerder, assistant secretary of defense for health affairs, insisted, "There is a moral question. Do you allow a person to commit suicide? Or do you take steps to protect their health and preserve their life? The objective in any circumstance is to protect and sustain a person's life."[63] Officials have defended the force-feeding of prisoners by claiming "it is our responsibility to make sure that the detainees are kept in good health."[64] To suggestions that the policy of force-feeding violates the ban on "outrages upon personal dignity, in particular humiliating and degrading treatment," of Common Article 3 of the Geneva Conventions, officials have responded by invoking the language of Common Article 3, which states "the wounded and sick shall be collected and cared for," to justify the force-feeding of prisoners.[65] While medical ethics and Defense Department guidelines allow for force-feeding only for cases in which immediate treatment is necessary to prevent death or serious harm,[66] the fact that the prisoners are healthy enough to need restraint suggests that force-feeding was being done well before the lives of prisoners were in danger.

Military officials also claim that hunger strikers are operating under a strategic logic, as agents of al Qaeda continuing their battle against the United States even while in prison. A *Time* magazine articles reports: "Harris [Defense Department spokesperson] argues the camp will be needed for the foreseeable future, and that refusing to eat is not a cry for help, but a ploy drawn from the al-Qaeda playbook calculated to attract media attention and force the U.S. government to back down." Harris is also quoted as saying, "The will to resist of these prisoners is high. They are waging their war, their jihad against America, and we just have to stop them."[67] The same article equates the hunger strikes with suicide attempts, arguing that both similarly seek to bring negative attention to Guantánamo so it will be shut down. Another spokesperson for Guantánamo Bay, Robert Durand, said, "The hunger strike technique is consistent with al-Qaeda practice and reflects detainee attempts to elicit media attention to bring international pressure on the United States to release them back to the battlefield."[68] Durand also denied that the hunger strikers have made any specific demands or requests. Officials have declared the hunger strikes to be "acts of war." The framing of hunger strikes as part of the "al-Qaeda playbook" indicates the instability of the prisoners' new status as a quasi-population. This line of argument keeps the logic of both biopower and sovereign power in play. Against arguments that force-feeding is an abuse of sovereign power, the idea of hunger strikers as enemies and terrorists can be invoked. Against arguments of violating the human rights of prisoners, the biopolitical logic of preserving the lives of prisoners under the care of the United States may be invoked. Thus, the force-fed hunger strikers occupy an unstable position as not-fully-terrorist enemies but not fully members of a population to be managed either.

While doctors have been involved in the force-feeding of prisoners at Guantánamo Bay from the beginning, ostensibly to ensure the safety of the prisoners, they have also led the charge against the practice of force-feeding hunger-striking prisoners under the banner of human rights. More than 250 medical professionals have signed an open letter to the *Lancet,* a British medical journal, demanding an end to force-feeding as a violation of the medical ethics of the American Medical Association and the World Medical Association. According to the codes of ethics of both organizations, force-feeding is considered an "assault on human dignity" so long as the prisoners or patients are capable of making an informed decision.[69] This view is premised upon understanding hunger strikes not as a form of suicide but as a form of political protest. Medical ethicists have also condemned the force-feedings by specifying the duties doctors have to patients who decide to undergo hunger strikes: above respecting the sanctity of life and the health of the detainees, physicians are obliged to respect the autonomy of patients who freely choose to go on hunger strikes and understand the consequences of their actions.[70] The labeling of force-feeding as torture per se, aside from the brutal measures used in its execution, is premised upon the Enlightenment view of the subject as an autonomous will that controls the body. It is also premised upon a juridical subject that is *homo œconomicus,* with preexisting preferences and interests that the government cannot prevent him from pursuing. Medical ethicists insist that the refusal of food in this context is a matter not of pathology, psychological or otherwise, but of free choice. Medical ethicists consider force-feeding of competent persons, which intervenes in this control over the body, to constitute torture through an abridgement of the rights of hunger strikers.

In the discourse of medical ethics, hunger strikers are positioned as patients (as opposed to enemy combatants continuing their battle in prison) for whom certain rules govern relationships with doctors. The main object is the prisoner/patient and his subjectivity as a rational bearer of rights. Force-feeding, medical ethicists insist, is permissible only when it is first of all necessary for the health of the patient who is unable or refusing to eat and, second, when the refusing patient has been deemed mentally impaired and unable to understand the consequences of not eating and drinking. Force-feeding becomes a matter of psychiatry, in which doctors must determine if the patient is sufficiently rational to freely make the choice to refuse food. This medical discourse is inseparable from a liberal discourse of individuals as rights-bearing subjects.

However, the discourse of force-feeding articulated by the military doctors and government spokespersons suggests not an autonomous subject with rights but rather a deranged subject who needs to be protected from himself. By force-feeding the hunger-striking prisoners at Guantánamo Bay, military personnel are not so much violating liberal principles of a subject's rational control over his or her own body but producing the detainees as irrational and "insane," in need of care and management. Judith Butler argues that the indefinite detention of the prisoners at Guantánamo Bay is comparable to the indefinite detention of patients in mental institutions.[71] Some hunger strikers are held in Guantánamo Bay's psych ward as suicidal and are under constant surveillance.[72] If the indefinite detention of mental patients is a suitable model for the indefinite detention of prisoners, then there is a corresponding analogy to the mental status of both kinds of patients. While no pictures of the restraint chairs have been released, an advertisement from the company that makes them is accompanied by the slogan "It's like a padded cell on wheels."[73] Force-feeding through nasal tubes is widely used with comatose patients or those suffering from psychiatric diseases. In these situations, it is not seen to be problematic, because such persons are deemed incapable of making rational decisions on their own behalf.

If the mental status of the hunger strikers is unfathomable and outside the bounds of accepted, civilized thought, then the detention and force-feeding can be justified. However, it is not the preexisting mental status of the prisoners that leads to their indefinite incarceration and force-feeding; rather, it is the practices of detention and force-feeding that produce the prisoners as subjects of irrationality and unfathomability. This is consistent with the production of "terrorist" subjectivity, but with an added dimension of social responsibility. When we consider the military discourse of hunger striking as a tactic of war, the fact of hunger striking is not what is produced as unfathomable or unknowable; it is the minds of the prisoners themselves as agents of al Qaeda that are produced as irrational and uncivilized. Once the prisoners and the hunger strikers in particular are produced as irrational subjects, then the state is authorized to intervene to "make live." The hunger strikers are figured not as dangerous but infantile, in need of the benevolence of the United States in order to remain alive. The production of hunger-striking prisoners into dependent figures of unfathomable moral and mental status not only has implications for the treatment of the prisoners but, perhaps more crucially, also has the effect of making the United States more comfortable with its exercise of sovereign power against its own liberal norms.

The dual techniques of sovereign power and biopower can be used to understand the transformation of the political status of American citizens. Aside from managing the prisoners, the force-feeding of hunger strikers serves to assure Americans that the technologies of biopower are safe — that they need not be concerned with interrogational torture nor suspect prisoners' rights are being violated by force-feeding. Months and years after September 11, 2001, instead of decrying the decadence and complacency of American society that helped allow the attacks to occur, the discourse shifted to recapturing a sense of urgency and unity of purpose in addressing the threat of terrorism. Two years after September 11, President Bush stated in a speech that "the enemy is wounded, but still resourceful and actively recruiting, and still dangerous. We cannot afford a moment of complacency. Yet, as you know, we've taken extraordinary measures these past two years to protect America."[74] Some of these extraordinary measures include authorizing torture. The war on terror, as officials frequently reminded Americans, is a long, if never-ending war. The threat of terrorism is to be considered ever present, and everyday life is to be rearranged around the prevention of terrorist attacks. As one official said, "It is just a fact of life and we have to deal with it."[75] Producing the prisoners as not only vaguely dangerous but also dependents in need of care makes Americans feel safe that the threat of terrorism is not only being managed but being managed in a humane way.

The act of force-feeding transforms the moral status of the hunger-striking prisoners from "enemy combatants" — figures outside any social contract — to humans susceptible to management, of minimal interrelations. While force-feeding suggests that there is something incurably pathological about the "terrorists," it does not necessarily indicate their exclusion from any body politic.[76] In sustaining the lives of hunger strikers by this means, the prisoners are included in the body politic in a way that produces them as figures of dependency. The threat of terrorism is thus managed by taking away freedom of speech in exchange for the speech of information. While medical ethicists attempt to assert that the prisoners are liberal subjects of rights, the continued force-feeding of hunger-striking prisoners makes the prisoners a symbol of diffuse danger on the border of political community. At the same time, it assures Americans that they are safe from the threat of terrorism because the terrorists are being managed competently. From this argument, we can read the Obama administration's delay in closing the prison at Guantánamo as based on not only operational difficulties but difficulties in assuring the American people as well as Obama's political opposition that the former Guantánamo Bay prisoners would pose no threat if housed domestically. Force-feeding gives rise to a new understanding of Senator John McCain's 2005 statement against torture in response to an admonishment about the nature of the terrorists: torture "is not about who *they* are. It's about who *we* are."[77]

Conclusion

Most debates about torture are concerned with arguing the ethical merits of this mode of political violence. Rather than enter this debate, I seek to open a space in which to ask why, despite its principles, does the United States continue to torture? The practice of torture and force-feeding tells us little about the people we torture but much about the troubled exercise of sovereign power in a liberal, biopolitical society. Torture and the force-feeding of hunger-striking prisoners not only strip the prisoners of subjectivity but remake U.S. subjectivity. By constituting the prisoners of Guantánamo Bay as figures of indefinite captivity and dependency rather than as killable enemies or untenable risks, the United States exercises its sovereign power in a way that assures its American audience of the safety and desirability of biopolitical techniques, thus reforming the political status of American subjects as well as the "terrorist" subjects who must be held but kept at bay, tortured yet kept alive.

NOTES

The author gratefully acknowledges the assistance of Nancy Luxon, Bud Duvall, Jennifer Lobasz, Shampa Biswas, and Zahi Zalloua as well as participants at the Minnesota International Relations Colloquium and the 2009 International Studies Association–Northeast conference, where previous versions of this essay were presented.

1 Carol Leonnig, "More Join Guantánamo Hunger Strike," *Washington Post,* September 13, 2005, section A.

2 Quoted in Steven H. Miles, *Oath Betrayed: Torture, Medical Complicity, and the War on Terror* (New York: Random House, 2006), 110.

3 Tim Golden, "Guantánamo Detainees Stage Hunger Strike," *New York Times,* April 9, 2007, http://www.nytimes.com/2007/04/09/us/09hunger.html.

4 Tim Reid, "One in Five Guantánamo Bay Detainees Is on Hunger Strike," *Times* (London), January 15, 2009, http://www.timesonline.co.uk/tol/news/world/us_and_americas /article5518812.ece.

5 Bob Woodward, "Detainee Tortured, Says U.S. Official," *Washington Post,* January 14, 2009, section A.

6 Marlise Simons, "Spanish Court Weighs Inquiry on Torture for 6 Bush-Era Officials," *New York Times,* 2009, http://www.nytimes.com/2009/03/29/world/europe/29spain.html (accessed August 18, 2009).

7 Michel Foucault, *The History of Sexuality: Volume 1: An Introduction,* trans. Robert Hurley (New York: Random House, 1978); Michel Foucault, *"Society Must Be Defended": Lectures at the Collège de France,* trans. David Macey (New York: Picador, 2003), 247.

8 Bob Brecher, *Torture and the Ticking Time Bomb* (Malden, Mass.: Blackwell, 2007); Alan Dershowitz, "Want Torture? Get a Warrant," *San Francisco Chronicle,* January 22, 2002, section A; Henry Shue, "Torture," *Philosophy and Public Affairs* 7, no. 2 (1978): 124–43; and Matthew Hannah, "Torture and the Ticking Time Bomb: The War on Terrorism as a Geographical Imagination of Power/Knowledge," *Annals of the Association of American Geographers* 96, no. 3 (2006): 622–40.

9 Quoted in Katharine Q. Seelye, "Some Guantánamo Detainees Will be Freed, Rumsfeld Says," *New York Times,* October 23, 2002.

10 Foucault, *Discipline and Punish,* 48.

11 This is not to say that prisoners have not died at Guantánamo Bay, or that they have not been intentionally killed. Three prisoners who had been reported to have committed suicide in June 2006 are suspected of being murdered based on testimony from prisoners and former military personnel. See Scott Horton, "The Guantánamo 'Suicides': A Camp Delta

123

DYINGDYING IS NOT PERMITTED

Sergeant Blows the Whistle," *Harper's,* January 18, 2010, http://harpers. org/archive/2010/01/hbc-90006368.

12 Foucault, *"Society Must Be Defended,"* 241.

13 Foucault, *Discipline and Punish,* 138–49.

14 Camp Delta Standard Operating Procedures, Joint Task Force Guantá-namo, March 28, 2003.

15 Michel Foucault, *Security, Territory, Population: Lectures at the Collège de France, 1977–78,* trans. Graham Burchell (Basingstoke, Hampshire, U.K.: Palgrave Macmillan, 2007), 45.

16 Mark Danner, "US Torture: Voices from the Black Sites," *New York Review of Books* 56, no. 6 (April 9, 2009).

17 Following a wave of abortion clinic bombings in 1984, the FBI refused to investigate the crimes as terrorism. As such, there was no coordinated federal effort to stop the violence for more than a decade. Philip Jenkins, "Fighting Terrorism As If Women Mattered: Anti-abortion Violence as Unconstructed Terrorism," in *Making Trouble: Cultural Constructions of Crime, Deviance, and Control,* ed. Jeff Ferrell and Neil Websdale (Hawthorne, N.Y.: Aldine De Gruyter, 1999), 319–46.

18 John Yoo, memorandum to William Haynes II, January 9, 2002, in *The Torture Papers: The Road to Abu Ghraib,* ed. Karen Greenberg and Joshua Dratel (Cambridge: Cambridge University Press, 2005), 49.

19 Ahmed Khalfan Ghailani was acquitted in a civilian court in November 2010 of all but 1 of 280 charges against him related to the 1998 U.S. embassy bombings after being held in various CIA black sites and Guantánamo Bay after his capture in 2004.

20 Steven G. Bradbury, memorandum to John A. Rizzo, "Re: Application of United States Obligations Under Article 16 of the Convention Against Torture to Certain Techniques That May Be Used in the Interrogation of High Value al Qaeda Detainees," U.S. Department of Justice, Office of Legal Counsel, May 30, 2005, http://luxmedia.vo.llnwd.net/ 010/ clients/aclu/olc_05302005_ bradbury.pdf.

21 Foucault, *Security, Territory, Population,* 7.

22 Darius Rejali, *Torture and Democracy* (Princeton, N.J.: Princeton University Press, 2007); Evan Thomas, "'24' versus the Real World," *Newsweek,* September 20, 2006, http://www.newsweek.com/id/45788; and James Glanz, "Torture Is Often a Temptation and Almost Never Works," *New York Times,* May 9, 2004, available at http://www.nytimes.com/2004/05/09/ weekinreview/the-world-torture-is-often-a-temptation-and-almost-never-works.html.

23 Peter Finn and Joby Warrick, "In 2002, Military Agency Warned Against 'Torture,'" *Washington Post,* April 25, 2009, http://www.washingtonpost.

com/wp-dyn/content/article/2009/04/24/ AR2009042403171.html (accessed August 17, 2009).

24 *Fouad Mahmoud al Rabiah v. United States.* Civil. Action No. 02-828 (CKK) http://www.pillsburylaw.com/siteFiles/News/1259B22146574C540A8 871C2C3131CA2.pdf; Andy Worthington, *The Guantánamo Files: The Stories of the 774 Detainees in America's Illegal Prison* (Ann Arbor, Mich.: Pluto Press, 2007); Andy Worthington, "A Truly Shocking Guantánamo Story," September 9, 2009, http://www.andyworthington.co.uk/2009/09/30/a-truly-shocking-guantanamo-story-judge-confirms-that-an-innocent-man-was-tortured-to-make-false-confessions/; and Peter Finn and Joby Warrick, "Torture of Abu Zubaida Produced False Leads," *Washington Post*, March 29, 2009.

25 See Adam Serwer, "Tortured Talking Points," *Guardian*, December 30, 2009, http://www.guardian.co.uk/commentisfree/cifamerica/2009/dec/30/torture-bomb-flight-253.

26 Rejali, *Torture and Democracy*, 446–50.

27 Foucault, *"Society Must Be Defended,"* 254–55.

28 Adriana Cavarero, *Horrorism: Naming Contemporary Violence*, trans. William McCuaig (New York: Columbia University Press, 2009), 31.

29 Page Dubois, *Torture and Truth* (New York: Routledge, 1991), 52.

30 Elaine Scarry, *The Body in Pain: The Making and Unmaking of the World* (New York: Oxford University Press, 1985), 35.

31 Ibid., 36.

32 Judith Butler, *Excitable Speech: The Politics of the Performative* (London: Routledge, 1997); Bibi Bakare-Yusuf, "The Economy of Violence: Black Bodies and Unspeakable Terror," in *Feminist Theory and the Body*, ed. Janet Price and Margrit Shildrick (London: Routledge, 1997), 232–311; Consuela Rivera-Fuentes and Lynda Birke, "Talking with/in Pain: Reflections on Bodies Under Torture," *Women's International Studies Forum* 24, no. 6 (2001): 653–68.

33 Paul W. Kahn, *Sacred Violence: Torture, Terror and Sovereignty* (Ann Arbor: University of Michigan Press, 2008), 42.

34 Convicted foreign terrorists in the Supermax prison include Zacarias Moussaoui, the so-called twentieth hijacker; Wadih el-Hage, of the 1998 embassy bombings; and Ramzi Yousef, leader of the 1993 World Trade Center bombings. See Carrie Johnson and Walter Pincus, "Supermax Prisons in the US Already Hold Terrorists," *Washington Post*, May 22, 2009.

35 Danner, "Voices from the Black Sites"; and Dana Priest, "CIA Holds Terror Suspects in Secret Prisons," *Washington Post*, November 2, 2005, http://www.washingtonpost.com/wp-dyn/content/article/2005/11/01/AR2005110101644.html.

36 Steven G. Bradbury, memorandum to John A. Rizzo, May 30, 2005.

37 Detainees have also reported being beaten at Guantánamo as well as other detention camps. These forms of abuse were intended to be kept secret and, unlike tactics such as sensory deprivation, stress positions, and waterboarding, have not been justified as crucial for information gathering.

38 Steven G. Bradbury to John A. Rizzo, memorandum, 10 May 2005, "Re: Application of 18 U.S.C. §§ 2340-2340A to the Combined Use of Certain Techniques in the Interrogation of High Value al Qaeda Detainees," U.S. Department of Justice, Office of Legal Counsel, http://luxmedia. vo.llnwd.net/o10/clients/aclu/olc_05102005_bradbury46pg.pdf.

39 Darius Rejali, "Modern Torture as Civic Marker: Solving a Global Anxiety with a New Political Technology," *Journal of Human Rights* 2, no. 2 (2003): 153–71.

40 Danner, "Voices from the Black Sites."

41 John Yoo, memorandum to Alberto Gonzales, U.S. Department of Justice, Office of Legal Counsel, August 1, 2002, http://www.usdoj.gov/olc/docs/memo-gonzales-aug1.pdf.

42 Miles, *Oath Betrayed*, 50–67.

43 Steven G. Bradbury, memorandum to John A. Rizzo, May 30, 2005.

44 Quoted in Ron Suskind, *The One Percent Doctrine: Deep Inside America's Pursuit of Its Enemies Since 9/11* (New York: Simon and Schuster, 2006), 100.

45 Miles, *Oath Betrayed*, 71.

46 Ayaz Nanji, "Report: 108 Died in U.S. Custody," March 16, 2005.

47 Physicians for Human Rights, *Break Them Down: Systemic Use of Psychological Torture by US Forces* (Cambridge, Mass.: Physicians for Human Rights, 2005), http://physiciansforhumanrights.org/library/documents/reports/break-them-down-the.pdf.

48 Foucault, *Security, Territory, Population*, 66.

49 Worthington, *The Guantánamo Files*, 271–76.

50 William Glaberson and Margot Williams, "Officials Report Suicide of Guantánamo Detainee," *New York Times*, June 3, 2009, http://www.nytimes.com/2009/06/03/us/politics/03gitmo.html.

51 Michael Melia, "Yemeni Official: Gitmo Inmate Died of Asphyxiation," *Associated Press*, August 1, 2009, http://abcnews.go.com/International/wireStory?id=8229664.

52 Quoted in Horton, "The Guantánamo 'Suicides.'" This report strongly suggests that the three men who had been reported to have committed suicide were in fact murdered. If they were murdered, the subsequent efforts to cover up the killings indicate that such deaths were considered impermissible, in contrast to the publicly acknowledged and defended "enhanced interrogations" and force-feeding.

53 Foucault, *"Society Must Be Defended,"* 247–48.

54 Rudi Williams, "Detainees Eat Well, Gain Weight on Camp Delta's Muslim Menu," *American Forces Press Service.* Press release dated July 3, 2002. Available online at http://www.defenselink.mil/ned ws/newsarticle. aspx?id=43686 (accessed August 18, 2009).

55 Mana Raju, "Graham: Detainees Get Better Treatment than Nazis," *Hill,* June 12, 2008, http://thehill.com/leading-the-news/graham-gitmo-detainees-get-better-treatment-than-nazis-2008-06 12.html (accessed August 12, 2009).

56 David D. Kirkpatrick, "Senators Laud Treatment of Detainees in Guantánamo," *New York Times,* June 28, 2005.

57 Ibid.

58 Miles, *Oath Betrayed,* 110.

59 Ben Fox, "Guantánamo Hunger Strikers Say Feeding Tubes Employed as Punishment," *Associated Press,* October 20, 2005.

60 Josh White, "Guantánamo Force-Feeding Tactics Are Called Torture," *Washington Post,* March 1, 2006, section A.

61 Adam Zagorin, "At Guantánamo, Dying Is Not Permitted," *Time,* June 30, 2006, http://www.time.com/time/nation/article/0,8599,1209530,00. htm.

62 Reid, "One in Five Guantánamo Bay Detainees."

63 Tim Golden, "Tough U.S. Steps in Hunger Strike at Camp in Cuba," *New York Times,* February 9, 2006.

64 Ibid.

65 Luke Mitchell, "Six Questions for Cynthia Smith on the Legality of Force-Feeding at Guantánamo," *Harper's,* June 4, 2009, http://harpers.org/ archive/2009/06/hbc-90005110.

66 Department of Defense, Medical Program Support for Detainee Operations, DoD instruction no. 2310.08E, June 6, 2006, http://www.dtic.mil/ whs/directives/corres/pdf/231008p.pdf (accessed April 11, 2010).

67 Zagorin, "Dying Is Not Permitted."

68 Melia, "More Gitmo Detainees Join Hunger Strike."

69 David Nicholl et al., "Forcefeeding and Restraint of Guantánamo Bay Hunger Strikers," *Lancet* 367 (March 11, 2006): 811.

70 David Nicholl, "Guantánamo and Medical Ethics," *Jurist,* June 13, 2006; and Physicians for Human Rights, "Forced Feeding of Gitmo Detainees Violates International Medical Codes of Ethics," September 16, 2005, http://physiciansforhumanrights.org/library/news-2005-09-16.html.

71 Judith Butler, *Precarious Life: Powers of Mourning and Violence* (London: Verso, 2004), 72.

72 Melia, "More Gitmo Detainees Join Hunger Strike."

73   This photograph accompanies Golden, "Tough U.S. Steps in Hunger Strike."

74   George W. Bush, "Remarks by the President on Homeland Security," Office of the Press Secretary, White House, September 10, 2003, http://georgewbush-whitehouse.archives.gov/news/releases/2003/09/20030910-6.html.

75   Richard Sheirer, quoted in Al Baker, "For Emergency Official Touched by 9/11's Horrors, Fears of Complacency," *New York Times*, May 21, 2002, section A.

76   See Allison Howell, "Victims or Madmen? The Diagnostic Competition over 'Terrorist' Detainees at Guantánamo Bay," *International Political Sociology* 1, no. 1 (2007): 29–47.

77   Quoted in Bob Herbert, "Who We Are," *New York Times*, August 1, 2005, http://www.nytimes.com/2005/08/01/opinion/01herbert.html.

5

THE TORTURE DEVICE

Debate and Archetype

Stephanie Athey

Military linguist Erik Saar served as an interpreter at Guantánamo Bay for six months beginning in December 2002. Leaked portions of the manuscript for his book *Inside the Wire* first revealed the use of fake menstrual blood and other sexualized assaults on detainees. As witness to and active participant in interrogations, Saar found these experiences both harrowing and shaming, and his writing struggles to describe the impact of such assaults on captors as well as captives. The book records other brutal treatment at the base—painful stress positions, frigid temperatures, sleep deprivation, and coordinated beatings that resulted in broken bones and brain injuries. While Saar finds the forms of physical and mental pain and suffering at Guantánamo to be shocking and inexcusable from moral and practical standpoints, he ultimately concludes this is not the kind of conduct "most people" would consider torture: "I didn't personally see anything that I would label torture as most people understand the word."[1] Do "most people"—does an American public—share a common image or conception of "torture"? What are the implications of such a claim?[2]

Professor Marcy Strauss of Loyola Law School ultimately relies on this conclusion to derive her working definition in "Torture," a 2004 article in the *New York Law School Law Review*.[3] Writing in the context of a growing media debate on torture, she notes that the media rarely define "torture," and what is more, no decision in U.S. case law offers an "all-encompassing definition": "at best the courts make passing reference to police behavior *as* 'torture' or *like* a 'rack and screw.'" Strauss says, "It's as though we all have the same working definition or conception of torture in mind. Do we?"

The answer, of course, might depend on the meaning of "we." It is unlikely that bystanders, perpetrators, and recipients of such abuse bear the same "working definition" of torture in mind. This essay explores the meanings ascribed to the word "torture" in news and legal writing from 2001 to 2005, paying particular attention to "the quintessential picture of torture" that emerges, to use Strauss's terms.[4] The features of that archetype have implications not only for policy and debate but also for the kind of community torture describes and divides.

Consider Ehab Elmaghraby, a New York restaurant owner and Muslim immigrant who had lived in the United States for thirteen years. He was apprehended along with hundreds of Muslim and Arab immigrants in the days after September 11, 2001, and held in the Metropolitan Detention Center Brooklyn, New York. He was jailed until 2003 and was among many who were charged only with financial crimes unrelated to terrorism and finally deported. Elmaghraby and fellow inmate Jvail Iqbal filed suit against the U.S. government. Among other things, they charged they were subjected to kicking and punching until they bled and "multiple unnecessary body-cavity searches, including one in which correction officers inserted a flashlight into [Elmaghraby's] rectum, making him bleed."[5] Theirs was not an isolated case. A Department of Justice review later denounced assaults at the Brooklyn facility during that period, many of them caught on videotape. The department's inspector general's 2003 report on the detention center found "widespread abuse of noncitizen detainees." On February 28, 2006, the *New York Times* announced that the U.S. government agreed to pay $300,000 to settle with Elmaghraby.

Rape in detention, which the *New York Times* described in Elmaghraby's case as an "unnecessary body cavity search," qualifies as torture. Torture, according to United Nations convention, involves acts by persons who as agents of the state or with the acquiescence or at the instigation of the state inflict severe pain or suffering, whether physical or mental, on persons in custody. Rape is a routine form of torture, and historically, a "search" is a common alibi for rape.[6] And yet, though a rape in a New York detention center by corrections officers falls well within the definition of state torture, the location, perpetrators, and act itself place it in a universe of similar violations that the United States is accustomed to recognize as police brutality or abuse rather than torture. The use of one term instead of another is more than a matter of euphemism or careful language crafted to evade prosecution. It is also indicative of the ways many U.S. citizens imagine torture, what they have come to believe torture is and is not.

This essay examines the public discourse of torture, particularly in the early debate, and uses aspects of Elmaghraby's ordeal to draw attention to three key arguments. It first considers an archetypal representation of torture circulating widely in speculative news and legal argument since 9/11. In arguments both for and against the use of torture, the unquestioned status and prevalence of an archetypal encounter between interrogator and subject have made it iconic, defining and limiting our understanding of torture, terrorist, and terror through its very repetition. It has helped promote a misrecognition of torture, past and present. For instance, Elmaghraby's torture, though it meets the UN definition, falls outside the circle defined by this archetypal instance. This iconic depiction is also far afield from, say, torture events at Abu Ghraib prison in Iraq or the circumstances alleged in the cases of the forty-five men suspected or confirmed to have been murdered in U.S. military custody, yet it has been and continues to be mobilized routinely in news writing.[7] Ultimately, the archetype functions, even in nuanced rejections of torture, to narrow our understanding of the systemic and communal nature of torture and to disconnect torture from its history of use in the United States: the use of torture in lynching and internal racial repression; its use in U.S. colonial wars and counterinsurgency programs in Cold War client states; and its use in policing contexts and prisons. These three lines of American descent are visible in the torture methods at issue in the war on terror today.

The first argument, therefore, traces the archetypal view of torture found in recent news and law suggesting the ways in which it closes off inquiry into the social nature of torture and its historical continuity. The second argument concerns the interplay between archetype and alibi, focusing in particular on one official alibi for torture that has proved very effective. To explain, more than a justification or rationalization offered before or after the fact, an alibi is often encoded in the very act of torture as one of its necessary elements. The flashlight used in Elmaghraby's torture is an instructive example. Aside from its ability to create pain, humiliation, and injury, the flashlight plays another strategic role. A flashlight is a common tool for use in a search, and it bears a commonsense association with the act of searching. Therefore, when a flashlight is used to rape, it also enacts the alibi in symbolic form; it is simultaneously a tool of torture and a powerful tool of misdirection.

Scholar Elaine Scarry produced a treatise on the practice of torture and the symbolic language of pain in 1985.[8] Drawing heavily on Amnesty International documentation from 1975–80 of torture in Greece, South Vietnam, Brazil, and the Philippines, *The Body in Pain* underscores the theatrical and representational essence of torture. The calculated display of weapons, wounds, and techniques to the prisoner, his or her family, or the public, the theatrical rituals of interrogation that accompany physical pain, all these are common symbolic elements that are important to torture's ends. Those symbols can be made, on the one hand, to tell a story of the torturer's power. On the other hand, they can be made to point to the suffering human body, isolated and destroyed by pain. While Scarry's narrative tells the latter story, that of the suffering body, she describes how torturers use the ritual and symbol of torture to weave a story that "converts pain into the fiction of the torturer's power." Ironically and necessarily, that fiction of power always conveys vulnerability as well. The subjects, though in custody, are made to represent an immediate and overwhelming threat to state power. And the state's vulnerability justifies a further exercise of state power.

In the ritualized language of torture, then, the flashlight is both a visual and a conceptual prop, an aspect of the symbolic structure of Elmaghraby's torture. It violates the prisoner but signals the converse, the prisoner's latent violence, the shiv or weapon or secret contained in his anus. Armed with a flashlight, the perpetrators may appear as if they truly are committed to nothing more than an especially diligent, thorough search of the body, a technique for seeking out Elmaghraby's violent potential. Perhaps out of an excess of zealousness or professionalism, the "search" went "too far." The flashlight rape offers a clear example of the way in which the very tools, rituals, and methods of torture establish their own alibi. While such an alibi may not be so effective as to make torture acceptable, it can serve to misconstrue and rename it. Indeed, the *New York Times'* description of the rape as an "unnecessary body cavity search" goes a long way toward proving this point.

As with the flashlight, the torture alibi is an important and integral part of the performance; it helps accomplish the act. In a similar way, but one harder to see, props and rituals associated with questioning prisoners have consistently invoked "interrogation" as an alibi for torture. In 1985, Elaine Scarry articulated "intelligence gathering" or "interrogation" as a powerful false motive for torture. That false motive, she wrote, was an alibi integrated into torture practice at the very level we have been describing. For Scarry, whose work is discussed more critically later, pain accompanied by ritual questioning is a specific type of torture, not a specific type of questioning. The torture debate has in no way really separated torture from the alibi of interrogation or considered torture's other ends, and the archetypal view further anchors our thinking to this alibi.

The third and final argument of this essay holds that just as the archetype reinforces the alibi, the archetype also complements a common assertion that recurs throughout the torture debate: that torture is a new and possibly necessary tool in the U.S. arsenal against terror. All sides in the U.S. torture debate have routinely asserted or implied that torture is something alien to the contemporary United States, not something thoroughly integrated into police work, domestic systems of punishment, or international security relationships.[9]

Ehab Elmaghraby and Jvail Iqbal and hundreds of other immigrant men rounded up in the first weeks after September 11, 2001, were, after all, among the first war-on-terror detainees. They were held in Brooklyn, before detention camps were established in Afghanistan, Guantánamo, and beyond, before Iraq. No new doctrine, or legal memos, executive orders, or Defense Department protocols were necessary to initiate the torture of Elmaghraby or the other men who suffered from "widespread abuse of noncitizen detainees." They were among the first to understand that, however "new" or unprecedented this war on terror, with respect to torture, it would build on old routines of detention and suppression.

Speculation on Torture

As a possibility and practice, torture has been proposed and discussed in the U.S. press since September 2001, first emerging in mid-September in news I call "speculative" as opposed to "investigative." Dozens of feature stories, news analyses, and commentaries debated the utility of torture in the war on terror in the pages of the *New York Times, Wall Street Journal, Washington Post, Newsweek, Time, Atlantic Monthly,* and *New Yorker.* Many features distinguish the speculative writing from the investigative reporting, but just a few of the titles that appeared from September 2001 to the end of 2003 will illustrate this point: "How Far Americans Would Go to Fight Terror," "Seeking a Moral Compass While Chasing Terrorists," "Security Comes Before Liberty," "Time to Think about Torture," "Agonizing Over Torture: Can Deliberate Hurt Be Justified in Times of Terror?" "No Tortured Dilemma," "A Nasty Business," "Should We Torture Qaeda Higher Ups?" "Making Terrorists Talk: America Doesn't Use Torture to Get Information Out of Terrorists; Perhaps We Just Need to Use the Magic Word: Mossad," "Make Them Talk," "Interrogation School — 30 Techniques . . . Just Short of Torture; Do They Yield Much?" "The Torturer's Apprentice," "Torture, Tough or Lite: If a Terror Suspect Won't Talk, Should He Be Made To?" "Word for Word: Psychology and Sometimes a Slap; The Man Who Made Prisoners Talk," "The Dark Art of Interrogation: The Most Effective Way to Gather Intelligence and Thwart Terrorism Can Also Be a Direct Route into Morally Repugnant Terrain; A Survey of the Landscape of Persuasion."

What are we to make of the speculative engine that began to turn as early as September 2001?

Two things are important to note. First, such speculative commentaries and features on torture have been prolific and sustained, gathering momentum *before* the November 2001 executive order on military tribunals signaled the scope of the U.S. administration's intentions toward captives, and they gained critical mass years before the 2004 photos from Abu Ghraib. That is to say, the speculative press was busily defining torture and imagining its uses well in advance of and alongside the classified torture memos and interrogation protocols quietly being drawn up inside the executive branch.

Second, hypothetical torture became a big news story while actual torture went unreported. It is striking that during the same period in which these speculations on torture occasioned lively response, indications and evidence that torture was already in use were met by near silence. Only a few, perhaps as few as seven, investigative pieces looked at brutal and illegal measures that characterized the actual practice of apprehending, handling, detaining, transferring, or interrogating prisoners.[10] One of the first of the investigative stories was a report on March 11, 2002, in the *Washington Post*, "US Behind Secret Transfer of Terror Suspects." Journalists Rajiv Chandrasekaran and Peter Finn describe in some detail the cases of eight persons who had been subject to extralegal arrest and rendition to a third country. Their discussion of torture and U.S. responsibility is frank:

> The suspects have been taken to countries, including Egypt and Jordan, whose intelligence services have close ties to the CIA and where they can be subjected to interrogation tactics — including torture and threats to families — that are illegal in the United States, the sources said. In some cases, U.S. intelligence agents remain closely involved in the interrogation, the sources said. "After September 11, these sorts of movements have been occurring all the time," a U.S. diplomat said. "It allows us to get information from terrorists in a way we can't do on U.S. soil."[11]

When the *Washington Post* returned to the topic nine months later, on December 26, 2002, it published a piece about treatment in U.S. custody titled "U.S. Decries Abuse but Defends Interrogations; 'Stress and Duress' Tactics Used on Terrorism Suspects Held in Secret Overseas Facilities." Writers Dana Priest and Barton Gellman identified U.S. strategies of physical violence and sensory manipulation in custody as well as third-country rendition. The report did not assign the term "torture" to the detainee treatment it recorded, preferring to examine the term and to walk around the notion with great care.

This scant handful of early investigative reports bears all the elements of the broader story on U.S. torture that would consume the press by mid-2004 in the wake of revelations from Abu Ghraib, minus only the nudity, dogs, corpses, and, of course, the photos. These early articles contain detailed observations and telling comments from government officials, but nevertheless they vanished without follow-up stories. What is more, the government's own near acknowledgment of torture in January 2004 set off no storm of curiosity. A one-paragraph press release issued on January 16 indicated in colorless language that an investigation into detainee abuse at a "coalition facility" was under way. The *American Journalism Review* counted only four newspapers and three networks that offered cursory reports on the release.[12]

When CBS broadcast visual evidence of torture at Abu Ghraib prison in Iraq three months later, in late April 2004, the investigative press was stirred to action and has since pursued a string of legal memos and executive protocols, revealing the trail of command documents that created the environment necessary for torture and attempted to establish zones of impunity.

Obsessed as we then became with one paper trail, we neglected to investigate another. The speculative news writing on torture has been broadly influential, shaping the larger discourse and setting the parameters of thought. It struck narrative postures, anointed experts, and lent terminology, propositions, and anecdotal evidence that were taken up and repeated in other arenas. In circular fashion, the speculative pieces generated, then echoed and publicized what has been termed "the torture debate" taking place in legal reviews and academic publishing as well. And prevalent in that debate has been a single archetypal depiction of torture.

The Torture Archetype

Despite valuable studies of media, terror, and violence, the outpouring of *speculative* commentary debating torture's desirability has received no critical attention in studies of the media response to 9/11. Nor has it received extended comment in the press's own self-critical reflections following the Abu Ghraib revelations. Yet there are patterns worthy of study. For instance, the speculative news writing can be sorted into three uneven groups in order to highlight common structures and approaches, namely, Hypothetical, Historical, and Heart of Darkness narratives. The Hypothetical stories use imagined scenarios to pose the "should we or should we not?" question to so-called specialists. The stories might elicit comment on a ticking-time-bomb scenario, or they may discuss results of opinion surveys or student quizzes on torture.[13] The Historical group ponders torture through two primary models. Not coincidentally, both are campaigns against Muslim populations: France's use of torture against Algerians and Israel's use of torture against Palestinians.[14] The third group of news speculation draws core elements from the Hypothetical and Historical stories, fusing them into a larger Heart of Darkness narrative. Here, a lone journalist sets forth to explore the practice and practitioners of torture. He exudes a calculated moral ambivalence and exhibits a powerful fascination with the torturer and his "dark arts," "hard questions," and "unthinkable choices."[15]

Among many other things, these formulaic structures promote certain views of history, for instance, weighing the utility of torture by conflating quite distinct land-based occupations and anticolonial struggles, in Palestine and Algeria, with a newer, specialized and Islamist strain of terrorist franchise. So, too, they ignore the United States' historical track record on torture and strike narrative postures that promote the reader's identification with the would-be torturers, or with the protected citizenry, but not with those subjected to torture. This last point is critically important. Speculative stories on torture must be weighed in light of the cultural and political work they do imagining and projecting a unified community that believes it has a stake in torture. While the most important aspect of these stories may be their attempt to fashion that community, I focus instead on a very simple but pervasive depiction of torture in news since 2001. This depiction also works in concert with the other narrative devices to manipulate historical understanding. While seeming to make torture visible, the archetype works to suppress historical memory of torture's trauma and enables its perpetuation in the present.

The explicit features of this device will seem immediately familiar, as if they were representational prerequisites that in themselves define torture. The first is a focus on specific techniques. The investigative pieces pursue these primarily: which techniques were authorized, which were out of bounds, which are torture, which are so-called torture lite, and so on. But in taking technique as its focus, the speculative writing on the utility of torture implicitly relies on a certain staging of the torture scene. The setting is an interrogation, a one-on-one encounter between the subject of questioning and a skilled, goal-oriented professional who inflicts calculated amounts of pain. The pain inflicted is managed by a technique that has a definite beginning and a specific duration, and the pain is produced in a controlled and incremental fashion (that is, one neither murders the subject outright nor begins with the most extreme pain).

Once the scene has been invoked, torture has been named, looked in the face, and we know what it's made of, as in Jonathan Alter's 2001 piece "Time to Think about Torture" or Peter Maas's 2003 "Torture Tough or Lite: If a Terror Suspect Won't Talk, Should He Be Made To?" The scene is so common, so iconic, that one element can imply another: the subject in "the fetid basement cell" and the technique or injury—"the teeth extracted," "limbs broken"—can together invoke the torturer and his demands. In a Historical piece such as Bruce Hoffman's "A Nasty Business" or a Heart of Darkness feature such as Mark Bowden's "The Dark Art of Interrogation," the struggle between potential torturer and subject is Manichean in tone and drives the structure of the report. The language lyricizes the torturer's dire world of urgency and ethical quandary or the subject's world of pain and isolation, or both.

The dual agonists of the iconic scenario obviously are underscored by the graphics that accompany these articles. The articles by Hoffman and Bowden, for instance, and most of the longer features carry sidebar illustrations that suggest a single perpetrator—a long shadow leaning in through a cell door—or a single victim, wrists dangling from shackles or a man blindfolded and strapped to a chair beneath a bare lightbulb, and the like. At times, the news writing may use the example of a single subject who is being implicitly worked over by many perpetrators whom the story renders as a larger entity: "the Philippine police" or "Jordan." Not only is a team personified as a single entity, but the group nature of the event may be underplayed or erased through passive voice construction that accents the technique, not the technicians: "teeth pulled," "limbs broken," and so on.

Archetype in Anti-torture Scholarship

Much of the legal argument as well as the speculative news debating torture in the wake of 9/11 have defined torture implicitly through this archetypal interplay between interrogator and subject, torturer and victim. Indeed, the ticking-time-bomb scenario, so prevalent in torture-debate articles by and responding to Alan Dershowitz, Sanford Levinson, Richard Posner, and the like, simply recombines features of the archetype, making artful enhancements to the motives of the key figures and the circumstances in which they meet. The archetype and the time bomb, however, are not identical. While the time-bomb scenario recasts the archetype in order to justify torture, even those who reject torture and do so absolutely often portray torture in the iconic mold, imagining the same duo locked in the same elemental battle. The key difference is they cast their lot with the subject.

Early examples of this in the modern campaign to end torture are instructive. For instance, Amnesty International's groundbreaking 1973 campaign to abolish torture opened its appeal to the public with selections from a Turkish survivor's testimony, which closely followed this formula: an isolated subject, a torturer, an array of graphic techniques. Amnesty reassessed its representational strategy a decade later, incorporating an empowered spectator acting to prevent torture, but the point here is the power and recurrence of the archetypal representation of torture.[16]

Elaine Scarry's *The Body in Pain* drew on the full complexity of Amnesty's documentation from the 1970s, not just the rhetoric of the opening appeal. A fascinating and careful argument based on Amnesty reports as well as literary and philosophical sources, Scarry's profound contribution exposes "interrogation" as an alibi that plays an integral role in the theatrical pantomime of torture. And yet, for Scarry, "the basic structure of torture" is the iconic scenario I have described; her analysis keeps torture structurally bound to the charade of interrogation and the archetypal depiction. Torture is "essentially a two-person event . . . premised on one-directional injuring."[17] To better delineate its features, she lifts the players out of historical and cultural space and time: "Torture has a structure that is as narrow and consistent as its geographical incidence is widespread." She further explains, "That structure entails the simultaneous and inseparable occurrence of three events . . . first, the infliction of physical pain; second, the objectification of the eight central attributes of pain; and third, the translation of those attributes into the insignia of the regime."[18] For Scarry, the "one-directional injuring" of torture relies upon the symbolic rituals of interrogation, but torture is not about eliciting speech and information. Instead, it uses speech to reduce the subject's voice either to silence or to an echo of the interrogator's. In eliminating the subject's ability to speak for himself or herself, torture destroys language, self, and the social world all at once. The pretense to interrogation is part of the ritual violence.

Defining torture, therefore, through this archetypal exchange between torturer and subject, Scarry concludes that torture is an extreme limit, the "condensed case," the "absolute model" of destruction, more exemplary of total destruction than war. An attack on the self, the voice, and social world, torture reverses the process of creative labor. It is civilization deliberately unmade.

Scarry's *The Body in Pain* has been widely influential, and she is cited in one of the most provocative and thorough legal rebuttals to the contemporary, post-9/11, time-bomb debate. In an essay published in the *Virginia Law Review* in December 2005, David Luban persuasively unravels the time-bomb scenario as a "jejeune" cheat, an "intellectual fraud."[19] His piece offers historical range on attitudes toward cruelty in liberal democracy; he urges us to look away from the mesmerizing time bomb and toward the "torture lawyers of Washington" and the legal apparatus they have attempted to establish for state torture. His essay points to torture as a practice that would require social networks to sustain it, but ironically his understanding of torture keeps pulling him back to the narrow archetypal dyad. Why is torture more repugnant than killing or war? Luban's response: "The answer lies in the relationship between torturer and victim." He explains with a stress on the two-ness of torture:

> Torture aims, in other words, to strip away from its victim all the qualities of human dignity that liberalism prizes. It does this by the deliberate actions of a torturer, who inflicts pain one-on-one, up close and personal, in order to break the spirit of the victim—in other words, to tyrannize and dominate the victim. The relationship between them becomes a perverse parody of friendship and intimacy: intimacy transformed into its inverse image, where the torturer focuses on the victim's body with the intensity of a lover, except that every bit of that focus is bent to causing pain and tyrannizing the victim's spirit. At bottom all torture is rape, and all rape is tyranny.[20]

Luban says, "Torture is a microcosm (raised to the highest level of intensity) of the tyrannical political relationships that liberalism hates the most."[21]

Philosopher David Sussman, too, defines torture in its elemental duality and diabolical intimacy in the *Case Western Journal of International Law.*

"For torture to occur," the antagonists must be "standing in a particular kind of relationship with one another, and understand that the other understands this as well."[22] This perverse relationship is a "living death," a kind of "anti-life," a "natural slavery."[23] For Sussman, torture inverts, again, at the highest level of intensity, the very principle of human dignity in social relations.

For Scarry, then, torture is the inverse of civilization, human labor, and creation, and for Sussman and Luban, torture is the inverse of human dignity or the liberal democratic social bond. For Columbia University law professor Jeremy Waldron, torture is the inverse of law itself. In his *Columbia Law Review* article of October 2005, Waldron argues that torture and its prohibition play an "archetypal function" within law, what he also describes as a "background function." Torture is an image and exemplum, persistently embodying and communicating a vital standard. It is a form of brutal violation so fundamental that its prohibition is the basis of all legal prohibitions; it "expresses and epitomizes the spirit . . . of the entire legal enterprise." The prohibition is "vividly emblematic of our determination to sever the link between law and brutality, between law and terror, and the enterprise of breaking a person's will."[24] As do Scarry and Luban, Waldron chooses examples that stress the interrogational setting of torture, and his language emphasizes the visual character and power of this legal archetype: the prohibition on torture "sums up or makes vivid to us" the point or purpose of law.[25]

Scarry, Luban, Sussman, and Waldron all reduce torture to this "basic structure," emblem, or model the better to enlarge it as a theory of pain and civilization, liberal democracy, or law. In warning against it, they lift the practice out of its historical, social, and institutional complexity and continuities. What is more, they install this image of torture as a threshold the United States has yet to cross: there is a before and an after to torture. For liberal democracy, permission to torture is a gateway to the new, a fall from innocence, a plunge into the unknown.

Looking Beyond the Archetype

All of these authors—journalists, academics, and jurists—mobilize an image of torture that is already a stylized image of interrogation, a one-on-one encounter, an archetype that has been presented repeatedly to the public in news commentary since 2001. What is fascinating is how far afield this iconic depiction is from actual interrogation, let alone torture. Even noncoercive questioning is not a one-on-one encounter. It involves questioners, translators, military guards, security contractors, and other observers.

Nor is torture itself secluded, a single identifiable act, or a one-on-one practice. Military investigations, military memoirs, detainee statements, and reporting details routinely indicate multiple persons at the scene of physical and psychological violence in custody. This is the case when group violence closely approximates recreation: the High Five Paintball Club of Camp Nama, in Baghdad, used prisoners for target practice.[26] Soldiers at Forward Operating Base Mercury in Iraq lined up to strike prisoners' knees and shins with a baseball bat and also assembled human pyramids à la Abu Ghraib.[27] Groups of guards at the detention center in Bagram Airbase in Afghanistan used severely painful and eventually fatal kneeing in the thigh because they were amused to hear the prisoner's cries of "Allah!" with each strike.[28]

The torture of sexual assault is also a group undertaking. Masquerading as a "security measure," it is a persistent feature of detention. Such was the case with those first detainees in the war on terror, men like Ehab Elmaghraby, who charged that "corrections officers inserted a flashlight into his rectum, making him bleed."[29] This form of rape follows a pattern of anal searches reported by detainees freed from Guantánamo and confirmed by military personnel. They are described as unnecessary because performed on men who had been under guard, their hands shackled far from the anus between "searches."[30] Interrogator Chris Mackey writes that at Bagram, these probes were preceded by the shout "Cavity search!" meant to further humiliate the individual and intimidate the group.[31]

The daily attentions of military police (MPs) can be unpredictable, violent, and humiliating. Some released detainees detail weeks and days of interminable softening-up activities or the violent and degrading contact surrounding daily needs. MPs function in pairs and teams while escorting, "controlling," caging, feeding, attending, and supervising prisoners' bathing and bathroom trips or depriving them of same.

When torture poses as interrogation, it, too, is a group event. At Baghdad airport, several U.S. Navy SEALs and CIA officers "interrogated" homicide victim Manadel Al-Jamadi in the so-called Romper Room "in a rough manner." When transferred to Abu Ghraib, two MPs, CIA officer Mark Swanner, and a translator worked together to lift and steady the battered prisoner into a "Palestinian hanging" position, in which he died.[32] Indeed, the shackling, overhead or otherwise, as well as forced standing and sleep deprivation, not to mention waterboarding or beatings, all require teamwork: to restrain, lift, position, or return the prisoner to consciousness.

Challenging the Archetype

These investigative news accounts and testimonials challenge the common archetype for torture in powerful ways. For one, isolating a technique, a moment, or a "basic structure" that constitutes torture is difficult in these accounts. What is more, though the iconic scenario diverts our thinking from this fact, torture is a group dynamic and occurs in a context marked by complicated group dynamics.[33] These accounts exist because spectators are present. As soldiers and intelligence officers observe prisoners, they also observe each other. Accounts by interrogators Chris Mackey and Tony Lagouranis, and military reports on "abuse" at Abu Ghraib by Major General Antonio M. Taguba, Major General George R. Fay, and Lieutenant General Anthony R. Jones, all point to the mystique, envy, and admiration with which the workers at Bagram, Abu Ghraib, and a U.S. base near Mosul watched the CIA or Special Operations personnel who moved among them. Electronic surveillance is an ever present feature of the environment and is multilayered. At Camp Nama, Special Ops personnel took care to watch their watchers, monitoring the e-mail and phone communications of their CIA or FBI colleagues.[34] Former army chaplain James Yee remarks that soldiers at Guantánamo talked circumspectly about the semi-clandestine total-surveillance environment, referring to the "secret squirrels" who could be watching and listening to a soldier's every move.

More intimate than electronic surveillance is the host of peers, colleagues, and supervisors involved at close range. Interrogator Mackey, writing about his time at Bagram, describes the populated detention camp as a setting organized by rank, clear division of labor, and complex sets of mixed agendas. Professional identities are asserted and formed in the context of peer groups who can be cooperative and also always highly competitive. Groups are attuned to their impact on detainees and how that impact might impress the others and their commanders. Workers are hyperaware of their own specialized task—scheduling, questioning, translating, writing reports, editing, and transmitting—but they also are hyperaware of negotiating roles among a hierarchy of players, including military police and multiple contractors, service branches, and intelligence services. MPs or military interrogators who spend time with prisoners are anything but isolated. Personnel respond to the close physical presence of coworkers and to their awareness of nearby soldiers, civilians, and prisoners. All the above examples of violence detailed in investigative news and military reports took place in such communal contexts. In the face of this, it can only seem strange that so many speculative news features as well as legal and philosophical arguments for and against torture scrub from the scene all onlookers, fellow participants, and other captives, leaving only the dyad of torturer and tortured in place.

This dyadic view of power or suffering may be a habit of mind and argument borrowed from Western philosophy or Enlightenment rhetoric of suffering.[35] While the origins of this iconic and dyadic formulation are beyond the scope of this essay, discussion of the political and cultural consequences of this archetype are not. First, the archetype narrowly defines torture and encodes an alibi for torture in that very definition. The archetype anchors the definition of torture to the act of interrogation, limiting recognition and analysis of violence that comes in other varieties and settings. Second, despite all evidence to the contrary, the archetype and alibi promote a dubious understanding of torture as a "means" to a single purported "end." In doing so, the archetype forecloses consideration of the multiple functions and effects of torture, such as securing power, authority, morale, or communal identities through ritualized violence; marking out a particular political, racial, religious, ethnic, or gender group for domination (by torture of representative members); and ensuring allegiance or subjugation of broader populations through fear. Third, the archetype telegraphs a scenario that removes from consideration the institutions, social structures, and communal energies that support the practice.

To begin with the third consequence, just as the nature of the archetypal duo closes down avenues of inquiry, simply reintroducing other players opens torture to different paths of analysis and political action.

It may be clear that a dyadic view of the "basic structure" of torture does not make a chain of command basic to that structure, although torture certainly is embedded in a chain of command. In fact, the dyad closes off from scrutiny all political, social, and economic networks that support the activity. These certainly include social and institutional arrangements designed to train and condition violence workers, such as those described in a recent study of Brazilian torturers or Tony Lagouranis's 2007 first-person account of torture in Mosul, Iraq.[36] Erasure of supporting networks also includes the supply chain that manufactures and equips state personnel with, say, tasers in the first place — like those used by four Special Ops officers disciplined for burning captives at Camp Nama and like those exported to our rendition allies annually.[37] In 2003, in the midst of all the speculative debate on the utility of torture in the war on terror, a single story in *U.S. News and World Report* noted that more than sixty American companies had obtained annual approvals to export stun batons, stun guns, thumb cuffs, and other devices to thirty-nine countries known to torture dissidents.[38] There are other devices, special and mundane, that come from somewhere at a profit: restraint chairs for force-feeding, trained dogs, shackles, flex cuffs, goggles, and hoods.

Torture requires a command structure, an infrastructure, and a supply chain. So, too, does it require group support. As Scarry has it, torture produces a fiction of state power, yet it produces as well a communal dynamic. Torture forges group or individual identities for perpetrators, supervisors, and bystanders. There is not only the semi-clandestine surveillance of soldiers' and civilians' activities to consider but also the physical and psychological dynamics of small- or large-group participation, the camaraderie and energy of people together, responding to, performing for, and competing with one another through violence. The "perverse parody of friendship and intimacy" described in the one-on-one exchange of anti-torture rhetoric must be revised in the light of this group participation. A view of the group calls attention to the real physical intimacy, energy, and eroticism forged among spectators and perpetrators of sexual, psychological, and physical violence.[39]

In the same way that perpetrators are not acting alone, subjects are not simply or only "isolated in their pain," as Scarry and Luban put it.[40] Those subjected to torture are assaulted together or forced to hear or witness the terror and shaming of others. To reorient our thinking and to reckon with torture as a communal assault on groups or aggregates obviously lays bare the range of functions, effects, and ends otherwise obscured by the archetypal depiction. That reorientation opens for consideration the relations among torture and racism, misogyny, religious persecution, and other oppressions that have been enacted historically through torture but rendered absent from the "basic structure" of the archetype. The fact that the Abu Ghraib torture photos implied that spectators were anticipated and essential was as profoundly disturbing to some as the corpses or brutalities depicted. That the Abu Ghraib tortures were community-building events, enacting, drawing, or securing lines of racial, gender, and religious division through forms of sexual and religious violence, was captured in some of the writing in 2004.[41] But this insight was fleeting and was not applied to torture in the general case. The dyadic view of torture was not remade in order to accommodate an understanding of torture as a communal rite. It is telling that when the crowded cell block of Abu Ghraib has been memorialized visually as "torture" on book jackets and elsewhere, it has been through the silhouette of a single hooded man, not the group silhouette of human backs, buttocks, and genitals exposed in a human pyramid or a masturbation circle of captives and captors.

Finally, to return to the first point concerning political and cultural consequences, the archetype's narrow definition of torture encodes its own alibi. Instead of bringing into view the multiple forms of torture and the environments in which it takes place, its complex institutional and communal conditions of possibility, and its breadth of impact, the archetype deliberately excises these, keeping torture bound to a scenario in which intelligence gathering is said to be its primary purpose and alibi.

Considering the power and prevalence of the archetype and its grip on the public imagination, perhaps only a momentous conceptual shift could prepare one to look beyond the "interrogation" alibi and fairly consider whether information gathering is really at stake in torture at all. Reviewing investigative reports and testimonials on torture from the current conflict, it seems clear that torture is not linked necessarily or even primarily to the interrogation booth. To the contrary, some detainees have described actual questioning as a period of respite from the mental and physical violence of "care" in detention.[42] What is more, no matter how far removed from the rituals and symbols of interrogation, the alibi of interrogation persists. All treatment in detention no matter how violent or bizarre becomes a preparation for interrogation, so-called softening up; nothing occurs that does not in some way refer back to and support the alibi.

Detainee accounts, together with participant memoirs by military personnel and detainees, suggest that torture is not an isolatable act or technique but a larger, more extensive condition, a mode of domination enacted through ritualized interaction in which time and space as well as other instruments are used against bodies for the purpose of creating severe pain and suffering, physical and mental. This altered understanding of torture comes into view when reading survivor testimony across many periods and geographical locations and when reviewing psychological and sociological documents on torture survivors and perpetrators. Nigel Rodley, former special rapporteur on questions relevant to torture for the United Nations' High Commissioner for Human Rights, locates the origin of torture in detention, not interrogation, specifically incommunicado detention prolonged for more than one day.

Nonetheless, news and legal scholarship persistently reinforce the mental link between the idea of torture and the pretense of intelligence gathering, even if only to point out, as does Jeremy Waldron, that it makes for lousy interrogation. Even so, in other speculative news and legal writing rejecting torture, the dyadic view has helped reinforce intelligence gathering as the underlying goal and continues to assert the interrogator's booth as the place where torture begins only to break free, "metastasize," or "run amok." We have lost Scarry's fundamental insight that this is a false motive, an integrated alibi. Torture masquerades as interrogation and has many other guises.

As argued by practitioners themselves, while questioning might devolve into physical and mental assault, it ceases to be effective questioning at precisely that point. It becomes merely assault. Scarry points out that ritual questioning may continue during assaults in order to reinforce the alibi and the personal humiliations. Abusive "questioning" while beating or freezing or hanging or drowning a prisoner is no more related to intelligence gathering than a flashlight in the anus is related to a search. Questioning prisoners for useful intelligence is a separate undertaking, requiring different skills.[43]

In the larger institutional sense, the focus on physical and mental violence undermines intelligence gathering. Darius Rejali repeatedly makes the point that torture saps energy and resources from modes of investigation that collect, follow, and develop information. In his terms, reliance on torture actually "de-skills" the intelligence or police services that use it. In the U.S. context, one can easily see that the necessary debates over intelligence gathering through torture have taken precedence over valid but neglected intelligence-gathering challenges—such as hiring, training, and retaining translators or designing and bringing online data management software with adequate search capacity for the FBI. Years after 9/11 exposed this fundamental failure in the U.S. intelligence service, the heralded connect-the-dots ware is still not in place.[44]

Too often in the speculative torture debate, one's willingness to face the "hard questions" and one's commitment to homeland protection have been measured in one's willingness to commit violence, instead of, say, one's willingness to improve investigation. The latter requires willingness to wage battle within a nation's bureaucracies, restructuring Washington's pathways of money and power. One could argue that far harder than deciding to torture suspected terrorists are the tasks of devising and implementing faster and more effective institutional routines for identifying and tracking terror cells; detecting the flows of funding, ammunitions, technology, and data that support terrorists; collecting, translating, and analyzing relevant communications; projecting possible terror scenarios and devising and funding new policies or practices to prevent those scenarios—and doing all this with speed and accuracy. The archetypal presentation of torture narrows not only our recognition and understanding of torture but also our understanding of neglected but necessary intelligence-gathering tasks.

One urgent conclusion is that our thinking and discussion about torture need to move much further out from under the shadow of the interrogator's booth and the spell of the archetype in order to see not only the varieties of torture but also its multiple functions and effects. Idelbar Avelar suggests we think of torture as ubiquitous instead of an accident or excess.[45] Put in other terms, having declared a state of war on a racialized, global enemy, violence is the rule of engagement; it is the *medium* of contact. Interrogational torture is but one ritualized and self-justifying form of that ubiquitous violence. Torture may occur in the interrogation booth, but it does not emanate from it. More critical energy must be mustered to attack the false link between interrogation and torture.

Further, archetype and alibi not only obscure the functions and effects of torture but also curtail responsibility for it. To remove suppliers, commanders, participants, multiple victims, survivors, and spectators from our basic representation of torture closes off avenues of thought that lead to theories of complicity and from these back to ourselves as news consumers, spectators, and participants in the debate, not to mention ourselves as beneficiaries of the protection (or profit) said to be generated by the practice. Luc Boltanski's work on morality, media, and politics argues that contemporary media shape positive moral and emotional response to suffering by mobilizing specific rhetorical forms, vignettes that "nourish the imagination and coordinate political response" across populations. The iconic representation of torture I have been discussing might be likened to one such vignette: it features a subject of suffering and an agent of pain but removes the reflective spectator that Boltanski takes to be crucial in vignettes that enlist a political response. Ervin Staub has argued that entire societies prepare in advance to commit the violence of torture or genocide. The iconic image circulated in news and legal debate has been a powerful vignette on this order, at worst a form of preparation for violence, at best a dead end for analytical thought and for political response to torture in all the ways suggested in this chapter.

Finally, in its depiction of torture as an isolated exchange cut off from communal dynamics and a history of training, supervision, torture technology, and supply, the archetype complements assertions that the use of torture in the U.S. war on terror augurs something exceptional and new. This contention is common among those who advocate torture's use; they depict torture as a new tool for fighting "a new kind of war." It is common as well among those who reject torture; they hold that the Bush administration's attempts to legalize the practice signaled a new era, bringing us to the "gateway by which the demonic and depraved enter into public life."[46]

These persistent assertions are odd, almost absurd, in their neglect or willful denial of this nation's long and intimate history with the practice of torture. Some may certainly see the George W. Bush and Dick Cheney administration as distinct in its claim to sweeping war powers for the president; its signing statements on anti-torture legislation, supported by the October 2006 Military Commissions Act, empower the executive to define and authorize torture at will. Some might also see as a grave departure the legal maneuvers that made a range of heretofore legally prohibited violence formally permissible. But consider: torture has always belonged to the state to define and deploy. We need not look far back in the *New York Times* to find reports of torture used against Al Qaeda suspects, for instance, in 1995 and 2000 against World Trade Center and U.S. embassy bombing suspects respectively, who were tortured under the supervision of the FBI, not the CIA.[47] In this light, it is indeed peculiar that the news writing I have discussed looks repeatedly to Israel and France for a torture track record, not to the United States in Latin America, the Philippines, or Vietnam. As with the made-in-America torture devices, we have deliberately developed, practiced, and exported U.S. torture know-how for most of the twentieth century.[48]

Indeed, torture's history of use in lynching and internal racial repression, in U.S. colonial wars and counterinsurgency programs in Cold War client states, and in policing contexts and prisons encompasses three lines of descent that are important for analyzing the practice as it is visible today, given, for example, the sexual, racial, and communal features common to lynching and now evident in the war-on-terror prison camps. Since the 1950s, U.S. agencies have developed not only torture techniques, manuals, and pedagogy but also transnational torture relationships and routines of deniability, all of which are evident in current rendition practice. While in 2001 and 2002, journalists and jurists such as Alan Dershowitz purported to broach torture as an unspeakably new idea whose time was right, U.S. police torture was also in the news: Abner Louima's last assailant was being retried and sentenced, and John Conroy continued his lonely, dogged reporting on the ongoing, obstructed prosecution of Chicago's Area 2 police torture team, led by Jon Burge, who brought electroshock tactics from his tour in Vietnam to the Chicago Police Department and used them on numerous Chicagoans during the 1970s and 1980s.[49] In this way, torture in the present reinvents and builds on the torture of the past. Torture is not everywhere and always the same, of course; however, personnel, techniques, rituals, rhetoric, and routines of denial or justification are passed on, borrowed and adapted for use in new contexts. It did not escape notice that Abu Ghraib's Charles Graner and Ivan Chip Frederick were seasoned guards from maximum security prisons who brought their expertise to bear in Iraq.

This all is to say that the representation, the imagining, of torture in speculative news and legal writing has not only closed off the communal and social nature of torture but also its historical continuity. Page Dubois would argue that torture is not a departure from democratic ideals but, rather, has been at the foundation of Western democratic life since classical Greece. U.S. history provides clear examples of torture as the accomplice and tool of civilizing and democratizing efforts at home and abroad.

Despite this fact, a denial of torture's historical role can be communicated even in smart, powerful arguments against the practice. The legal arguments of David Luban and Jeremy Waldron are instructive in this way. Both wrote in late 2005 and acknowledged the horrors of Abu Ghraib in many ways, but both preserved the sense of newness surrounding the idea of torture in the torture debate. They also preserved the sense of state-authorized torture as a threshold event, a point beyond which law collapses and a torture culture proliferates, tyranny abounds, and (as Scarry would put it) the world is unmade. In an important way, their arguments situate the current debate itself as exceptional, something new in U.S. history and a challenge to long-held principles of law and belief.

In one strong example, Slavoj Žižek has deplored the torture debate itself as a dangerous shift in fundamental assumptions: "Such legitimization of torture as a topic of debate changes the background of ideological presuppositions and options much more radically than its outright advocacy: it changes the entire field while, without this change, outright advocacy remains an idiosyncratic view."[50] While, on the one hand, Luban, Waldron, and Žižek nod toward torture events in the U.S. past, on the other, they reinforce the belief that across that history, our ideological presuppositions have moved decidedly against torture and that torture has been progressively eliminated. As a result, its emergence now — in debate and in practice — is encountered as something new. My point is that when torture or the idea of torture is preserved or reinforced as something new in this way, an exception in the national narrative, torture will not be analyzed as the story of the U.S. past and a practice woven deeply into the country's cultural ideas about state security, punishment, and necessary violence. The historical continuities that exist within torture routines suggest we need to look more carefully at the fundamental "ideological presuppositions" Žižek cites and the extent to which they have been consistent with torture.

This is to say that, perhaps, when we claim liberal democracy has progressively prohibited torture, what we mean to say or ought to say is that we believe we have relegated its practice to certain spaces and theaters of operation including, historically, certain (racialized) populations, certain colonial contexts and client states, and certain policing agencies or prisons. It is no coincidence that the recurring narrative devices and archetypes so pervasive in our debate collude to obscure precisely these three important U.S. lines of descent. The fact that Ehab Elmaghraby's flashlight rape in Brooklyn stands at the intersection of those three (obscured) strands of torture practice may make it *more* difficult to recognize his ordeal as torture. No memo from the secretary of defense or the Office of Legal Counsel was necessary to initiate his ordeal; it drew on old routines of suppression and violence.

Seen from this perspective, the United States has a dual history to consider with regard to torture: a long history of torture and, of equal importance, a long history of denial, even tolerance, for it. Surely fundamental to that tolerance are the terms, metaphors, and archetypes through which we imagine, define, and debate.

NOTES

1   Erik Saar and Viveca Novak, *Inside the Wire: A Military Intelligence Soldier's Eyewitness Account of Life at Guantánamo* (New York: Penguin, 2005), 247.

2   This essay substantially revises an earlier discussion of torture in the speculative press in Stephanie Athey, "Torture: Alibi and Archetype in US News and Law since 2001," in *Culture, Trauma and Conflict: Cultural Studies Perspectives on War,* ed. Nico Carpentier (Newcastle upon Tyne, U.K.: Cambridge Scholars Publishing, 2007).

3   Marcy Strauss, "Torture," *New York Law School Law Review* 48, no. 1/2, (2003/2004).

4   "The quintessential picture of torture in the United States" involves whipping or beating a suspect to secure confession, according to Strauss. While she tests that picture against an array of varied incidents drawn equally from Supreme Court decisions and from the highly imaginative speculative press I will discuss, the picture she arranges in the end reflects the familiar aspects of the archetype to be described here. In part, she says, because these definitions of torture remain "surprisingly blurry," she relies on the presumption of a shared mental image instead: "I will . . . only

use . . . 'torture' as a generic term when a more precise delineation is *not necessary*. . . . In those cases, the reader should simply bear in mind the type of abuse that most people would agree constitutes torture" (emphasis mine). Strauss, "Torture," 216.

5   Nina Bernstein, "U.S. Is Settling Detainee's Suit in 9/11 Sweep," *New York Times*, February 28, 2006.

6   Under international law, rape of an inmate by staff is considered to be torture. Other forms of sexual abuse violate the internationally recognized prohibition on cruel, inhuman, or degrading treatment or punishment. Rape and sexual assault violate U.S. federal and state criminal laws. See Amnesty International, "'Not Part of My Sentence': Violations of the Human Rights of Women in Custody," March 1999, http://www.amnestyusa.org/document.php?id=DoF5C2222D1AABEA80256900006 92FC4&lang=e (accessed December 21, 2009).

7   Since 2002, at least ninety-eight detainees have died while in U.S. custody. According to the U.S. military thirty-four are suspected or confirmed homicides. Human Rights First identifies eleven more cases in which physical abuse or harsh detention resulted in death, bringing its total to forty-five suspected or confirmed homicides in custody. John Sifton, "The Bush Administration Homicides," Daily Beast, May 5, 2009, www.thedailybeast.com/blogs-and-stories/2009-05-05/how-many-were-tortured-to-death/full/; and Human Rights First, "Torture: Quick Facts," www.humanrightsfirst.org/us_law/etn/misc/factsheet (accessed December 7, 2009).

8   Elaine Scarry, *The Body in Pain: The Making and Unmaking of the World* (New York: Oxford University Press, 1985).

9   Darius Rejali, "Modern Torture as a Civic Marker: Solving a Global Anxiety with a New Political Technology," *Journal of Human Rights* 2, no. 2 (2003): 153–71. Human Rights Clinic of Columbia Law School, "In the Shadows of the War on Terror: Persistent Police Brutality and Abuse in the United States," Report prepared for the United Nations Human Rights Committee on the occasion of its review of the United States of America's second and third periodic report to the Human Rights Committee, May 2006.

10   Eric Umansky, "Failures of Imagination," *Columbia Journalism Review* 45, no. 3 (September/October 2006): 16–31. Ricchiardi counted as few as six investigative pieces from 2001 to April 2004 that looked at brutal and illegal measures used in handling U.S. prisoners. Sherry Ricchiardi, "Missed Signals," *American Journalism Review* 26, no. 4 (August/September 2004): 22–29.

11   Rajiv Chandrasekaran and Peter Finn, "U.S. Behind Secret Transfer of Terror Suspects," *Washington Post*, March 11, 2002, section A.

12   Ricchiardi, "Missed Signals."

13   For quizzes and surveys, see Amy Argetsinger, "At Colleges, Students
      Are Facing a Big Test," *Washington Post*, September 17, 2001, section B;
      and Abraham McLaughlin, "How Far Americans Would Go to Fight Ter-
      ror," *Christian Science Monitor*, November 14, 2001. For other pieces in
      the Hypothetical vein, see John Blake, "Seeking a Moral Compass While
      Chasing Terrorists: How to React to Enemies Raises Tough Questions for
      People of Faith," *Atlanta Journal Constitution*, September 22, 2001, section
      B; Jay Winik, "Security Comes Before Liberty," *Wall Street Journal*, Octo-
      ber 23, 2001, section A; Jonathan Alter, "Time to Think about Torture,"
      Newsweek, November 5, 2001, 45; Jim Rutenberg, "Torture Seeps into
      Discussion by News Media," *New York Times*, November 5, 2001, section C;
      Sandi Dolbee, "Agonizing Over Torture: Can Deliberate Hurt Be Justified
      in Times of Terror?" *San Diego Union-Tribune*, November 23, 2001, section
      D; Jess Bravin, "Interrogation School Tells Army Recruits How Grilling
      Works — 30 Techniques in 16 Weeks, Just Short of Torture; Do They Yield
      Much?" *Wall Street Journal*, April 26, 2002, section A; E. V. Kantorovich,
      "Make Them Talk," *Wall Street Journal*, June 18, 2002, section A; and Peter
      Maas, "Torture, Tough or Lite: If a Terror Suspect Won't Talk, Should
      He Be Made To?" *New York Times*, Week in Review, March 9, 2003.

14   See Steve Chapman, "No Tortured Dilemma," *Washington Times*, Novem-
      ber 5, 2001, section A; Bruce Hoffman, "Nasty Business," *Atlantic Monthly*,
      January 2002, 49–52; Michael T. Kaufman, "What Does the Pentagon See
      in 'Battle of Algiers'?" *New York Times*, September 7, 2003; Drake Bennett,
      "The War in the Mind," *Boston Globe*, November 27, 2005, section K; and
      Mark Bowden, "The Dark Art of Interrogation," *Atlantic Monthly*, October
      2003, 51–70. In variations on this France-and-Israel pattern, Hoffman
      discusses potential U.S. techniques in the war on terror in the context
      of the French campaign in Algeria and the Sri Lankans' fight against the
      Muslim Tamil Tigers, and Bowden discusses Israel and France and then
      reviews aspects of England's torture of Irish Republican Army suspects in
      the 1970s.

15   See Hoffman, "Nasty Business," 49–52. Also see "Word for Word: Psychol-
      ogy and Sometimes a Slap; The Man Who Made Prisoners Talk," Week in
      Review, *New York Times*, December 12, 2004; Bowden, "The Dark Art of
      Interrogation"; and Joseph Lelyveld, "Interrogating Ourselves," *New York
      Times Magazine*, June 12, 2005, http://www.nytimes.com/2005/06/12/
      magazine/12TORTURE.html (accessed June 15, 2005).

16   Eric Prokosch, "Amnesty International's Anti-torture Campaigns," in *A
      Glimpse of Hell: Reports on Torture Worldwide*, ed. Duncan Forest, for Amnesty
      International (New York: New York University Press, 1996), 26–35

17 Scarry, *The Body in Pain*, 20.

18 Ibid., 9.

19 David Luban, "Liberalism, Torture and the Ticking Bomb," in *The Torture Debate in America*, ed. Karen J. Greenberg (New York: Cambridge University Press, 2006), 35–83.

20 Ibid, 39.

21 Ibid.

22 David Sussman, "Defining Torture," *Case Western Reserve Journal of International Law* 37 (2005): 225–30.

23 This last quote is from David Sussman, "What's Wrong with Torture," in *The Phenomenon of Torture*, ed. William Schulz (Philadelphia: University of Pennsylvania Press, 2007), 178–79.

24 Jeremy Waldron, "Torture and Positive Law: Jurisprudence for the White House," *Columbia Law Review* 105, no. 6 (2005): 1727.

25 Ibid.

26 Eric Schmitt and Carolyn Marshall, "In Secret Unit's 'Black Room' a Grim Portrait of U.S. Abuse," *New York Times*, March 19, 2006, http://www.nytimes.com/2006/03/19/international/middleeast/19abuse.html.

27 Human Rights Watch, "Leadership Failure: Firsthand Accounts of Torture of Iraqi Detainees by the U.S. Army's 82nd Airborne Division," September 22, 2005, http://hrw.org/reports/2005/us0905; and Michael Hirsch, "Truth about Torture: A Courageous Soldier and a Determined Senator Demand Clear Standards," *Newsweek*, November 7, 2005.

28 Tim Golden, "Years After Two Afghans Died, Abuse Case Falters," *New York Times*, February 13, 2006, section A.

29 Bernstein, "U.S. Is Settling Detainee's Suit."

30 Shafiq Rasul, Asif Iqbal, and Rhuhel Ahmed, "Detention in Afghanistan and Guantánamo Bay," Center for Constitutional Rights, July 26, 2004, http://ccrjustice.org/files/report_tiptonThree.pdf; and James Yee, *For God and Country: Faith and Patriotism under Fire* (New York: Public Affairs, 2005).

31 Chris Mackey, *Interrogator's War: Inside the Secret War on Al Qaeda* (Boston: Little Brown, 2004).

32 With six broken ribs, he was left hanging from wrists shackled behind his back. The cause of death was asphyxiation, "as in a crucifixion," according to Dr. Michael Baden, chief forensic pathologist for the New York State Police. As a CIA official, Swanner has so far avoided penalty or prosecution (Jane Mayer, "A Deadly Interrogation," *New Yorker*, November 15, 2005).

33 Ervin Staub, "Torture: Psychological and Cultural Origins," in *The Politics of Pain: Torturers and Their Masters*, ed. Ronald Crelinsten and Alex P. Schmid (San Francisco: Westview Press, 1995), 99–112.

34   Schmitt and Marshall, "In Secret Unit's 'Black Room.'"

35   Luc Boltanski, *Distant Suffering: Media, Morality, and Politics* (New York: Cambridge University Press, 1999).

36   M. K. Huggins, M. Haritos-Fatouros, and P. G. Zimbardo, *Violence Workers: Police Torturers and Murderers Reconstruct Brazilian Atrocities* (Los Angeles: University of California Press, 2002); and Tony Lagouranis and Allen Mikaelian, *Fear Up Harsh: An Army Interrogator's Dark Journey through Iraq* (New York: New American Library, 2007).

37   Schmitt and Marshall, "In Secret Unit's 'Black Room.'"

38   Danielle Knight, "Trade in Tools of Torture," *U.S. News and World Report*, November 24, 2003.

39   Yee describes the rituals of the Initial Reaction Force (IRF) at Guantánamo, from initial huddles, chanting and "pumping up" prior to an attack on a "resistant" detainee, to the adrenalized high fives and chest-to-chest body slams afterward. One company exchanged information on attack counts at shift changes, "How many IRFings did you do today?" (Yee, *For God and Country*, 71–73).

40   "Torture isolates and privatizes." "The world of the man or woman in bad pain is a world without relationships or engagements, a world without an exterior. It is a world reduced to a point, a world that makes no sense and in which the human soul finds no home and no response" (Luban, "Liberalism, Torture and the Ticking Bomb," 39).

41   Hazel Carby, "A Strange and Bitter Crop: The Spectacle of Torture," OpenDemocracy, October 11, 2004, http://www.opendemocracy.net/media-abu_ghraib/article_2149.jsp (accessed June 28, 2010); Allen Feldman, "Abu Ghraib: Ceremonies of Nostalgia," OpenDemocracy, October 18, 2004, http://www.opendemocracy.net/media-abu_ghraib/article_2163.jsp (accessed June 28, 2010); and Susan Sontag, "Regarding the Torture of Others," *New York Times Magazine*, May 23, 2004. See also Joanna Bourke, "Sexy Snaps," *Index on Censorship* 1 (2005): 39–45

42   Rasul, Iqbal, and Ahmed, "Detention in Afghanistan and Guantánamo Bay."

43   This is not a fringe view among interrogation practitioners. See Intelligence Science Board, "Educing Information: Interrogation; Science and Art" (Washington, D.C.: Center for Strategic Intelligence Research, National Defense Intelligence College, 2006), available online at Federation of American Scientists, http://www.fas.org/irp/dni/educing.pdf/. Also see Mackey, *Interrogator's War*, and discussion by Michael Gelles of the Navy Criminal Investigative Service in Charlie Savage, "Split Seen on Interrogation Techniques: Navy Official Says Many Back Stance against Coercion," *Boston Globe*, March 31, 2005, http://www.boston.com/news/

world/latinamerica/articles/2005/03/31/split_seen_on_interrogation_
techniques/ (accessed January 30, 2011).

The CIA's KUBARK counterintelligence interrogation manual says
pain is counterproductive in interrogation, and FBI specialists hold that
techniques other than pain, so-called abuse, and coercion are likewise
"ineffective, counterproductive and unlikely to produce reliable information" (*Boston Globe*, February 25, 2005). See also Paisley Dodds, "FBI Letter
Alleged Abuse," *Boston Globe*, December 7, 2004, section A.

44   Jason Miller, "FBI's Case Management Project Remains on Shaky Ground,"
      November 11, 2009, Federal News Radio, http://federalnewsradio.com/
      index.php?sid=1809819&nid=35&_hw=FBIs+Case+Management+Projec
      t+Remains+on+Shaky+Ground%94 (accessed December 7, 2009). Dan
      Eggan and Griff Witte, "The FBI's Upgrade That Wasn't: $170 Million
      Bought an Unusable Computer System," *Washington Post*, August 18, 2006,
      section A.

45   Idelbar Avelar, "Five Theses on Torture," *Journal of Latin American Cultural
      Studies* 10, no. 3 (2001): 253–71.

46   Waldron, "Torture and Positive Law, 1681–1750.

47   The torture of terrorist Abdul Hakim Murad in 1995 has since 9/11 been
      widely used to demonstrate that torture works, a contention that readily
      falls apart under scrutiny. Murad was tortured in the Philippines with FBI
      collaboration (Stephanie Athey, "The Terrorist We Torture: The Tale of
      Abdul Hakim Murad," in *On Torture*, ed. Thomas C. Hilde [Baltimore:
      Johns Hopkins University Press, 2008], 87–104). In 2000, three of the
      four defendants brought to trial for the 1998 embassy bombings in Kenya
      and Tanzania argued they had signed confessions only after physical coer-
      cion (Benjamin Weiser, "Asserting Coercion, Embassy Bombing Suspect
      Tries to Suppress Statements," *New York Times*, July 13, 2000, section B,
      and Benjamin Weiser, "U.S. Faces Tough Challenge to Statements in Ter-
      rorism Case," *New York Times*, January 25, 2001, section B; see also Athey,
      "The Terrorist We Torture").

48   Alfred W. McCoy, *A Question of Torture: CIA Interrogation, from the Cold War
      to the War on Terror* (New York: Metropolitan Books, 2006); and Kristian
      Williams, *American Methods, Torture and the Logic of Domination* (Cambridge,
      Mass.: South End Press, 2006).

49   See the following works by John Conroy: *Unspeakable Acts, Ordinary People:
      Dynamics of Torture* (New York: Knopf, 2000); "Annals of Police Torture:
      What Price Freedom?" *Chicago Reader*, March 2, 2001, 1; and "Tools of
      Torture," *Chicago Reader*, February 4, 2005.

50   Slavoj Žižek, "From Homo Sucker to Homo Sacer," in *Welcome to the Desert
      of the Real* (New York: Verso, 2002), 104.

6

SPECTERS OF THE *MUSELMANN*

Guantánamo Bay Penalogical Theme Park
and the Torture of Omar Khadr

Joseph Pugliese

On September 8, 2006, the guerrilla artist Banksy staged another of his politico-artistic interventions, installing an inflatable doll dressed as a Guantánamo Bay detainee on the grounds of Disneyland, in Anaheim, California. Banksy has achieved international fame as both a street and a guerrilla artist. His graffiti projects have commented on everything from the Iraq war to the wall built by Israel on Palestinian land. He has also, as guerrilla artist, made significant interventions that have called into question the cultural politics of museums and art galleries by clandestinely installing "fake" paintings and pseudo-archaeological artifacts that have often remained on gallery walls for days before being discovered by museum staff.[1] Banksy's work consistently brings into focus the often effaced or naturalized relations of power and violence that underpin "legitimate" social sites and established cultural practices.

This essay fleshes out the complex mesh of politico-cultural significations that inscribe Banksy's installation of an inflatable doll dressed as a Guantánamo Bay detainee in Disneyland. In particular, it brings into focus the relations between subjects and sites that might otherwise appear to stand in absolutely dichotomous positions: Guantánamo Bay detainees and inflatable dolls; Guantánamo Bay military prison, Cuba, and Disney-land theme park, California. Driving this analysis of seemingly untenable systems of relations between graphically incommensurable subjects (real prisoners and inflatable dolls, an entertainment theme park and a military prison) is a desire to address what I think is magnetized and brought to the surface through Banksy's provocative guerrilla gesture of installing the simulacrum of a Guantánamo detainee within a site that is charged with "the inflammatory power of Disneyland as cultural metaphor."[2]

In the course of my analysis, I read Banksy's tactical intervention in terms of the rhetorical figure of the apostrophe. In rhetorical terms, an apostrophe instantiates a break in either a narrative or a discourse for the purpose of addressing the reader or spectator. It marks, in other words, a rupture of the narrative or discursive flow in order to bring a particular issue into sharp focus. The abrupt nature of the apostrophe ensures that the writer grabs the reader's attention. In this essay, I read the specific site in which Banksy installed his Guantánamo detainee, Big Thunder Mountain Railroad in the Frontierland section of Disneyland, in social semiotic terms; as such, Big Thunder Mountain Railroad, Frontierland, will be construed in both narratological and discursive terms. As a narratological construct, Disneyland's Frontierland bespeaks a story of heroic pioneers carving civilization out of a wild and savage wilderness. This narrative, embedded within the spatiotemporal coordinates of the site and its multiple historical reconstructions, is, in turn, discursively inscribed and structured. The discourses of colonialism and empire, embodied in the ideology of Manifest Destiny (as discussed below), enable the teleological narrative of the heroic clearing of the land and the forced removal of its uncivilized indigenous inhabitants, precisely as they mark the labor of establishing the foundations for the future-oriented imperial visions of Tomorrowland, with its promise of the conquest of other alien lands and uncivilized spaces.

Situated within this narratological and discursive configuration, Banksy's startling insertion of the simulacrum of a contemporary figure, which iconically signifies the violent prerogatives of empire and its attendant impunities, rends the seamless flow of the historical scene in question. As an apostrophic gesture, Banksy's Guantánamo detainee in Disneyland disrupts the narrative fabric of the site in order to enunciate to its audience/spectators two critical questions: What historico-political genealogies are at once ruptured and sutured through this figure? What occlusions can be brought to light only by the rhetorical force of this apostrophe? The latter part of this essay examines these questions by focusing on the ongoing incarceration of a juvenile, Omar Khadr, in Guantánamo. Khadr at once embodies the violent effects of Banksy's apostrophic intervention precisely as he dramatizes the unsettling figure of the Muslim prisoner as a qualified, contemporary reincarnation of the *Muselmann*.

In situating my analysis of Guantánamo Bay prison in the context of the camp, I delineate a number of parallels between the Nazi concentration camps and contemporary sites such as Guantánamo. While the two sites are, in many fundamental respects, incommensurable, I also attempt to trace those aspects of the camp that continue to be reproduced across different historical and geopolitical spaces. In particular, I focus on the contemporary reincarnation of the haunting figure of the *Muselmann*. The *Muselmann*, in the charged context of the camp, is that subject who has been stripped of his or her human-rights-bearing status and has been reduced to a mere figure of subhuman waste that can be killed by the state and its operatives with absolute impunity. In marking the politico-discursive cross-hatchings that establish lines of connection between two critically different sites (Nazi concentration camps and Guantánamo prison) and figures (Jews and Muslims), I attempt to materialize the points of intersection that are embodied by the specter of the *Muselmann*. Even as the contemporary embodiment of the *Muselmann* differs in fundamental ways from the *Muselmann* of the Nazi camps, it is both animated and serially inflected by biopolitical forces (premised on racism, necropower, and the exercise of state violence) that need urgently to be marked and addressed. By invoking the ultimate term—*Figuren*, or doll—by which the Jewish *Muselmann* was completely stripped of her or his human-rights-bearing status in the Nazi camps, I return, in the conclusion of this essay, to Banksy's Guantánamo doll in Disneyland in order to underscore the murderous operations of this contemporary penalogical system.

Guantánamo Bay Penalogical Theme Park

Soon after Banksy's guerrilla intervention at Disneyland, he released a short video on YouTube that tracked in detail the process of making and installing his Guantánamo Bay inflatable doll.[3] Banksy's video begins with a line of real Guantánamo prisoners, dressed in their now iconic orange jumpsuits and black hoods, being marched by U.S. soldiers. Superimposed on this image is the text "Disneyland 2006." The video then cuts to a nondescript room in which Banksy, his face pixelated, is shown dressing his inflatable doll in the orange jumpsuit and hood. Once the doll has been dressed, he stashes it in his backpack. The viewer is then taken on a car journey to Disneyland. Banksy is seen negotiating the security check at Disneyland's entrance, with a guard rummaging through his backpack and then giving him the all-clear to enter. Banksy's walk through the grounds of the amusement park is set, satirically, to the soundtrack of the Disneyland classic "It's a Small World." He is then shown sitting on a bench, where he removes the doll and proceeds to inflate it. Once the doll is inflated, he places it over the stockade-like fence that surrounds the Big Thunder Mountain Railroad in the Frontierland section of the park. The Big Thunder Mountain train is shown careering into the shot, with the visitors abruptly confronted by the incongruous sight of a Guantánamo Bay prisoner in a diagonal relation to a Christian cross staked in the river. The doll remains in place for ninety minutes before the voice of a Disneyland official is heard to say: "Sorry, folks, due to some security reasons, we have to stop our ride." The ride is closed to the public while the figure is removed. The last shot of the video is of the entrance plaque to Disneyland: "Here you leave today and enter the world of yesterday, tomorrow and fantasy."

If nothing else, in his positioning of a simulacrum of a Guantánamo prisoner in the grounds of Disneyland, Banksy brings into focus the possibility that an entertainment theme park, Disneyland, is politically and culturally connected to its absolute other, Guantánamo Bay military prison, and that, furthermore, both sites can be viewed through the specialist lens of the theme park.[4] If Disneyland is a theme park oriented both by the practices of leisure and consumption and by its moralizing narratives of imperial U.S. history, then Guantánamo Bay military prison must be viewed as another type of theme park altogether. Even as Guantánamo stands as the obverse of Disneyland, it can also be seen to be coextensive with Disneyland's theme park logic of spectacle, control, and moralizing didactics.

The logic of both sites is predicated on the construction of absolutely quarantined space: in radically different ways, both sites function as types of camps, in which the points of ingress and egress are tightly controlled, the disposition of space is carefully mapped, and the movement of subjects is regulated. Guantánamo Bay camp is surrounded by razor wire fences that isolate it from the outside world and imprison its detainees. In Disneyland, a massive berm surrounds the theme park, enclosing its visitors and blocking any views to the outside world.[5] Furthermore, if the disposition of space and the governing principles of Disneyland's architecture are fundamentally informed by principles of "security [and] restraint,"[6] then precisely the same spatial and architectonic principles are operative at Guantánamo.

In Guantánamo Bay carceral theme park, the detainees are transformed, through costume, into instantly identifiable characters of "evil": they are the absolute other of Mickey Mouse. Between Guantánamo and Disneyland there is a line of connection that pivots on categorical representations of good and evil. Remarking on how California's Disneyland was built and opened in the context of the Cold War and McCarthyist America, Erika Doss underscores the labor expended in order to establish "clear demarcations between the forces of good and evil (Snow White vs. the Wicked Queen, Peter Pan vs. Captain Hook, etc.), thereby heightening, perhaps, American desires for (or expectations of) moralistic simplicity in an age of increasing sociocultural and political complexity."[7] In its Disneyland landscape, Banksy's Guantánamo detainee brings into focus an unsettling symmetry between these categorical representations of good and evil. With prosthetically augmented ears (earmuffs), enlarged unblinking eyes (blackened goggles), a snout (surgical mask) instead of a mouth, and oversize padded paws (thick synthetic gloves) instead of hands, the Guantánamo Bay doll-prisoner emerges as a grotesque mirror image of Mickey Mouse. Whereas in Disneyland the animal characters (mice, dogs, ducks) are stripped of the alterity of their animality and are domesticated and anthropomorphized so as to create a magical affinity between humans and animals, in Guantánamo Bay the human prisoners are animalized in order to mark their preclusion from the legal category of (human-)rights-bearing person. The Guantánamo guards clinically record in their entry for December 20, 2002: "Began teaching the detainee lessons such as stay, come, and bark to elevate his social status up to that of a dog. Detainee became very agitated."[8]

Whereas in Disneyland the anthropomorphized animals have free run of the theme park, in Guantánamo Bay the animalized subhumans are, in Suvendrini Perera's words, imprisoned in "exposed chain-link pens more reminiscent of cages than cells."[9] Murat Kurnaz, imprisoned for five years in Guantánamo only to be found innocent and eventually released, writes: "An animal has more space in its cage in a zoo and is given more to eat. I can hardly put into words what that actually means."[10] This series of politico-juridical inversions is perhaps most graphically evidenced by the fact that while the detainees at Guantánamo Bay are denied basic legal rights, the iguanas that inhabit the camp are protected by U.S. law under the Endangered Species Act. As Mahvish Rukhsana Khan, a lawyer who volunteered to translate for the prisoners, remarks: "The prisoners at Guantánamo are entitled to fewer protections than an iguana."[11]

In his harrowing account of his time as a prisoner at Guantánamo Bay, Moazzam Begg documents the manner in which the prison guards viewed their prisoners: "I convince myself each day," says one guard, "that you guys are all subhuman."[12] Reflecting on the logic of representation engendered within the space of camps of imprisonment, Jean-Luc Nancy argues that what unfolds in such spaces is "the devastation of representation and/or the reduction of representation to mockery."[13] The penalogically prostheticized theme park figure that is the Guantánamo Bay detainee attests to the perverse effects of this representational logic, and Banksy's guerrilla intervention tactically amplifies this reduction of representation to a queer mockery. In her discussion of Guantánamo Bay prisoners as exempla of what she terms "terrorist assemblages," Jaspar Puar asks: "Are these bodies queer?" As "ungendered, un-raced, un-sexed, [and] un-nationalised" entities, they constitute, Puar concludes, "the subject formation of *homo sacer*," that is, queer forms of bare life that can be tortured and sacrificed with impunity.[14]

The conceptualization of Guantánamo Bay military prison in terms of a penalogical theme park—what Mahvish Khan aptly terms "an eerie Neverland"[15]—can be elaborated by bringing into focus the various "themed" sections that characterize the toponomy of the prison. The themed sections of Disneyland—Frontierland, Tomorrowland, Main Street U.S.A., and so on—have their perverse equivalent in Guantánamo Bay prison: Camp Delta, Camp Iguana, Camp X-Ray, Camp Eskimo, Camp Echo (the maximum-security isolation block), the Secret Squirrel (in which prisoners are secretly squirreled away in an isolation room without the other prisoners being aware of their whereabouts), and so on. "Guantánamo Bay," Begg sardonically observes, "is effectively a large, working American town," with its own Starbucks, KFC, and McDonald's.[16] Prisoners who agree to "confess" their terrorist connections and crimes are, furthermore, rewarded with a "McDonald's Happy Meal or a Twinkie."[17] The practice of penalogical entertainment is documented by the ex-detainee Begg in his description of the guards, and their attack dogs, as hunters playing with their prey: "Hey, do you want to chase some orange meat?"[18]

As with any self-respecting theme park, Guantánamo Bay penalogical theme park has its own souvenir shop.[19] The penalogical souvenirs on offer are inscribed by the spectalist commodification of the prisoners and their suffering. "In Guantánamo," writes Begg, "there was a rodent nicknamed the Banana Rat, the size of a domestic cat, with long rat-like tail. Some of the soldiers and interrogators would wear orange T-shirts depicting these animals as detainees. . . . I had it confirmed because other people were talking about buying these T-shirts and taking them home as souvenirs."[20] Banksy's Guantánamo figure in the Disneyland landscape materializes that long-standing U.S. tradition of intermixing festivity with cruelty, torture, and violence and of interlacing public executions with theater, while selling souvenirs of the event. I refer here to the "festivals of violence" that accompanied public lynchings of African Americans, the trade in souvenir body parts, including shards of bone, teeth, and the genitals of the tortured, burned, and/or lynched victims, and the traffic in postcards and photographs depicting the lynchings.[21] This festival of violence has found its contemporary reincarnation in places like Abu Ghraib, where torture, sexual assault, and murder were intertwined with entertainment, visual spectacle, and the trade in souvenir photographs and screen savers depicting the tortured and executed prisoners.[22] Banksy's Guantánamo Bay figure in Disneyland channels this cultural history and gives it yet another contemporary guise.

American Gulags: Colonial and Imperial Palimpsests

Banksy's Guantánamo Bay figure in Disneyland generates a politico-cultural charge that accrues from the fact that, like "the Grand Canyon or Chicago or the Golden Gate Bridge, Disneyland is a key American place-marker, an icon."[23] Precisely as the Guantánamo prisoner functions as

164

an icon of "the terrorist," or iconic figure of "bare life"—deprived of due legal process and fundamental human rights—Guantánamo Bay is also another (in)famous American place-marker: the military camp situated beyond the purview of the rule of law, the off-shore prison imprisoning mere subhuman detritus.[24] Through his tactical superimposition or, more accurately, collision of two seemingly polarized icons and place-markers, Banksy draws attention to the relations that hold between seemingly dichotomous sites and subjects.

Banksy's Guantánamo prisoner stands, in the context of Disney's Frontierland, as a mute figure in the landscape, destitute of speech and denied any right of reply. Yet this totemic figure silently embodies the form of an accusation, precisely as it sets in train a polemical transvaluation of received values: this site of leisure, it accuses, is a site of effaced and disavowed violence. Couched in rhetorical terms, Banksy's Guantánamo Bay doll in Disneyland functions as an apostrophe in the landscape. As apostrophe, this figure instantiates a coup de théâtre that generates a series of unsettling rhetorical effects, including the disruption of the mise-en-scène, the rupture of the narrative fabric, and the enunciation of what Giorgio Agamben describes as "a call that cannot be avoided."[25] The apostrophic effects of Banksy's figure come into being because of the charged semiotics of place that accrue from the signs "Disneyland," in general, and "Frontierland," in particular.

In her cultural history of Disneyland, Karal Ann Marling explains how the Anaheim theme park was specifically designed "to provide comfort and refuge from that world of woes. . . . His [Disney's] park was built behind a berm to protect it from the evils that daily beset humankind on all sides. It aimed to soothe and reassure. . . . Disneyland is about . . . the overarching reassurance that there is order governing the disposition of things."[26] In the context of Disneyland's landscape of reassurance, with its ordered disposition of things, Banksy's Guantánamo figure instantiates a breach that imports the evils of the outside world into the quarantined space of the entertainment theme park, disrupting the seamless narrative fabric of reassurance; simultaneously, this apostrophic figure demands that points of connection be established between this quarantined and controlled space, the internal and effaced world upon which the park was built and now stands, and the external world held at bay by the park's berms.

Banksy's installation of his Guantánamo figure in the context of Frontierland, "one of the icons of Disney's world,"²⁷ brings into focus a number of effaced genealogies of colonial and imperial violence that mark the site even as they have been invisibilized by the power of the hegemonic narratives that organize the theme park. Walt Disney's decision to build his theme park in California is inscribed with the mythic resonances of the West in white America's history. In his detailed analysis of tourism in the twentieth-century American West, Hal Rothman draws attention to the manner in which the burgeoning industry of recreational tourism in the West was marked by the "power of conquest embodied in Manifest Destiny."²⁸ The West emerges, Rothman argues, as a space at once marked by the violence of colonial conquest of Native Americans and their lands and by the concomitant erasure of this violence through the scripting of the West as a place of "mythic purpose" and "expiation": "To Americans the West is their refuge, the home of the 'last best place' . . . home to the mythic landscapes where Americans become whole again in the aftermath of personal or national cataclysm."²⁹ In the schema of American providential teleology and eschatology, the figure of the Guantánamo prisoner signifies a type of absolute subhuman detritus that cannot be teleologically dialecticized or eschatologically redeemed. Marked by the fusion of charged triple indices—Arab, Muslim, terrorist—that collectively spell "un-American," this figure embodies the unfreedom constitutive of the racialogically inflected liberal democratic state. "White supremacy, colonialism, and economic exploitation," writes Andrea Smith, "are inextricably linked to U.S. democratic ideals rather than aberrations from it. The 'freedom' guaranteed to some individuals in society has always been premised upon the radical unfreedom of others."³⁰

Banksy's Guantánamo figure, as a form of visual apostrophe, disrupts this narrative of historicidal forgetting and expiation. As a figure embodying stories of torture, violence, and sexual assault, its location in Frontierland generates points of connection with California's violent colonial history. In the work of Antonia Castañeda, the West (and, coextensively, Frontierland, as geopolitical concept metaphor for the West) is mapped as the site of double empires, Spanish and white American, and as the colonized space within which the colonizers exercised their imperial prerogatives on the colonized subjects: "Amerindian women and men were both regarded as inferior social beings, whose inferiority justified the original conquest and continued to make them justifiably exploitable and expendable in the eyes of the conqueror."[31] The relations of sexual violence, abuse, and torture that were operative in the colonial conquest of the West can be seen to resonate with what has unfolded at Guantánamo Bay. "Thus Guantánamo is a location," writes Amy Kaplan, "where many narratives about the Americas intersect, about shackled slaves brought from Africa, the important role of Cuba in U.S. history, and U.S. intervention in the Caribbean and Latin America."[32] Both geopolitical sites have borne witness to the transmutation of the captive subject into subhuman object that can be violated, sexually assaulted, or killed with impunity. Banksy's Guantánamo doll instantiates a type of visual chiasmus in which past imperial histories cross through this totemic figure of contemporary imperial subjection. The symbolic lexicon of the Wild West folds over into the contemporary war on terror and its cowboy language of "smoking out" the "bad guys": "[T]here's an old poster out West," former president George W. Bush declared soon after the 9/11 attacks, "that said, 'Wanted, Dead or Alive.'"[33]

Writing of his experience in Kandahar prison, Afghanistan, before he was transferred to Guantánamo Bay, Moazzam Begg brings into focus this point of intersection between colonialism and the contemporary war on terror:

One of the MPs I often spoke to was Cody, an Irish American who had been brought up on a Cherokee reservation in North Carolina. . . . [H]e identified more with them than with white America. He said to me once, "When I see you people here, it reminds me of *my* people. They were treated the same way. Their lands were invaded, they were slaughtered and imprisoned, their language and religion were not understood, and they were depicted, until recently, as savages and murderous heathens."[34]

Banksy's act of placing a mannequin in Frontierland, with its Big Thunder Mountain train ride, works to resignify the mise-en-scène of the tourist park into a type of contemporary diorama, thereby accentuating its effaced colonial genealogies and significations. In the nineteenth century, visitors to the colonial exhibitions and world fairs would take train rides through live exhibits and dioramas that "brought far-flung territories and exotic peoples near," transmuting them into objects of colonial fixity and visual consumption.[35] The colonial logic of the diorama was predicated on objectifying Europe's others and marking their status as "proto-humans," "silent specimens in a frozen zoo."[36] Banksy's carceral mannequin in Frontierland brings far-flung Guantánamo Bay and its exotic inhabitants home, suturing past imperial histories to the contemporary U.S. colony in Cuba. For the brief duration of ninety minutes, every circuit of the Big Thunder Mountain train will bring its passengers face-to-face with an apostrophic "security breach" that disrupts the Disneyfied tourist narrative. The colonial frontier–as–post is jarringly compelled to assume the dimensions of a "live" imperial present every time the shackled and hooded Guantánamo prisoner careens into view.

The Big Thunder Mountain train, as the fabled "machine in the garden" that rends the reassuring spectacle of a pastoral America, "changes the texture" of the scene: "Now tension replaces repose . . . arous[ing] a sense of dislocation, conflict and anxiety."[37] As the train speeds past the Frontierland stockade with its Guantánamo detainee, the Disneyland spectator is confronted with the sight of a fluorescent orange apostrophe in the landscape that generates a momentary derangement of the field of vision and its visual cues. Banksy's apostrophic gash in the landscape flies in the face of the "Disney Realism" outlined by Disneyland's planners: "we program out all the negative, unwanted elements and program in the positive elements."[38] The temporality of nostalgia for a simpler and better time past, symbolized by this train journey through the Wild West, is disrupted by this dissonant shackled figure.

This figure generates a type of relational rupture and dis/continuity as it emblematizes a genealogy of tortured and imprisoned subjects—the native, the slave, the anticolonial insurgent—while also bringing into focus a palimpsest of colonial camps of imprisonment, beginning with the same "Caribbean island [Cuba] that gave birth to the institution of the concentration camps in the late nineteenth century."[39] For the duration of the time it remains in place in Frontierland, Banksy's Guantánamo detainee magnetizes a series of temporal retentions and protentions: the past (the colonial project of the Wild West), the present (the camp at Guantánamo Bay), and the future (the imperial war on terror that unfolds without an end in sight) all collide, overlap, and disjoin. Simultaneously, as the figure brings into focus this palimpsestic matrix, it resignifies it with the irruptive force of its own unique historicity, a historicity gathered under the imprimatur of the contemporary war on terror.

As apostrophic figure, Banksy's doll enunciates a seemingly impossible address: Guantánamo Bay, Disneyland. This uncanny coupling of two apparently opposed geopolitical sites (Guantánamo Bay and Disneyland) and of two seemingly irreconcilable "spaces of exception" (prison and theme park) is underpinned by the fact that the space of exception is, in Giorgio Agamben's terms, structurally imbricated with the actual rule of law in the civil spaces and practices of everyday life so that the state of exception and the exercise of "juridical rule enter into a threshold of indistinction."[40] Agamben's work underscores the seamless manner in which the space of leisure and recreation (a football stadium, cycle-racing track, or hotel) can be transmuted into a camp of imprisonment and torture.[41] Indeed, in radically different ways, both Guantánamo Bay and Disneyland self-represent as spaces of exception, with Disneyland designating itself as an "exceptional place," a "magic kingdom" protected and isolated from the outside world by its berm.[42] If "Disneyland is symbolic that all is right with the world," so that "the guest walks through an atmosphere of order and cleanliness and comes away feeling that things must be right, after all,"[43] then, situated in this context, Banksy's tactical installation of his Guantánamo detainee inside this iconic theme park breaches the berm that quarantines Disneyland from the outside world: the excluded and disavowed exteriority of white America's absolute other is thereby brought home to roost in this most identifiably American of all landscapes. Banksy's Guantánamo prisoner in Frontierland graphically embodies Alexander Solzhenitsyn's unforgettable words: "there is where the Gulag country begins, right next to us, two yards away from us."[44]

If the perverse representational logic that inscribes the space of the camp is, as Nancy argues, generative of devastation and/or mockery,[45] then Banksy's Guantánamo doll pushes this logic to its limits. The doll can be seized but not arrested; it can be stripped but cannot be rendered naked; it can be detained but not interrogated; it can be deflated but not tortured. In a fragile and ephemeral way, Banksy's tactical intervention in Disneyland discloses the constitutive, if limited, impotencies of authoritarian regimes, their irreflective blind spots, their vulnerability to ethical gestures of evasion, silence, mockery, and symbolic contestation. And the "authoritarian regimes" invoked here include both the U.S. government, as a regime that has "legally" sanctioned torture,[46] and the corporate governance of Disneyland. The corporate governance of Disneyland is distinguished by its quasi-fascistic control over all aspects of the park (in the words of one of Disneyland's executives, "Any ad libs [by park workers] must be approved before use"[47]) and by its exercise of the "iron hand of dictatorship, repression masked in smiles and mouse ears."[48] Precisely what Banksy's guerrilla tactic infracts is Disneyland's policy on what it terms "undesirables": "To 'restrict undesirables' and generally intimidate troublemakers, Disney recruited a special type of security guard" and deployed a screening process at the gates "to scrutinize visitors to make sure, like the hosts and hostesses onstage and backstage, they conformed to Disney's 'good grooming code,' as well as to ensure that nobody gained entrance who might cause problems for the park and its other customers."[49]

Haunting Banksy's detainee in Disneyland and his parody of the genre of amateur "terrorist" videos is yet another specter of exclusion, detention, and travesty of justice: the indictment of "five Muslim men of Middle Eastern origin in Detroit on charges of conspiring to support terrorist attacks in the United States."[50] Evidence used to prosecute the so-called Detroit terror cell included "recovered video and audio tapes in which those charged appear to be surveilling key American landmarks for possible attack, including Disneyland in California."[51] The recovered video, screened on global television, looks like nothing more than a conventional tourist video of one's travels in Disneyland. A federal judge later dismissed the terrorism charges, admitting "widespread prosecutorial misconduct in the case."[52] The case illustrates the endemic racialization of space and technologies in the current war on terror, as it begs the question as to who can traverse spaces of leisure and recreation and simultaneously record their experiences without fear of being branded terrorists.

Situated in this charged context, Banksy's apostrophic tactic emerges as a form of literal and symbolic travesty. It literally travesties the logic of the theme park—specifically, Disneyland and its "'sanitized' vision of America"[53]—by importing a figure of carceral violence and terror into this space of fun and leisure. Simultaneously, it symbolically draws attention to the travesty of juridical justice that this Guantánamo Bay figure embodies in his militarized space of exception.

Childhood's End and the Specters of the *Muselmann*

On July 15, 2008, a Guantánamo Bay interrogation video was released. The video shows a sixteen-year-old boy, Omar Khadr, being questioned by a Canadian Security Intelligence agent.[54] Released by Khadr's Canadian lawyers, the video was made by U.S. government agents using a camera hidden in a vent and was originally classified as secret. In the closing section of this essay, I discuss this video by situating it in relation to Banksy's Guantánamo Bay doll in Disneyland.

Unbeknownst to the general public, Guantánamo Bay holds child detainees, in direct violation of the United Nations Convention on the Rights of the Child, to which the United States is a signatory.[55] At various stages, Guantánamo has imprisoned children as young as twelve, thirteen, fourteen, fifteen, and sixteen years old.[56] "[I]n early 2004 three minors between 13 and 15 years old were freed," writes Michael Ratner, president of the Center for Constitutional Rights. "In response to pressure from human rights groups, the United States now imprisons most children at a separate detention facility called Camp Iguana, but children 16 years and older continue to be held captive with the adult detainees at Camp Delta."[57] Khadr is one of the children imprisoned in Camp Delta. In his detailed documentation of the case histories of all the Guantánamo prisoners, Andy Worthington writes of Khadr:

> One dubious example of a "fighter" captured as this time was Omar Khadr, who was shot three times by US soldiers during a firefight near Khost on July 27, 2002, and is nearly blind in one eye as a result of his injuries. According to the US military, he killed a US soldier during the fight, and as a result, even though he was seriously injured, his interrogation began as soon as he was taken into custody. His case was later mentioned by a US official, who claimed that prisoners were so scared of abuse by US soldiers that they would talk without prompting. . . . According to Khadr, the abuse was all too real. During his detention in Afghanistan, he "asked for pain medication for his wounds but was refused," and was "not allowed to use the bathroom and was forced to urinate on himself." Like many other prisoners, he was also hung from his wrists, and he explained that "his hands were tied above a door frame and he was forced to stand in this position for hours."[58]

Worthington cites further testimony from Khadr on the torture and ritualized humiliation and degradation he has had to endure in Guantánamo:

> Short-shackled and left in a room for six hours, he [Khadr] said that "occasionally a US officer would enter the room to laugh at him." Once, the guards left him until he urinated on himself, and then "poured a pine scented cleaning fluid over him and used him as a 'human mop' to clean up the mess." As if further humiliation was required, he added that he was "not provided with clean clothes for several days after his degradation."[59]

The practices of torture and ritualized humiliation that Khadr has been forced to endure operate to transmute him into the embodiment of "waste"; as such, he is precluded from occupying the sentient and rights-bearing category of the "human."

For many reasons, Khadr's interrogation video is harrowing to watch. The secret video was filmed through the opened slats of a Venetian blind. Khadr's body is segmented by the out-of-focus slats. The grid of the blind materializes a number of critical visual relations and effects. On one level, the grid of the blind functions as a metonym for the embedded series of cages, bars, and prisons that constitute Khadr's everyday conditions of existence. On another level, the slats mark a symbolic bar that separates the free spectator from the imprisoned Khadr. The persistence of this bar in the field of vision forecloses the possibility of the filmic lens or spectator's eye being transparent and invisible. It materializes the voyeuristic relation of this "peephole" looking into the anguish of the target subject, thereby bringing into scopic focus the asymmetries of power that mark this relation; in this asymmetrical scopic relation, Khadr has no visual right of reply to his unknown and invisibilized spectator.

As the video of Khadr's interrogation unfolds, it becomes evident that the interrogating agent is clinically detached from Khadr's plight. In the course of his interrogation and his unsuccessful pleas for help, Khadr abruptly lifts the top of his orange jumpsuit and points to the scars that mark his body, scars from wounds he received in the battlefield as a child soldier, and says that he has requested medical help but has received none. Khadr's corporeal gesture marks the limits of his speech act and also its failure. In the penal colony of Guantánamo Bay, Khadr's body attests to the dermographic inscription of a violent history that would otherwise remain unspeakable and that can be evidenced only by the thick materiality of his scars. This gesture, however, only serves to mark a rift between speech and body, specifically between a subject who is being verbally compelled to confessional speech by his interrogator and a body that remains mutely traumatized, signifying unintelligible ciphers or scars that fail to be interpreted as they are beyond the hermeneutic purview of the uninterested interrogating agent.

This rift between speech and body becomes even more graphic as the interrogation continues. The disjunctive nature of the two speech acts, of interrogator and interrogated, becomes unbridgeable in the moment that Omar Khadr, while crying, exclaims, "I lost my eyes, my feet, everything . . . " and the interrogator coolly replies, "No, you still have your eyes and your feet are still at the end of your legs, you know. Look, I want you to take a few minutes . . . I want you to get yourself together . . . relax a bit, have a bite to eat and we'll start again." Enunciated in Khadr's cry is the psychic toll of torture, isolation, and indefinite detention. Enmeshed within the psychic and physical violence of torture, Khadr's body is fragmented, dispersed, and "lost." His cry bespeaks a suffering so intense that it causes the dissolution of the borders that encompass his sense of a corporeal self that is whole and integrated. The impact of past and ongoing trauma violently truncates Khadr's sensorium so that it no longer works to connect all the parts of his body to his sense of self as unified embodied subject in the world. In her acute analysis of the "structure of torture," Elaine Scarry traces the destructive dimensions of this feedback loop: "as the prisoner's sentience destroys his world, so now his absence of world . . . destroys his claims of sentience."[60] The disabling of his sensorium and the loss of his sensate knowledge of the contours and limits of his body reproduce the chronic deprivation of sensory input—sound, sight, and touch—effected by the Guantánamo Bay prisoners being forced to wear sound-blocking earmuffs, surgical masks, padded gloves, and blackened goggles.[61]

Khadr attests through his cry of loss to a psychic amputation that is at once also symbolically corporeal. In the face of Khadr's attestation of his trauma of fragmentation and loss, the interrogator replies with a clinical observation that fails to register the psychic reality of Khadr's suffering: "No, you still have your eyes and your feet are still at the end of your legs, you know." Inscribing this moment are multiple levels of disjunction: perceptual, psychic, and temporal. Precisely as Khadr marks the trauma of the fragmentation and dissolution of his sense of embodied reality, the interrogator replies with a sense of disciplinary normativity ("get yourself together"), instrumentalizing hospitality ("have a bite to eat"), and recursive inquisition ("we'll start again") that effectively negate Khadr's testimony through their neutralizing violence. A fault line opens between the two discourses: I have lost my body—no, you're body is there. The bar that separates the two speakers marks the violent rupture between irreconcilable levels of perceptual and experiential reality.

As the video unfolds, the interrogator temporarily leaves the room, and Khadr, unaware that he is being filmed, begins to cry in Arabic for his mother: "*Ya ummi.*" He buries his head in his hands, sobs, and pulls at his hair. Khadr's somatic cries are not mere supplements to his oral testimony. Rather, they emerge as enunciative gaps that rupture the disciplinary order of inquisitorial language and underscore its violence. In this schema, Khadr's cries are so much non-sense and non-knowledge for the interrogator. Excess to the functionalist demands of the interrogator, they mark the superfluous status of Khadr's body, of his somatic testimony as useless waste. The video recorder is left running after the interrogator has left the room, in the hope that something "meaningful" will be confessed or captured, but Khadr offers nothing more than the articulation of his pain. Khadr's spoken and somatic testimony evidences a temporality of incessant suffering, what Maurice Blanchot calls "a time without respite that he [the subject] endures as the perpetuity of an indifferent present."[62] Caught in the vise of an incessant suffering that must be endured as the perpetuity of an indifferent present, Khadr is transmuted into a "no body" ("I lost my eyes, my feet, everything") that becomes utterly coextensive with the experience of unrelieved trauma. Blanchot captures this acutely paradoxical logic in his discussion of the victims of the Nazi concentration camps: "The one afflicted no longer has any identity other than the situation with which he merges and that never allows himself to be himself; for as a situation of affliction, it tends incessantly to de-situate itself, to dissolve in the void of a nowhere without foundation."[63] Khadr emerges as a subject transfixed in the event horizon of incessant suffering; his organs and limbs, as the coordinated sensorial ensemble that would allow him to establish a perceptual foundation in the world, have been absorbed into what one scholar of jurisprudence has termed a "legal black hole" of unrelieved trauma and affliction.[64]

The harrowing temporality of this event horizon of suffering without a future is evidenced by many of the testimonies of the inmates of Guantánamo, where the sense of a present without a future emerges as a key burden of their suffering. Jumah al-Dossary, imprisoned for more than five years, and having attempted suicide twelve times, writes: "Oh, those days and nights. I felt that time had ended at that time and did not want to move forward. I felt that the whole world with its mountains and all its gravity was bearing down on my chest." The temporal structure that al-Dossary articulates here is marked by the torsions of paradox: time ceases yet persists, enduring without movement or progress or future, a time without time that crushes the subject in its immovability. Al-Dossary relates how "he has lived for years alone in cells . . . and has been told by the military that he will live like that forever. All he can see is darkness."[65] Blanchot delineates this present of infinite suffering without future:

Time is as though arrested. . . . [T]he present is without end, separated from every other present by an inexhaustible and empty infinite, the very infinite of suffering, and thus dispossessed of any future: a present without end and yet impossible as a present. The present of suffering is the abyss of the present, indefinitely hollowed out and in this hollowing indefinitely distended, radically alien to the possibility that one might be present to it through the mastery of presence . . . time that can no longer redeem us, that constitutes no recourse. A time without event, without project, without possibility . . . an unstable perpetuity in which we are arrested and incapable of permanence, a time neither abiding nor granting the simplicity of a dwelling place.[66]

The simplicity of a dwelling place is what is foreclosed in the psychic withdrawal of the body's limbs and perceptual organs: there is no place in the world left to inhabit; rather, there is only a perpetuity of suffering, without locus or ground, to endure. In one of his suicide notes, al-Dossary writes: "The purpose of Guantánamo is to destroy people, and I have been destroyed."[67]

Blanchot's writing on suffering in the Nazi concentration camps effectively illuminates the lived experience of many of the inmates of Guantánamo. Mahavish Khan, who worked as translator for many of the prisoners in Guantánamo, has also documented the parallels between the two camps, including the use of serial numbers instead of names for cataloging and referring to all the prisoners and the manner in which "soldiers at Gitmo shaved the beards of the Muslim prisoners to punish them for minor infractions. What stronger image does this evoke than that of the Third Reich and the Nazi shaving of the beards and heads of the Jews?"[68] Other scholars have drawn attention to the structural parallels between Guantánamo and the Nazi concentration camps without, however, reflexively marking the significant differences between the two.[69] I want to pursue these structural parallels between Guantánamo Bay and the Nazi concentration camps by focusing, in particular, on the figure of the *Muselmann*. Before proceeding, however, I want to underscore that the relations that hold between the two camps are marked by both similarities and fundamental differences; precisely what I do not want to argue is that one, Guantánamo, is simply the same as the other, Auschwitz, for example, and that there is a simple homology between the two camps. This move would effectively reproduce its own form of epistemic violence, flattening and erasing the enormity of historical, geopolitical, and racial differences that mark the two camps. Guantánamo is not Auschwitz. Rather, I want to focus on the structurality of the camp, specifically on those features of the camp that appear to be constitutive of its operating logic and that, across different spatiotemporal configurations, continue to be reproduced.[70] Situated in this context, I want specifically to examine the figure of the *Muselmann* and its relational status across two historically different sites and geopolitical embodiments.

In his *Remnants of Auschwitz*, Giorgio Agamben spends some time tracking the figure of *der Muselmann* in the Nazi death camps.[71] The word *Muselmann*, according to testimonies of the camps' survivors, referred to those prisoners who had completely given up on hope and life. As Primo Levi explains, "the term *Muselmann*, 'Muslim,' [was] given to the irreversibly exhausted, worn-out prisoner closer to death. Two explanations for it have been advanced, neither very convincing: fatalism, and the head bandages that could resemble a turban."[72] Catatonic, indifferent to pain and suffering, no longer interested in food or drink, the *Muselmann* embodied the figure of the living dead. As such, the *Muselmann* was viewed with revulsion and even ostracized by the other prisoners of the Nazi camps; in the words of one of the survivors: "No one felt compassion for the Muslim, and no one felt sympathy for him either. The other inmates . . . did not even judge him worthy of being looked at. . . . [F]or the SS, they were merely useless garbage. Every group thought only about eliminating them, each in its own way."[73]

In his attempt to elucidate the emergence of the term in the camps, Agamben suggests that the "most likely explanation of the term can be found in the literal meaning of the Arabic word muslim [*sic*]: the one who submits unconditionally to the will of God."[74] Regardless of the term's origins, Agamben concludes, "it is certain that, with a kind of ferocious irony, the Jews knew that they would not die at Auschwitz as Jews."[75] The "ferocious irony" that Agamben draws attention to is, however, inscribed by yet another level of ferocity that remains unspeakable throughout his book. Despite the fact that Agamben devotes a substantial chapter to his analysis of the *Muselmann*, at no point does he name the racism that inscribes this term, specifically the Islamophobia and Arabophobia that constitute its very conditions of enunciation and signification. Rather, he refers only to the "deprecatory sense of the term in European languages," "concerning Islam's supposed fatalism."[76] In Anna Pawelczynska's text on Auschwitz, the translator, Catherine Leach, includes the word *Muselmann* in the glossary of terms, where it is defined as follows: "German for 'Moslem.' In the camps the word carried no religious connotation whatsoever. Used by the prisoners and the SS alike, it signified a prisoner who showed symptoms of the advanced stages of starvation."[77]

Although the term was purged of any "religious connotation whatsoever," the question remains as to why the word "Muslim" was, in the end, deployed to describe the camp's living dead. Levi's explanation, which he suggests is unconvincing, that it was due to "the head bandages that could resemble a turban," resonates on both racialogical and historical levels and, indeed, opens up other, non-European histories of this term. In his analysis of the term "Musalman" in the context of both pre- and post-unification India, Shahid Amin maps the way in which the word has insistently been used in order to mark "the resident-Indian Muslims as 'the other.'"[78] Amin analyzes the manner in which, in the Indian context, the Turkish cap, invested with the burden of signifying the unassimilable alterity of the Muslim within the body of the Indian nation, "is made to stand for an essential marker of the otherness of things 'Muslim.'"[79] Tracking the historical permutations of the Musalman across a range of Indian texts, Amin concludes: "It is the belief in the Musalman as someone recognizably different that counts and endures variedly."[80] This doubly other history of the *Muselmann* brings into focus what remains constant across radically different historical and geopolitical uses of the term: that whoever is designated as a *Muselmann, Musalman,* or Muslim is compelled to wear the burden of absolute alterity. Despite irreconcilable spatio-historical differences, this semantic kernel continues to signify.

The significant lacuna to which I have drawn attention haunted me as I read Agamben's text, and the complex dimensions of this denegation were finally crystallized in my reading of Parvez Manzoor's essay "Turning Jews into Muslims: The Untold Saga of the *Muselmänner*":

> There can be little doubt, then, that the contemptible image of the fatalist Muslim predates the arrival of the pitiable figure of the *Muselmann* at Auschwitz. And even if at the camp it surfaces from the netherworld of Jewish consciousness, it was the Islamophobic European imagination that gave birth to it in the first place. Be that as it may, it is disconcerting to learn that even for the inmates of the camp, the Muslim was the *Untermensch*, the lowest of the low. This is certainly what Agamben has in mind when he, in a moment of brutal encounter with the truth, seeks refuge in "the postmodern irony" and belittles the import of this realization: "In any case, it is certain that, with a kind of ferocious irony, the Jews knew that they would not die at Auschwitz as Jews" (45). For others, there's no escaping the perverse logic of the Holocaust: While the Nazis killed the Jews, the Jews in turn sacrificed the "Muslims" (*die Muselmänner*)![81]

Manzoor meditates on the symptomatic repetition of this lacuna across Holocaust studies, suggesting that the "disregard of any Muslim stake at Auschwitz is part of the awesome silence that the victims of the Holocaust [are] always entitled to exercise."[82] "Nevertheless," Manzoor contends, "the Jewish 'christening' of the 'damned of the camp' as *Muselmänner* does implicate the Muslim in the Holocaust. And it does so brutally and scornfully, neither in the name of the executioners, nor in that of the victims, but as the victims of the victims; it implicates them in the name of the living-dead, the non-men whose death cannot be called death."[83]

In the wake of Manzoor's critical work, I want to transpose the figure of the *Muselmann* onto the Muslim inmates of Guantánamo Bay in order to bring into focus certain genealogical relations and discursive cross-hatchings that emerge from the locus of the camp. As contemporary reincarnations of *Muselmänner*, the Muslim inmates at Guantánamo are compelled to live, in a critically qualified way, the *ontotautology* of the Muslim *Muselmann*. In the context of Guantánamo, the Muslim prisoner literally lives and dies as "*the* Muslim" as he is simultaneously transmuted into the haunting figure of the *Muselmann*. In the context of Guantánamo, the Muslim inmate does not, I underscore, incarnate the Nazi specter of the "living dead"—the two figures are caught in radically different biopolitical regimes. Critically, the Nazi regime had the end goal of the attempted genocide of an entire people; no such genocidal biopolitical program underpins Guantánamo. Rather, in the context of the operational logics of the camp, one can discern the symbolic reproduction of the term through the literal effects that this biopolitical figure exacts from its target subjects. In the case of Guantánamo, the Muslim inmates resonate with their Jewish counterparts along the limited lines of reproducing, among other things, the shuffling gait of the *Muselmann* because of their shackled feet, legs, and arms; they also effectively embody subjects who can be tortured with impunity. Traversing historical divides and politically unique trajectories, the one, the *Muselmann*, through the instrumentalizing and serializing logic of the camp, inflects the symbolic production of that other figure: Guantánamo's Muslim prisoner. In keeping with the operational logic of the camp, a logic underpinned by an anomic violence that respects no categorical borders or limits, the Jew-become-*Muselmann* is spectrally interwoven into the Muslim-become-Jew-become-*Muselmann*.

Yet the irreconcilable outlines that haunt this moment of superimposition mark the specificity of historical determinations that cannot be assimilated: the one is also *not* the other, even as the assimilative forces of the camp labor to erase difference through the production of the serial figure of the *Muselmann*. In the context of the serializing and assimilative forces constitutive of the violent operations of the camp, I want to emphasize the fundamental difference between the Jewish *Muselmann* of the Nazi camps and the Muslim *Muselmann* of Guantánamo. Unlike the selective imprisoning of Muslim subjects at Guantánamo in the waging of the war on terror, the serial production of the Jewish *Muselmann* in the

Nazi camps was driven by the totality of the apparatuses, both repressive and ideological, of the German state, a totality predicated on achieving the complete liquidation of Europe's Jews. As Anna Pawelczynska, an Auschwitz survivor, writes: "The objective of a [Nazi] concentration camp was the biological destruction of prisoners."[84] Through the systematic deployment of "assembly-line-style death," the Nazis put in place "the operation of industrial genocide."[85]

The convoluted structure of the paleonymic formation, *Muselmann* as Muslim-become-Jew-become-Muslim, that I have attempted to trace is marked by a complex weave of categorical oppositions and racist sedimentations that collide, affiliate, and cleave, precisely as they (re)constitute their target subject and attempt to erase the traces of these unspeakable contradictions through an historicidal logic in which the other is serially assimilated into the same. Like the Jews in the Nazi camps, the Guantánamo prisoners are "catalogued and referred to by a serial number as a way of dehumanising them."[86] The literal and symbolic violence of the Muslim *Muselmann* ramifies across a number of levels at Guantánamo Bay. As a contemporary embodiment of *homo sacer*, the Muslim prisoner of Guantánamo marks the *Muselmann* "threshold in which man passe[s] into non-man."[87] "I convince myself each day," says one Guantánamo guard to the prisoners, "that you guys are all subhuman."[88] One of the ex-detainees, Murat Kurnaz, terms Guantánamo "a fully constructed project of dehumanisation."[89]

In the process of crossing the threshold from human to nonhuman, the *Muselmann*, Agamben writes, was also compelled to be known by a number of other dehumanizing appellations: "the thing itself," "donkeys," "cretins," "camels," "tired sheiks," and "trinkets."[90] At once animalized (donkeys), disabled (cretin), and repeatedly branded with other Arabophobic slurs (camels, tired sheiks), the *Muselmann* can be effectively left to die without those responsible feeling any sense of guilt or remorse. Within the schemas of anthropocentric/speciesist, ableist, and racist taxonomies, the linguistic transmutation of a Jew into a Muslim/Arab-cretin-animal enables the recalibration of her or his position down the different hierarchies to, in every instance, the very bottom rung, the "lowest of the low."[91] The bottom rung of these hierarchies becomes coextensive with the "space of the camp, where," in Perera's words, "the category of the 'citizen' is no longer operative"; it is also "the space where the claims and limits of the 'human,' what remains of the residue of the 'citizen,' are tested and revealed in lethal form."[92] The bottom rung marks the site from which an "ontological hygiene"[93] can be implacably exercised in order to dispatch target victims beyond the purview of the due process of law and justice.

In closing, I want to focus on one more constitutive aspect of the *Muselmänner* that both enabled and facilitated their torture and extermination with impunity: "we know from other witnesses," writes Agamben in a parenthetical aside, "that under no circumstances were they to be called 'corpses' or 'cadavers,' but rather simply *Figuren*, figures, dolls."[94] The naming of the *Muselmann* inmate as "doll" compels a return to the opening concerns of this essay, specifically, the ramifications of Banksy's installation of a Guantánamo detainee doll in Disneyland. The *Muselmänner* of the camps, writes Agamben, were said to be characterized by "faces rigid as masks";[95] they embodied a "faceless presence," an "anti-face."[96] Figurally, Banksy's Guantánamo doll and the prosthetically defaced Guantánamo detainees are transmogrified into one specter: *Muselmann Figuren* or dolls. Forced to wear blackened goggles, earmuffs and a surgical mask, the face of the Muslim detainee becomes the rigid mask of a doll that precludes the face-to-face relation because it is faceless, gazeless, and speechless. In invoking the face-to-face relation, I draw upon the work of Emmanuel Levinas, who formulates the ethical relation between humans as founded principally in proximity with the other's face. In so doing, Levinas draws attention to the irreplaceable alterity of the other: every face is unique, and to deface the face of the other instantiates the possibility of murdering the other by stripping away her or his personhood.[97] "The facelessness of the men at Guantánamo makes their abuse palatable," writes Sabin Willet, a lawyer working at the camp.[98]

For Levinas, the face incarnates more than the unique alterity of the other. "The absolute nakedness of a face, the absolutely defenceless face" articulates "the possibility of encountering a being through an interdiction. The face is the fact that a being affects us not in the indicative, but in the imperative"; this imperative invokes the command "Thou shalt not kill": "it is the impossibility of killing him [or her] who presents that face."[99] Yet, as Levinas makes clear, the power of the face in enunciating the interdiction not to kill is not based on its own disavowed violence. Rather, the power of this interdiction rests on something else altogether:

The opposition of the face is not the opposition of a force, is not a hostility. It is a pacific opposition, but one where peace is not a suspended war or a violence simply contained. On the contrary, violence consists in ignoring this opposition, ignoring the face of a being, avoiding the gaze, and catching sight of an angle whereby the *no* inscribed on a face by the very fact that it is a face becomes a hostile or submissive force.[100]

Stripped of his faciality, and prosthetically transmuted into an anti-face, the Muslim prisoner of Guantánamo becomes the contemporary, yet critically qualified, embodiment of "the *Muselmann*, the 'core of the camp,'" "the being whose death cannot be called death, but only the production of a corpse."[101] At Guantánamo Bay, the production of corpses is driven both by murder (Mahvish Khan has documented the unresolved forensic anomalies that haunt particular "suicide" cases[102]) and suicide through penalogical forces that are, in truth, forms of "letting die." As the "insignia of biopower,"[103] letting die evidences the reach of state biopolitical power into the very fibers of life. Guantánamo's penal apparatus pivots on the exercise of a virtually unfettered state power that can produce murder and corpses with impunity. The ontotautological transmutation and reduction of the Muslim inmates into *Muselmänner, Figuren*, and dolls facilitates the murderous operation of this penalogical system. As so many nonhuman dolls, the Muslim inmates of Guantánamo emerge as a "kind of absolute biopolitical substance" that can be dispatched beyond the legal purview of the person and her or his attendant human rights.[104]

For the brief duration of ninety minutes, a Guantánamo Bay doll is installed in the recreational surrounds of Disneyland. Instantiating a dissonant and scandalous rupture in the fantasy landscape of the theme park, Banksy's doll magnetizes the disavowed violent histories that stratify that place. As an apostrophe of empire, this Guantánamo doll testifies to regimes of biopolitical violence that suture the past to the present. As contemporary conjuration of the *Muselmann*, Banksy's Guantánamo doll stands as an apostrophic figure that rends the consoling fables of empire, exposing economies of violence that breach the prophylactic berms of the theme-park nation through the articulation of a seemingly impossible address: Guantámamo Bay, Disneyland.

Postscriptum: The Exigencies of Empire

Soon after Barack Obama was elected U.S. president, he ordered the closure of Guantánamo Bay prison. Yet, in the wake of this impending closure, "A freed Guantánamo prisoner has said that conditions at the US detention camp have worsened since President Barack Obama was elected, claiming guards wanted to 'take their last revenge.'"[105] In addition, in keeping with the brutal exigencies of empire, even as it appears that Guantánamo might finally be closed, it is being reported that the Obama administration is considering displacing Guantánamo to yet another offshore prison site, the secretive military prison at Bagram Airbase in Afghanistan, where it can continue to torture and abuse prisoners as they would not be situated on U.S. soil and would thus be beyond the purview of U.S. law.[106] Bagram, indeed, has already served as the first site of torture for many of the prisoners currently being held at Guantánamo.

NOTES

1   See Banksy, *Wall and Piece* (London: Century, 2005).

2   Nicholas Olsberg, foreword to *Designing Disney's Theme Parks*, ed. Karal Ann Marling (Paris and New York: Flammarion, 1998), 9.

3   "Banksy at Disneyland 2006"; YouTube video; 2 minutes, 6 seconds; http://www.youtube.com/watch?v=jkZoC6dwRqE.

4   Guy Debord, *Society of the Spectacle*, trans. Ken Knabb (London: Rebel Press, 2006), 10.

5   Karal Ann Marling, "Imagineering the Disney Theme Parks," in *Designing Disney's Theme Parks*, 29.

6   Erika Doss, "Making the Imagination Safe in the 1950s: Disneyland's Fantasy Art and Architecture," in *Designing Disney's Theme Parks*, ed. Marling, 180.

7   Doss, "Making the Imagination Safe," 182.

8   Alfred W. McCoy, "The Punishment of David Hicks," *Monthly*, June 2006, 24.

9   Suvendrini Perera, "What Is a Camp . . . ?" *Borderlands* 1, no. 1 (2002), http://www.borderlandsejournal.adelaide.edu.au/vol1no1_2002/perera_camp.html.

10   Murat Kurnaz, *Five Years of My Life: An Innocent Man in Guantánamo Bay* (New York: Palgrave Macmillan, 2007), 99.

11   Mahvish Rukhsana Khan, *My Guantánamo Diary: The Detainees and the Stories They Told Me* (Carlton North, Australia: Scribe, 2008), 40.

12   Cited in Moazzam Begg, *Enemy Combatant: A British Muslim's Journey to Guantánamo and Back* (London: Free Press, 2006), 165.

13   Jean-Luc Nancy, *The Ground of the Image*, trans. Jeff Fort (New York: Fordham University Press, 2005), 49.

14   Jasbir K. Puar, *Terrorist Assemblages* (Durham, N.C.: Duke University Press, 2007), 158.

15   Khan, *Guantánamo Diary*, 60.

16   Begg, *Enemy Combatant*, 286.

17   Michael Ratner and Ellen Ray, *Guantánamo: What the World Should Know* (White River Junction, Vt.: Chelsea Green Publishing, 2004), 43.

18   Begg, *Enemy Combatant*, 200.

19   David Rose, *Guantánamo: The War on Human Rights* (New York: New Press, 2004), 89.

20   Begg, *Enemy Combatant*, 243.

21   See Stewart E. Tolnay and E. M. Beck, *A Festival of Violence: An Analysis of Southern Lynchings, 1882–1930* (Urbana: University of Illinois Press, 1995); Philip Dray, *At the Hands of Persons Unknown: The Lynching of Black America* (New York: Modern Library, 2003); and James Allen et al., *Without Sanctuary: Lynching Photography in America* (Santa Fe, N.Mex.: Twin Palms Publishers, 2005).

22   Joseph Pugliese, "Abu Ghraib's Shadow Archives," *Law and Literature* 9, no. 2 (2007).

23   Marling, "Imagineering Disney Theme Parks," 29.

24   Perera, "What Is a Camp?"; and Ricardo L. Ortíz, "On (Our) American Ground: Caribbean-Latino-Diasporic Production and the Postnational 'Guantanamera,'" *Social Text* 94, no. 261 (2008): 18.

25   Giorgio Agamben, *Remnants of Auschwitz*, trans. Daniel Heller-Roazen (New York: Zone Books, 2002), 54.

26   Marling, "Imagineering Disney Theme Parks," 83.

27   Ibid., 74.

28   Hal K. Rothman, *Devil's Bargain: Tourism in the Twentieth-Century American West* (Lawrence: University of Kansas Press, 1998), 44.

29   Ibid., 14, 15, 43.

30   Andrea Smith, *Conquest: Sexual Violence and American Indian Genocide* (Cambridge, Mass.: South End Press, 2005), 184.

31   Antonia I. Castañeda, "Sexual Violence in the Politics and Policies of Conquest: Amerindian Women and the Spanish Conquest of Alta California," in *Building with Our Hands: New Directions in Chicana Studies*, ed. Adela de la Torre and Beatríz M. Pesquera (Berkeley: University of California Press, 1993), 26.

32   Amy Kaplan, "Violent Belongings and the Question of Empire Today:

Presidential Address to the American Studies Association, October 17, 2003," *American Quarterly* 56 (2004): 13–14.

33 Cited in Andy Worthington, *The Guantánamo Files: The Stories of the 774 Detainees in America's Illegal Prison* (London: Pluto Press, 2007), 1.

34 Begg, *Enemy Combatant*, 124–25.

35 Anne Maxwell, *Colonial Photography and Exhibitions* (London: Leicester University Press, 1999), 36.

36 Lynette Russell, *Savage Imaginings* (Melbourne: Australian Scholarly Publishing, 2001), 46.

37 Leo Marx, *The Machine in the Garden* (Oxford: University of Oxford Press, 2000), 16.

38 Cited in John M. Findlay, *Magic Lands: Western Cityscapes and American Culture after 1940* (Berkeley: University of California Press, 1993), 69–70.

39 Paul Gilroy, *Postcolonial Melancholia* (New York: Columbia University Press, 2005), 22.

40 Giorgio Agamben, *Homo Sacer: Sovereign Power and Bare Life*, trans. D. Heller-Roazen (Stanford, Calif.: Stanford University Press, 1998), 174.

41 Ibid., 174.

42 Findlay, *Magic Lands*, 267.

43 Ibid., 78.

44 Cited in Mark Dow, *American Gulag: Inside U.S. Immigration Prisons* (Berkeley: University of California Press, 2004), 12.

45 Nancy, *Ground of the Image*, 49.

46 See Joseph Pugliese, "Geocorpographies of Torture," *Australian Critical Race and Whiteness Studies Association Journal* 3, no. 1 (2007).

47 Cited in Findlay, *Magic Lands*, 77.

48 Marling, "Imagineering Disney's Theme Parks," 85.

49 Historically, this screening of "undesirables" was also premised on white supremacist criteria that "mainly employed attractive, white young men and women who could be easily assimilated into the company's design"; see Findlay, *Magic Lands*, 74, 82.

50 GlobalSecurity.org, "Terror/Indictment," 2002, http://www.globalsecurity.org/security/library/news/2002/sec-020828-2f5d9e89.htm.

51 Ibid.

52 "Judge Throws Out Terror Convictions," *USA Today*, 2004, http://www.usdatoday.com/news/washington/2004-09-01-terror-doi_x.htm.

53 Neil Harris, "Expository Expositions: Preparing for the Theme Parks," in *Designing Disney's Theme Parks*, ed. Marling, 27.

54 The video is available at http://www.youtube.com/watch?v=aQHFFbD_-Pg. (accessed July 21, 2008).

55 See Michael Ratner, "The Guantánamo Prisoners," in *America's Disap-*

peared, ed. Rachel Meeropol (New York: Seven Stories Press, 2005), 42; and Ratner and Ray, *Guantánamo*, 68–69.

56 Worthington, *Guantánamo Files*, 252–53.

57 Ratner, "Guantánamo Prisoners," 42–43.

58 Worthington, *Guantánamo Files*, 185–86.

59 Ibid., 196.

60 Elaine Scarry, *The Body in Pain: The Making and Unmaking of the World* (New York: Oxford University Press, 1985), 38.

61 For a detailed discussion of the historical precedents of this form of sensory-deprivation torture, see Alfred W. McCoy, *A Question of Torture: CIA Interrogation, from the Cold War to the War on Terror* (New York: Metropolitan Books, 2006), 35–36; and for a discussion of the use of "sonic assault" on Guantánamo inmates, see Anne Cranny-Francis, "Sonic Assault to Massive Attack: Touch, Sound and Embodiment," *SCAN: Journal of Media, Arts, Culture* 5, no. 3 (2008), http://scan.net.au/scan/journal/display.php?journal_id=1244.

62 Maurice Blanchot, *The Infinite Conversation*, trans. Susan Hanson (Minneapolis: University of Minnesota Press, 2003), 131.

63 Ibid., 131–32.

64 George F. Fletcher, "Black Hole in Guantanamo Bay," *Journal of International Criminal Justice* 2 (2004): 121–32.

65 Cited in Khan, *Guantánamo Diary*, 226–27, 221.

66 Blanchot, *Infinite Conversation*, 44.

67 Cited in Khan, *Guantánamo Diary*, 212.

68 Ibid., 264.

69 See Agamben, *Remnants of Auschwitz*; Rose, *Guantánamo*; and Joshua Comaroff, "Terror and Territory: Guantánamo and the Space of Contradiction," *Public Culture* 19, no. 2 (2007): 383.

70 See Agamben, *Homo Sacer*; and Perera, "What Is a Camp?"

71 Agamben, *Remnants of Auschwitz*, 41.

72 Primo Levi, *The Drowned and the Saved*, trans. Raymond Rosenthal (London: Abacus, 1998), 77.

73 Cited in Agamben, *Remnants of Auschwitz*, 43.

74 Ibid., 45.

75 Ibid.

76 Ibid.

77 Anna Pawelczynska, *Values and Violence in Auschwitz*, trans. Catherine S. Leach (Berkeley: University of California Press, 1979), 146.

78 Shahid Amin, "Remembering the Muselam," in *Fussing Modernity: Appropriation of History and Political Mobilization in South Asia*, ed. Kotani Hiroyuki, Fujii Takeshi, and Oshikawa Fumiko (Osaka: Japan Center for Area Studies and National Museum of Ethnology, 2000), 76.

79   Ibid., 79.

80   Ibid., 82.

81   Parvez S. Manzoor, "Turning Jews into Muslims: The Untold Saga of the Muselmänner," *Islam21*, no. 28 (2001): 4.

82   Ibid., 5.

83   Ibid., 6.

84   Pawelczynska, *Values and Violence in Auschwitz*, 44.

85   Ibid., 53, 79.

86   Khan, *Guantánamo Diary*, 264.

87   Agamben, *Remnants of Auschwitz*, 47.

88   Cited in Begg, *Enemy Combatant*, 165.

89   Kurnaz, *Five Years of My Life*.

90   Agamben, *Remnants of Auschwitz*, 44.

91   For a detailed discussion of the racial hierarchies that structured the inmates of the Nazi concentration camps, see Pawelczynska, *Values and Violence in Auschwitz*, 54–55; and Robert Joseph White, "IG Auschwitz: The Primacy of Racial Politics" (PhD diss., University of Nebraska, 2000), 61–109.

92   Perera, "What Is a Camp?" 2.

93   Elaine L. Graham, *Representations of the Post/Human* (Manchester, U.K.: Manchester University Press, 2002), 35.

94   Agamben, *Remnants of Auschwitz*, 54.

95   Primo Levi, *Survival in Auschwitz*, trans. Stuart Wolfe (New York: Summit Books, 1985), 90.

96   Agamben, *Remnants of Auschwitz*, 45, 53.

97   See Joseph Pugliese, "Necroethics of Terrorism," *Law and Critique* 21 (2010): 218.

98   Cited in Khan, *Guantánamo Diary*, 265.

99   Emmanuel Levinas, *Collected Philosophical Papers*, trans. Alphonso Lingis (Dordrecht, Netherlands: Martinus Nijhof, 1987), 21.

100   Ibid., 19.

101   Agamben, *Remnants of Auschwitz*, 81.

102   Khan, *Guantánamo Diary*, 153–56.

103   Agamben, *Remnants of Auschwitz*, 155.

104   Ibid., 156.

105   "Guantanamo Gets Worse," *Sydney Morning Herald*, March 9, 2009, 9.

106   Michael Evans, "Bagram Prison in Afghanistan May Become the New Guantánamo," *Times Online*, March 22, 2009, http//www.timesonline.co.uk/tol/news/world/us_and_americas/article7070460.ece.

7

THIS FRAGILE BODY

Susan Crile's *Abu Ghraib: Abuse of Power*

Julia A. Ireland

W hen the Abu Ghraib torture photographs first became public in April 2004, they met with an array of mostly predictable responses. These responses ranged in tone from the vehemence of moral outrage, to the defeated confirmation that "this is to be expected within the context of an illegitimate war," to the strategies of dismissal that acknowledged evidence of torture only to casually deflect it onto some version of human nature, thereby demonstrating a willingness to confuse behaving badly with acting immorally and even criminally.

Yet it is by no means clear what the Abu Ghraib photographs themselves *are.* They are certainly not documentary photography in the normal sense in which we understand documentary as neutrally and transparently providing factual evidence.[1] Some of the photographs were purportedly taken to extort confessions from prisoners and their family members by showing detainees naked and in sexually compromising positions—a strangely misguided innovation in the public structure of humiliation for its willingness to conflate the exposure of a consensual act with one coerced for the camera. The intention to humiliate not only makes this particular subset of photographs inseparable from the acts of torture that they do not just "depict" but also actively participate in the use of the camera to coerce by forcing bodies into view reveals a knowledge of violation that underlies *all* the Abu Ghraib photographs. And though there is something correct about the comparison of the images with pornography, this arguably has as much to do with the cognitive dissonance generated by what the eye perceives as an amateurish yet stylized simulation of real events as it does with sexual content, something that gives even the non-sexualized photographs a feeling akin to performance art.[2]

Whatever the precise circumstances under which they were taken, the visual and conceptual confusions generated by perpetrators of torture taking pictures of themselves looking at torture inevitably comes to frame the way that torture is seen in the photographs. This gives the photographs the peculiar effect of reading their own interpretive ambiguity back onto the person who views them, who may or may not *actually see* torture being perpetrated in the photographs. Viewers may or may not *actually see* themselves participating in the act of torture in the photos or see their viewing of the photographs as problematic in any way. ("Tell me what you see in the Abu Ghraib photographs, and I will tell you who you are.")

As such, the photographs not only beg certain questions about the relationship between representation and reality already familiar to postmodern criticism; the use of photography to torture seems to almost willfully collapse the distinction between the infliction of pain and its representation. Bodily suffering isn't so much being "captured" in the photographs as being approached from the vantage of its being posed as though *for* the camera. This remains the case even in those photographs that show prisoners in legally authorized "stress positions," in which the ongoing nature of their suffering so clearly extends beyond the instant the photo was taken.

The feeling that the torture being shown in the photographs has somehow been posed has the effect of undercutting the immediacy through which pain is made visually manifest by those undergoing it and is confirmed by the visceral, which is to say, *spontaneous* and *bodily* response of the person looking at the photographs. The entire visual orientation of the photographs thus serves to preempt the experience of sympathy evinced at the sight of suffering that Susan Sontag identifies as the distinguishing feature of war or "shock" photography and which gives it its ethical potential not through a misplaced identification with another's pain but as the "spark" for understanding the viewer's own relation to—and even responsibility for—that pain.[3] Yet this is not because we have been made insensitive as a culture through an excessive exposure to images of violence but because the Abu Ghraib photographs are direct about their own enactment of a complicit seeing: the photographs put the intentional coercion of pain and suffering on view in order to be seen as substituting an appropriately affective response for the act of taking a picture.[4] Such self-reflexive awareness is certainly not only an aspect of how the camera is transformed into an instrument of torture at that moment the photographs were taken; the photographs frame—frame in order to freeze and reiterate through the photographs themselves—the act of perception through which we become capable of *actually seeing* and being moved by the suffering of bodies.[5]

This makes viewing the Abu Ghraib photographs far more complicated than it at first appears. For if what the photographs show is perpetrators of torture regarding the intentional infliction of pain in order to be seen *not* to be seeing it as pain, the question becomes how we can look at the photographs without reiterating the perceptual and affective disposition that the photographs themselves compel. How can we recuperate a sympathetic response to the immediate suffering of the bodies in the photographs *against* the photographs' own structuring of a complicit seeing? Still further, what sense of ethical and political responsibility might such a response open up in considering the effects of the United States' policy on torture under the George W. Bush administration?

These are the questions posed by American artist Susan Crile, whose highly unusual project *Abu Ghraib: Abuse of Power* seeks, by drawing the photographs, to recuperate the possibility of the viewer's experience of sympathy for the prisoners being tortured.[6] As Crile writes in her artist's statement in the Italian exhibition catalog that accompanied the series:

> The Abu Ghraib photographs are particularly disturbing since they were taken with the intent *not* to have an empathic connection to the suffering of the prisoners—to "the horror of it all"—but are meant to show his weakness in the face of might. . . . By recasting now familiar signs of power and ideology in the Abu Ghraib photos, by exposing them as markers of brutality and viciousness, and by turning those abused objects of degradation and contempt back into human beings, I have tried to elicit the viewer's empathy.[7]

JULIA A. IRELAND

Quite unexpectedly, then, it is art—and, in particular, Crile's intuition about the nature of drawing in relation to the fragile outline of the body and the viewer's own sense of touch—that restores the immediate and affective connection between the individual bodies of those suffering in the photographs and the viewer's own body as providing the opening for the viewer to assume ethical responsibility in response to another's pain.

Crile is unique in this regard. Where the artists Richard Serra in *Stop Bush* (2004) and Gerald Laing in *American Gothic* (2004) have capitalized on the iconic feel of individual Abu Ghraib photographs for the purpose of branding the Bush administration's policy on torture, and Fernando Botero has allegorized the photographs in his series of paintings *Botero Abu Ghraib*, Crile straightforwardly bases each of her drawings on the original photographs.[8] She thus assumes that viewers have seen the photographs in order to challenge and expose their underlying framing—and this includes the viewers' first encounter with the photographs, what they saw and didn't see—by making the violated bodies of the prisoners the very site for the restoration of their humanity. This radical, if not also obvious, shift in visual orientation allows the viewer of the drawings to make a critical self-reflexive turn with respect to the way seeing is being framed in the torture photographs; this turn is neither ironic nor generalized but instead takes place through the viewer's sympathetic response to the suffering of bodies and the sense of ethical responsibility that follows from it.

This essay begins by laying out in greater detail how the Abu Ghraib photographs enact a complicit seeing by comparing them with lynching photographs taken in the United States during the 1920s and 1930s. My intent in developing this comparison is to contextualize Crile's specific artistic decisions by juxtaposing this analysis to her drawing *Crouching in Terror* (2005), which presents viewers with a choice concerning the position from which they see the drawing—prisoner or guard—that directly implicates their own spectatorship. Next, through the two drawings *Panties as Hood* (2005) and *Erotic Humiliation* (2005), I make a series of points about Crile's use of white chalk to communicate the fragility of bodies and the various ways in which she seeks to evoke the viewer's sense of touch. Finally, I offer an interpretation of Crile's drawing of the infamous (and also interpretively overdetermined) photograph showing Private First Class Lynndie England with a prisoner on a leash, suggesting that Crile's sensitivity to the intimate relation between bodies offers a different way in which to understand the logic of torture.

Before turning to my analysis, however, it is important to clarify a terminological distinction that has philosophical import and that poses itself as something of a temptation within Crile's project, for where I use the word "sympathy," Crile uses the word "empathy." While Crile's drawings are clearly about recuperating the possibility of an affective response that takes place through the viewer's own body, there is a significant difference between empathy and sympathy: empathy is predicated upon an *identification* with the other's pain as my own pain. This collapses the difference between self and other, as the other's pain becomes my pain purely through my ability to be affected by it—to literally "feel their pain"—which gives the appearance of doing all of the ethical work when, in fact, doing none of it. But the other's pain is, of course, not my pain (even as I show myself capable of being moved by it), and it is this distinction that the word "sympathy" attempts to capture as the opening onto the ethical relation with the other's pain and, critically, with the other's difference.

The publication of the Abu Ghraib photographs was accompanied by the almost immediate impulse on the part of writers, journalists, and intellectuals to contextualize the visual uncanniness of the images by searching for precedents.[9] Individual torture photographs have been compared to iconographic representations of Christ's crucifixion in great works of art, to the Statue of Liberty, to the sportsman's souvenir trophy shot, and, less imaginatively, to sadomasochistic and gay porn. Where these comparisons have operated primarily on the level of visual composition, the unusualness of including perpetrators of torture as also spectators of torture has led a number of commentators—Luc Sante first and Susan Sontag most famously—to compare the Abu Ghraib photographs to lynching postcards that were taken in the United States during the 1920s and 1930s.[10] While later critics have gone on to stress the very different racial, social, and power dynamics under which the pictures were taken, there is something importantly correct about this comparison in going beyond similarities in composition to the manner in which both sets of photographs enact a complicit seeing.[11] And in both cases, the crucial clue proves to be the ways those in the photographs are shown to look *for* the camera.

Inevitably, the first thing the viewer sees in the photographs are the eyes and smiles that look out beyond the frame of the picture and directly at the camera, which is where the action of the photographs is taking place in apparent disconnection with the violence being done to the bodies. The viewer of the photographs is also quite blatantly being shown how to interpret this gaze through the use of hands (the accusatory index finger, the congratulatory thumbs-up), which direct the viewer's eye toward the bodies being tortured, not in order to make them the focus of attention, but to make visible its own way of seeing through the self-disclosive gesture of a pointing finger. By contrast, Crile, in her rendering of the Abu Ghraib photographs, tends either to crop out the sight line of the torturers or to obscure the directness of their gaze so that hands are made to refer to bodies—they nearly always suggest a menacing touch—and not to the act of seeing.

This direct eye contact made by those in the photographs collapses the distance between the viewer and the photographer, and has the peculiar visual effect of placing the viewer at the scene of the photographs in looking at it from behind the camera so that the viewer's seeing becomes the actual foreground of the photographs.[12] As British photographer and documentary filmmaker David Modell implies in referring to a "triangle of communication," there is a strange kind of interpolation of gazes that takes place between those looking at the camera, the photographer, and the viewer, as the viewer does not simply meet the gaze of those in the photographs but is also anticipated by it in a manner that compels consent to and reciprocation of how seeing is being staged *within* the photographs, yet *within* the photographs as *for* the camera.[13]

There are two important and internally connected points to be made here. First, the immediate reciprocation of direct eye contact compels the viewer to look past the violence being done to bodies as the viewer's gaze is directed through the eyes and hand gestures of those in the photographs back to the viewer's own seeing, which is made indistinguishable in the photographs from that of the camera. This is what gives so many of the Abu Ghraib photographs their distinctive three-dimensional or holographic quality. In direct violation of Sontag's insistence that photography is a *way* of seeing, the collapsing of the viewer into the photographer allows the photographs to present themselves as though they are, in fact, capturing "seeing itself."[14] For it is in appearing to reflect back to the viewer the viewer's own seeing through the eyes of those in the photographs that the photographs actually *impose* this seeing onto the viewer as though it were the viewer's own — they impose this seeing onto the viewer in order to, in the same instant, confirm this seeing through the very act of the viewer's looking at the photographs. This means that the photographs not only enact a complicit seeing, but that they are directly coercive; the photographs attempt to construct the viewer's seeing by reiterating through their very framing the perceptual and affective disposition that the photographs themselves compel.

This leads to the next point: the transformation of the viewer's seeing into the foreground of the photographs has the disorienting visual effect of making the bodies of those being tortured withdraw to the position of incidental background within the frame of the photographs. In what is no doubt their most cognitively dissonant aspect, both the lynching and the Abu Ghraib photographs are seen to force the intentional infliction of pain into view in order to show those in the photographs looking away not in horror or moral repugnance, but to smilingly pose their seeing *for* the camera. This self-reflexive awareness thus not only comes to substitute for the immediacy of a sympathetic response to the other's pain, its further effect on viewers is to actively obscure their ability to see the bodies in the photographs as *suffering* bodies. Quite tellingly, Luc Sante describes first looking at the Abu Ghraib photograph depicting the pile of naked Iraqi prisoners and thinking it was a montage, the relationship between Specialist Charles A. Graner Jr. and Private First Class England's thumbs-up appears so utterly disconnected from the sculptural staticness of the naked bodies.[15] (Laing's *American Gothic* actually does turn this photograph into a montage, pasting the pile of bodies on top of his ironic rendering of Grant Wood's *American Gothic*.) Although both the lynching and the Abu Ghraib photographs are necessarily, and even *irreducibly* about the violence being done to bodies, the true object of the photographs — and what the photographs themselves *are* — is this being seen *not* to be seeing, which regards the intentional infliction of pain from the position of banal spectacle. This point is made sadly vivid by lynching photographs that were reproduced by the thousands as postcards.[16]

Crile prompts the viewer to make a different kind of self-reflexive turn in *Crouching in Terror* (fig. 7.1), her drawing of an Abu Ghraib photograph showing a prisoner being menaced by a dog. In comparing the drawing to the original photograph, the first thing the viewer notices is Crile's decision to place the prisoner at the center of the viewer's visual field, which

7.1   Susan Crile (United States), *Crouching in Terror*, 2005; 34 × 33 in.
Printed with permission of the artist. Photo: Ellen Page Wilson

requires her to crop out the guard with the dog, reducing his body to a forearm, gloved hand, and the barest suggestion of a toe. This not only shortens the perspective of the camera shot (the photograph's landscape view is made into a square); it also reorients the entire visual framing of the original photograph by eliminating the sight line of the photographer, who, in standing at the right-hand corner of the scene, is physically aligned with the guard along the wall, but visually aligned with the guard restraining the dog. This oblique orientation generates an odd and perceptually confusing double perspective as the photographer looks at the guard with the dog menacing the prisoner, who looks back at the guard in obvious terror. At the same time, however, the photographer's physical positioning places him on the same side as the guard along the wall with whom he looks on in also assuming the position of casual spectator. The viewer of the photograph is thus compelled to regard the prisoner's terror from the perspective of the two guards simultaneously—from the one guard who is the source of that terror, as well as from the other who, in direct contrast to the photographer, is shown within the photograph to casually disregard that source.

Crile's elimination of the photographer's direct sight line changes where the source of the visual action originates, even as it leaves the viewer to contend with the looking-on of the guard along the wall. The large, 34-inch by 33-inch, format places the viewer who encounters the drawing in a gallery setting roughly at eye level with the crouching prisoner. This means that the viewer is put into the position of starting from the prisoner's gaze and outstretched hand in order to visually trace out what, from the prisoner's perspective, he is attempting to so forcefully and so vulnerably STOP.

In contrast to the original photograph, whose vanishing point creates the illusion of the prisoner receding into the corridor of the cell block, in the drawing the prisoner's eyes and hands direct—if not *push*—the viewer's gaze away from his body, back into the foreground of the visual field, and even out beyond the paper's left edge. And it is in being pushed away from the prisoner's body that the viewer's gaze is directed along the prisoner's sight line toward the gloved hand and lunging dog, whose menace and black mass are emphasized in seeming to come out of nowhere—a nowhere that viewers are now made to understand that they share with the torturers. Crile is explicit about what she hopes to achieve in this. She writes, "Tertiary or grayed-out colored papers increase the institutional barrenness of the space—the chill of the cement prison floor. The frame of the empty page is like the cell or the cage. The figures brush against its limit—the edge. This is the space of torture and abuse."[17] The sensuous impact of this effect in *Crouching in Terror* is decidedly dramatic, as the original photograph's oblique perspective is accentuated and rendered uncanny in making the drawing appear to come at (and even over) the viewer, who is included under the glare and drab relentlessness of its decontextualized space.

This reframing of the viewer's visual orientation is essential for understanding the contrast between the structure of complicit seeing enacted by the original photograph and what Crile is attempting in this particular drawing, as both the photograph and the drawing are about the viewer *seeing* seeing. Where the original photograph compels the viewer to adopt the perspective of the two guards simultaneously, collapsing them into each other in placing the viewer into the position of the photographer, Crile's cropping out of the guard with the dog enables her to expose the photograph's confused double perspective by putting into its place a different double perspective. In starting with the prisoner's body and moving to the dog's coming out of nowhere, the viewer of the drawing is viscerally made to feel the terror and vulnerability of the prisoner's STOP. Yet in keeping with the original perspective of the photograph, the viewer remains ever so slightly aligned with the guard along the wall, who does not stop the prisoner from being terrorized but is instead shown looking on from the position of casual spectator. This is key: the side-by-side juxtaposition of these two perspectives puts the viewer of the drawing's seeing in tension with itself by initiating the possibility of the viewer making a critical self-reflexive turn with regard to his or her own spectatorship. (Here it is important to note that Crile's recuperation of distance preempts the collapse of self into other that takes place in empathetic identification.) While this critical self-reflexive turn necessarily originates with the prisoner's body, it is in Crile's staging of the viewer's *next* seeing the guard's looking-on that the viewer is called upon to reflect on the relationship between his or her own seeing and the guard's seeing. Is the viewer's seeing the same as the guard's seeing? Is the viewer looking at the terrorized prisoner from the position of casual spectator? What would distinguish the viewer's looking at the drawing from the guard's looking-on?

In direct contrast to the self-reflexive awareness of the camera operative in complicit seeing, the critical self-reflexive turn initiated in Crile's drawing offers the viewers a choice by presenting them with two possible *ways* of seeing, each alongside the other and each holding the other in suspense. It is in the tension generated by these two *ways* of seeing that the drawing critically exposes how the original photograph attempts to both coerce and construct the act of perception by presenting itself as capturing "seeing itself." Even more important, however, viewers of the drawing's *seeing* of the structure of complicity directly and explicitly implicate their own seeing without thereby determining what comes next—that is, without thereby determining whether and how viewers follow out the immediate claim that the prisoner's terrified STOP places on them. In ethical terms, the structure of implication initiated by this critical turn would be the beginning of responsibility, as the viewer's experience of sympathy would, to adopt Sontag's language, "spark" the next step of action in response to the prisoner's suffering. In political terms, it would be the occasion for viewers to reflect on the nature of their still deeper complicity with the United States' formal policy of legalized torture.

Beyond making the prisoners her visual focus, the effectiveness of Crile's drawing in eliciting sympathy lies in the way she marks the presence of the body in calling forth a full range of sensuous experience. This includes not only the bodies of the prisoners but the bodies of the guards, and—very importantly—the body of the viewer. The insubstantiality and powerlessness of the prisoner in *Crouching in Terror* is made apparent not only in his ghostlike, floating presence but in his diminutive size. And his diminutive size accentuates, and is accentuated by, an impossibly large hand. Though this appears exaggerated in the drawing, in the original photograph the prisoner's outstretched hand does, indeed, appear *that* large—as large as the prisoner's head, which he is pulling down into his body in a desperate effort to protect himself by folding his body back onto itself. It is clear that in her rendering of the prisoner's hand, Crile is calling attention not just to its large size but also to its specifically human distinctness as it gestures STOP. For although the body of the guard with the dog has been mostly cropped out, his physical presence is nonetheless retained in being reduced to a black-gloved hand whose indistinctness calls forward the act of torture in being made to appear simply as an extension of the black dog. This is the inverse of the marked physical presence of the guard along the wall, whose casual spectatorship is in part indicated by his having his hands in his pockets, which in Crile's drawing curiously makes him appear to have no hands.

Interestingly, the only exposed flesh of the guards that is visible is the ear of the guard standing along the wall; its curve seems to vaguely echo the posture of the crouching prisoner. Crile remarks in her artist's statement that the dominant sense in prison is not sight but sound. Yet in evoking the viewer's hearing, this ear does not call attention to what is heard in the prison so much as it reminds the viewer of the absence of the prisoner's voice — his no doubt also screaming in terror — as well as his inability to directly testify to his experience and be heard, confronting the viewer with the terrible responsibility of hearing the silence that engulfs the entire drawing.

The vulnerability of the prisoner in *Crouching in Terror* is in part achieved through Crile's use of white chalk, which is the dominant visual element that connects the drawings in the series. As she describes in her artist's statement, it is intended to communicate the fragility and insubstantiality of the bodies of the tortured prisoners while at the same time calling to mind a set of visual resonances that suggests the bodily, human imprint left at scenes of violent devastation:

> In the photos from Abu Ghraib, the prisoners have no weight; like Raggedy Ann dolls or balloons they lack balance or gravity. When the body is subjected to torture, the protection of the skin dissolves and the self no longer has a safe container; it is afloat and defenseless. I use white chalk to designate the fragility of the victims, who are like the ash-covered figures fleeing the World Trade Center, the body shells from Pompeii or the chalk outlines that mark the place of dead bodies at crime scenes. It takes me days to get the white chalk line to show the particular sense of humiliation of a particular man, to reveal the exact sense of his terrible pain.[18]

While Crile's filling in of the body of the prisoner in *Crouching in Terror* gives him a ghostlike, floating presence, some of her most affecting drawings depict the bodies of prisoners in pure outline form. Of these, the most disturbingly beautiful is *Panties as Hood* (fig. 7.2), which shows a prisoner in a legally sanctioned stress position. What is so immediately arresting about this particular drawing is the way that its beauty calls

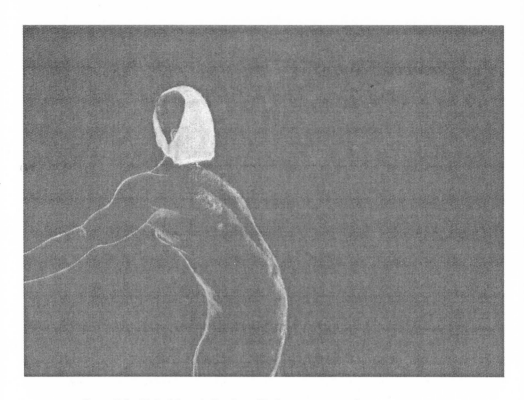

7.2 Susan Crile (United States), *Panties as Hood*, 2005; 27.5 × 39 in.
Reprinted with permission of the artist. Photo: Ellen Page Wilson

forward—and thus highlights—the intentional degradation of the prisoner achieved precisely in the use of panties as a hood. In order to achieve this effect, Crile edits out both the bed frame and the bars of the prison cell, which together create a jumbled and distracting network of intersecting vertical and horizontal lines. This allows her to bring forward the unnatural gracefulness of the body's outward arc, as the prisoner's single arm is rigidly pulled back and outside the field of the drawing. Though the viewer cannot actually see that the prisoner is bound (this is also true of the original photograph), the sense that the prisoner has been forced into this position is poignantly suggested by the flap of skin at the level of his shoulder blade, which interrupts the body's curve. Where the original photograph appears to be shot from above, as though the photographer were standing on the lower bed rack looking down, Crile emphasizes the feeling of horizontal movement generated by the body's arc by turning the photograph's portrait view into an asymmetrically executed horizontal framing. The drawing measures a wide 27.5 inches by 39 inches, and the expanse of blank space on its right-hand side contributes to the effect of the prisoner's being stretched, as the experience of his pain is shown to extend beyond the boundary of his body and continue on into an empty, and perhaps even infinite, space.

Whereas *Crouching in Terror* exposes the structure of complicit seeing by creating the possibility that the viewer will make a critical self-reflexive turn, *Panties as Hood* is by far the more challenging drawing for the way its arresting and fragile beauty positively invites the viewer's gaze. And, indeed, this is Crile's intent. While the original photograph is a quick snapshot, Crile's effort to capture the "exact pain" of particular bodies calls on the viewer to visually trace out with his or her eye the white chalk outline of the prisoner's body. This not only serves to restore something of the temporality of the prisoner's pain in the stress position; the act of visually tracing out the movement of a line has the further—and unexpected—effect of evoking the viewer's own sense of touch, which is the sense originally violated in the act of torture. Crile, whose artistic background includes work in textiles, is deeply aware of this connection: "Drawing, the use of chalk and charcoal, the texture of the paper speaks to our sense of touch. Touch slows down the hungry and impatient appetite of the eye and allows the body—our body—to respond empathetically."[19] The connection between drawing and touch is essential for understanding the insight that underlies the entire collection as what Crile also titles "Works on Paper." The materiality of drawing as a medium allows the viewer's body to respond sympathetically because the elements specific to drawing are uniquely able to capture the fragility of the human body as subject violation: the tactility of the paper reveals the prisoner's naked and exposed skin as the pure surface of *impressionable* flesh; the white chalk outline contains the body at the same time it calls attention to it in its fragility as *permeable* boundary.

Yet there is a still further point to be made here that reveals the greatest risk Crile takes as an artist. For the viewer's act of tracing the outline of the prisoner's body has the effect of returning to it its violated integrity—the literal sense in which it is self-contained, individual, and *whole*—by granting the prisoner the dignity of his pain precisely within the context of his body's intentional degradation. This is accomplished through the viewer's responsive touch, which gestures toward the undoing of the original perversion of touch that underlies the act of torture at the same time that it affirms the prisoner's suffering as separate. It would be easy to regard this gesture as salvific or even invasive, which perhaps says something about how uncomfortable we are today with the vocabulary of dignity and the unique sense of self-contained and bodily beauty through which it is communicated. However, Crile's drawings show that it is this experience of being responsively touched by the prisoner's violated dignity that alone reveals the irreducible vulnerability of the body as the site of a common humanity. And it is exactly this common humanity that the torture shown in the photograph not only denies but also exploits in order to falsify by treating the prisoner *first* as an Iraqi, an Arab, an enemy, a terrorist, and so on—anything but a human being subject to pain and wounding.

Crile's sensitivity to the outline of the body is used to quite different effect in the drawing *Erotic Humiliation* (fig. 7.3). Where the focus of the original photograph is clearly the coerced staging of mock fellatio in which the prisoner standing along the wall just happens to be included, Crile's effort to capture the bodily postures of the prisoners in a single white line creates a series of visual resonances that not only incorporates that prisoner into the formal composition of the drawing but makes him its key in appearing to comment on the scene of staged humiliation that he is nonetheless unable to see.

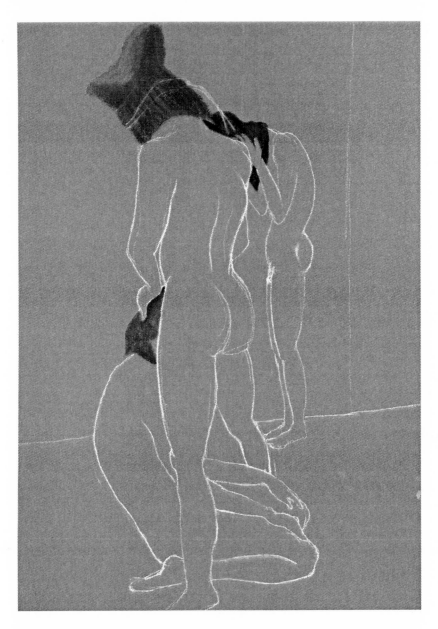

7.3 Susan Crile (United States), *Erotic Humiliation*, 2005; 39 × 27 in.
Reprinted with permission of the artist. Photo: Ellen Page Wilson

In first looking at the drawing, the viewer starts with the hooded and downcast head of the prisoner standing at its center in order to then trace the outline of the curved back of the prisoner being forced to kneel between his legs, continuing this line through the curve of the back of the prisoner standing along the wall, who completes the visual circuit of the drawing in being shown holding his head between his hands. While the viewer of the photograph takes in the strange disconnectedness of this tableau all at once, Crile slows the viewer's eye in tracing the continuous outline of the prisoners' bodies, incorporating the prisoner standing along the wall by calling attention to the way that his bodily posture echoes aspects of the postures of the other two prisoners simultaneously: his verticality, together with the positioning of his feet, make him appear to be less an independent figure than an exteriorized projection of the interior experience of humiliation of the prisoner standing at the center of the drawing, who is denied the gesture of holding his head between his hands by being forced to hold the other prisoner's head between his legs. Similarly, the curving back of the prisoner along the wall brings forward the curve of the back of the kneeling prisoner, whose posture does not so much embody the self-withdrawal of humiliation as slump well beyond it to a place of utter passivity and dejection.

While the bodily posture of the prisoner along the wall makes it appear as though he is responding to the scene taking place in front of him, the black hood makes viewers aware that, in contrast to the viewers themselves, he cannot *actually see* what is being staged in front of his eyes. Crile uses this fact to recast the way that hoods operate within the drawing, and it has the effect of both underscoring the disconnected interiority of each of the prisoners in relationship to one another and revealing the true perversity of this posed scene of mock fellatio. If the experience of humiliation implies the coerced exposure of self before the eyes of an other, as well the capacity to positively withdraw from that exposure into a protective interior by being seen to avert one's eyes, then an aspect of the torture in the photograph is the denial of the prisoners' ability to show themselves as withdrawing from view, which would be to retract the conditions of their exposure. (Indeed, this is the significance of what it means for the prisoner along the wall to put his head in his hands.) Still further, the original photograph in its extreme psychic violence puts on display for a digital eternity this inability to withdraw from view by constantly reenacting the exposure of the prisoners to the gaze of others through the medium of the photograph itself. Where *Crouching in Terror* stages the possibility of the viewer's making a critical self-reflexive turn, here the viewer's looking at the prisoner along the wall averting his eyes from a scene that he *cannot* see invites viewers to consider what they *can* see, and to do what the photograph itself does not: protect the prisoners from humiliation by looking away—in shame. Sympathy responds while again preserving distance and separateness.

Crile's use of the neutral, empty space of the paper to communicate the decontextualization of the bodies being tortured takes on a markedly different inflection in her rendering of what is no doubt the most interpretively overdetermined of all the Abu Ghraib photographs, which shows Private First Class Lynndie England with a prisoner on a leash (fig. 7.4). The photograph, which England claims her superiors told her to pose for, has become emblematic of the United States' abuse of power. And it was able to become emblematic because the posing of the photograph reveals not just an awareness of the relative hierarchical positions that define power (guard-prisoner, male-female), it also dramatizes that awareness in a manner that is at once assertive and parodic. Within the staging of this photograph, the conspicuously theatrical inversion of the power relationship between male and female through the use of the leash is being borrowed on to positively assert the power of guard over prisoner. What is transgressive, and even liberatory, in subverting the dominant hierarchical relationship between male and female within the highly stylized context of sadomasochistic play becomes within the context of the prisoner-guard relationship license for the sheer domination of transgressive violence.

The visual—and also visually interpretive—effect of this framing in the original photograph is twofold. First, the tortured prisoner's compelled submission is being both highlighted and masked insofar as a dimension of his torture is his being forcibly posed for the camera as *playing at* submission. Though this does not show up well in the photograph, the prisoner is, in fact, leashed to himself. The violent realization of what is being passed off as a fantasy of transgression creates—and must create, if its purpose is to humiliate—the illusion of agency.[20] (This is also an aspect of the scene depicted in *Erotic Humiliation*.) The man's seemingly willing surrender to domination by a woman thus serves to cover over the

7.4 Susan Crile (United States), *Private England, with Prisoner on a Leash*, 2005; 33 × 33 in. Printed with permission of the artist. Photo: Ellen Page Wilson

actual domination of a prisoner by a guard, which is rendered ambiguous in appearing to be just part of an act that reveals itself to be well aware of the dynamics of both power and transgression. Second, the posing of the photograph makes it inevitably about England's gender, which is not simply being "lent" to this scene in order to compound the tortured prisoner's humiliation but is instead being performed as violently dominating. According to certain feminist interpretations, the body that shows up as being originally violated is *hers*, which should be incapable of torture on either biologically essentialist grounds or as the result of a heightened social awareness generated by her own reductive exploitation as a body.[21]

Crile's simple attention to the spatial relationship between bodies radically recontextualizes how power relations can be seen to operate in the original photograph. As she did in *Crouching in Terror*, Crile crops out most of England's body in order to bring forward the body of the tortured prisoner. (Interestingly, the original photograph was already cropped by Specialist Graner, who was also the photographer, to edit out the presence of another female guard who was shown watching the scene.)[22] This removes both the distraction of England's gender—what is most noticeable about "her" is the living fleshiness of a naked arm—and the domination of her downward gaze, which takes its orientation not from the body of the prisoner attached to the end of her leash but from the camera. Though the viewer of the drawing is clearly aware that what is being shown here is a scene of violation, Crile's emphasis on space creates a feeling of both quiet and passivity. This has the effect of exposing not only the gratuitousness of the act of staged domination but also its uncomfortable intimacy. And it is this intimacy that makes this overly familiar image surprising.

The elimination of England's sight line, together with the absence of lines indicating the physical setting of a room, once again have the effect of giving the drawing a peculiar dimensionality. Where the black diagonal line created by the leash seems to confirm its initial appearance as flatly two-dimensional, Crile's inclusion of the outline of England's boot toe moves her back within the unmarked spatial field of the drawing. This both gives England a verticality that towers upward in its solid mass and makes the body of the prisoner seem to float forward and toward the viewer as it threatens to float outside the right-hand frame of the drawing. (One thinks of Crile's comparison of the weightless bodies of the prisoners to "balloons.") The sense that the prisoner is floating toward the viewer interrupts his or her natural way of "reading" the drawing (right to left, up and down) by making the viewer engage with what appears to be visually closest—namely, the prisoner's outstretched arm—in order to move backward: the viewer's gaze starts with the prisoner's arm, travels upward through the black diagonal created by the leash to England's arm, and then travels back down to extend through the white tether that attaches the prisoner's wrist to his own body.

It is in tracing the diagonal movement of the leash backward and *then* forward that Crile calls attention to the symmetries between arms and the tethers that connect bodies to bodies, offering the viewer a different way of understanding power relations in the original photograph. In following the strong diagonal that cuts through the entire drawing, the viewer becomes aware that what England is, in fact, being shown to hold in holding her leash is the power to bind the body of the prisoner to himself through the coerced experience of pain and humiliation. Here, Crile uses the visual logic of the drawing to bring forward a deeper insight into the logic of torture. For torture dominates by making the prisoner subject to his own body through the intentional infliction of pain, which undoes him as a human being in order to turn him into something that he never is on his own—just a body. Yet this emphasis on the photograph's underlying symmetries has the effect of exposing its organizing asymmetry, which is the contrast between open and closed circuits within a space of willed disconnection. This is evident not only in the difference between the leash (which demarcates open spaces within the field of the drawing) and the tether (which reveals the body as a closed circuit of pain) but in the small space of skin that separates the black leash from the black watchband that encloses England's wrist. Thus, where England holds the connection that binds the prisoner's body to itself, he does not hold a connection to her; the tethers that connect bodies to bodies in the drawing would seem to move in one direction only.

It is at this juncture that Crile does something unexpected, and that goes beyond what she would have been able to actually see in the original photograph. While she is careful to show the break of skin between England's hand holding the black leash and her black watchband, she continues the visual line of the leash through her faint, dark tracing of the veins in England's own arm. In so doing, Crile brings forward the presence of England's physical body in relation to the act of torture, suggesting that England's arm is an extension — if not the actual source — of the leash. Yet in showing what is just beneath the surface of England's skin, Crile succeeds in simultaneously communicating the vulnerability of England's body, bringing forward the intimacy of her bodily connection to the prisoner even within the space of her willed disconnection from him. It is finally this shared vulnerability that connects *him* to her even in the face of her power to deny it.

The affective power of Crile's drawings lies in her attention to the prisoners' bodies, making the viewer aware of the extent to which the singularity of their suffering has been left out of the discussion of the Abu Ghraib photographs in particular and the United States' policy on torture in general. This begs what is perhaps the only pertinent question here: Could we torture if we *really saw* the fragility of the body as a shared human condition, when *really seeing* implies undergoing the immediate claim to sympathy itself evoked by the insight into the vulnerability of *all bodies* as subject to pain? Could the dual insight into singularity and a shared vulnerability STOP torture?

Understood from this perspective, Crile's effort to "recast" and "expose" the dynamics of power underlying the original torture photographs is certainly a political act. She concludes her artist's statement by expressing her hope that "accountability does not lag far behind empathy."[23] Her sensitivity to the singular suffering of particular bodies enables her to avoid the didacticism of art intended to morally or politically instruct — a didacticism she nonetheless risks with each artistic choice she makes in her rendering of the original photographs. This shows us something about Crile's deeper sensitivity to the fragility of bodies and the sense of restraint that a vigilantly responsive attention to particularity imposes. For the restoration of the viewer's sense of touch that is the beginning of sympathy starts with Crile's eye and the relationship between that eye and the hand that holds the white chalk as she labors "to show the *particular* sense of humiliation of a *particular* man, to reveal the *exact* sense of his terrible pain" (my emphasis). Though this certainly does not undo the experience of torture for the prisoners who suffered it, Crile's attention to the singularity of their suffering restores for the viewer the perverted sense of connection — eye, hand, implement, touch — that becomes disconnected, instrumentalized, rationalized, and made into something finally inhuman through the act of torture. Art cannot save us from ourselves. One hopes, however, that in tracing Crile's fragile outlines, we remain vulnerable to letting it restore.

NOTES

1   Though problematic in combining interviews with dramatic reenactments and overdone scene setting, Errol Morris's 2008 documentary *Standard Operating Procedure* is nonetheless helpful in clarifying basic facts surrounding both the torture of prisoners at Abu Ghraib and the specific circumstances under which particular photographs were taken. Of the three guards taking photographs in express violation of signs forbidding photography within the prison, Sabrina Harman alone understood herself to be documenting evidence of torture. (During the interview with Morris, she repeatedly says that she wanted to "just show what was going on, what was allowed to be done.") With the exception of pictures showing the dead prisoner wrapped and iced in a body bag, Harman's photographs of prisoners in stress positions were found by investigators to show "standard operating procedures" rather than torture. At the same time, however, that Harman was documenting these legal acts of torture, she was also consenting to pose with prisoners who had been arranged in sexually humiliating positions. For more about how Harman understood her role as photographer, see Philip Gourevitch and Errol Morris, "Exposure: The Woman Behind the Camera at Abu Ghraib," *New Yorker*, March 24, 2008.

2   Though a sustained discussion exceeds the scope of this chapter, the connection made between the Abu Ghraib photographs and pornography was immediate and revealed important tensions as feminist writers struggled to make sense of the role that women played in the acts of torture at Abu Ghraib. For two different perspectives on the relationship between the Abu Ghraib photographs and pornography, see Susan J. Brison, "The Torture Connection: When Photographs from Abu Ghraib Can't Be Distinguished from 'Good Old American Pornography,' It's Not Just the Torture We Should Be Questioning," *San Francisco Chronicle*, July 25, 2004; and Rochelle Gurstein, "The Triumph of the Pornographic Imagination," *Arts and Opinion* 7, no. 1 (2008). Italian feminist philosopher Adriana Cavarero challenges aspects of these readings by calling attention to the photographs' feeling of simulation; see *Horrorism: Naming Contemporary Violence*, trans. William McCuaig (New York: Columbia University Press, 2007), 106–15.

3   Sontag lays out the ways in which war or "shock" photography affects the viewer in *On Photography* (New York: Farrar, Straus and Giroux, 1977) and *Regarding the Pain of Others* (New York: Farrar, Straus and Giroux, 2003). She is clear, however, that, on its own, the feeling of sympathy is not a sufficient response to the pain and suffering of others. As she writes in *Regarding the Pain of Others*: "Our sympathy proclaims our innocence as well as our impotence. To that extent, it can be (for all our good intentions) an impertinent—if not an inappropriate—response. To set aside the sympathy we extend to others beset by war and murderous politics for a reflection on how our privileges are located on the same map as their suffering, and may—in ways we might prefer not to imagine—be linked to their suffering as the wealth of some may imply the destitution of others, is a task for which the painful, stirring images supply only a spark" (102–3). For a critical engagement of Sontag's approach, see Judith Butler, *Frames of War* (London: Verso, 2009), 63–100. While I am persuaded by aspects of Butler's critique (this is particularly true of her analysis of embedded reporting), I am skeptical about understanding *all* photography as "visually interpretive" (e.g., already situated within a frame, and itself framing in a manner that is reality constituting). This follows from Butler's understanding of photography as representation (does it have to be?) and informs her resistance to Sontag's claim that photographs need narratives to "'make us understand'" (69). On this score, I'm inclined to agree with Sontag.

4   Certainly, one of the more remarkable moments in Morris's *Standard Operating Procedure* is a video showing Sabrina Harman looking down at the 'viewfinder' of her camera, photographing a pile of naked detainees as she is being videotaped.

5   In her analyses of the Abu Ghraib photographs, Judith Butler calls particular attention to the way in which the photographs "frame" the act of perception, challenging, among other things, Sontag's understanding of photography as documentary rather than already interpretive. While my own understanding of framing is indebted to Martin Heidegger's elaboration of the "as"-structure in *Being and Time* and "Origin of the Work of Art," Butler's recent work on the precariousness of life has been important for clarifying my approach to Crile's drawings, even if I do not engage Butler directly in this piece. For Butler's interpretation of the Abu Ghraib photographs, see her "Photography, War, Outrage," *PMLA: Theories and Methodologies* (2005): 822–27; the chapter "Torture and the Ethics of Photography: Thinking with Sontag," in *Frames of War*, is an expanded version of this essay.

6   When this essay was written, Crile's "Abu Ghraib: Abuse of Power" series included thirty-two works on paper, with possible plans to continue with

more drawings as other photographs were released. All of the drawings are executed in chalk, charcoal, pastel, and conte. Crile's most recent work includes drawings of prisoners held in black sites, and is based on written testimony found in the International Committee of the Red Cross depositions. Susan Crile, e-mail to author, April 6, 2009.

7   Susan Crile, *Abu Ghraib: Abuse of Power* (Rome: Gangemi Editore, 2007), 29.

8   David Ebony's introduction to the exhibition catalog *Botero Abu Ghraib* is useful for documenting a variety of artistic responses to the Abu Ghraib photographs. While the Botero paintings are compelling (the series does include some drawings), they tend to be composites rather than based on the actual Abu Ghraib photographs. As Ebony writes, "Botero based his Abu Ghraib compositions on written testimony as much as on the photographic material" (*Botero Abu Ghraib* [Munich: Prestel Verlag, 2006], 15). There is something important about the singularity of the bodies of those being tortured in the photographs that is lost in this approach and that Crile understands her drawings as recovering. Here, I would also risk making the further point that the materiality of drawing—the tactile presence of the paper and the body in outline form—is uniquely well suited to communicating the fragility of the body in pain. Painting, by contrast, fills up the surface of the canvas and fills in the outline of the body, turning it into a figure. The significance of the materiality of drawing is addressed later in this essay.

9   In his book *The Abu Ghraib Effect* (London: Reaktion Books, 2007), Stephen F. Eisenman lays out the connection between the viewer's experience of the photographs' visual uncanniness and Freud's theory of the uncanny, writing: "On seeing the photographs from Abu Ghraib prison, many critics, art historians and others experienced the disorientation of the uncanny because they saw in the hierarchic disposition of bodies, the mock-erotic scenarios, and the expressions of triumphant glee on the faces of the captors, something that was disturbing and intensely familiar, but could not be named or fully recalled to consciousness. What they recognized but quickly forgot . . . is in fact a key element of the classical tradition in art. . . . That feature of the Western classical tradition is specifically the motif of tortured people . . . who appear to sanction their own abuse" (16).

10   See Luc Sante, "Tourists and Torturers," *New York Times*, May 11, 2004, Opinion section. Sontag makes this connection in "Regarding the Torture of Others," pointing out that "snapshots in which executioners placed themselves among their victims are exceedingly rare" (*At the Same Time: Essays and Speeches* [New York: Farrar, Straus and Giroux, 2007], 132). Sontag had already briefly addressed the lynching photographs in *Regarding the*

Pain of Others, 91–93. For a full discussion and complete collection of the lynching postcards, see James Allen, *Without Sanctuary: Lynching Photography in America* (Santa Fe, N.Mex.: Twin Palms Publishers, 2003); the collection is further supplemented by the Web site www.withoutsanctuary.org.

11   Dora Apel lays out the important differences between the lynching and Abu Ghraib photographs in "Torture Culture: Lynching Photographs and the Images of Abu Ghraib," *Art Journal* 64, no. 2 (Summer 2005): 88–100.

12   It is worth noting that only the lynching photograph, with its inclusion of a white border denoting day and place, makes this relationship between frame and the viewer's seeing visible and thus interpretively available. The digital medium of the Abu Ghraib photograph is, by contrast, effectively limitless, filling in so as to absorb any outer edge, and punctually unlocatable as even capturing a real event unfolding in real time.

13   As Modell eloquently writes in his post "Viewpoint: The Power of Abuse Pictures," for the BBC News: "The pictures from Abu Ghraib are fundamentally different [from documentary]. They are not snatched, clandestine images taken to uncover the truth and disseminate it. In the almost perfect compositions it is obvious that they were taken in a perversely relaxed atmosphere—emphasized by the demeanor of the troops. And this reveals an appalling reality—that the photographs are a deliberate part of the torture. The taking of the pictures was supposed to compound the humiliation and sense of powerlessness of the victims. The photographer was the abuser. When we view the pictures, we are forced to play our part in this triangle of communication. The photographs were taken to abuse, by exposing the victim at their most vulnerable. By looking at the images we become complicit in the abuse itself. It is what makes them intolerable for the viewer and why they are so destructive to a war effort built on the spin of 'liberation'" (BBC News, May 13, 2004, http://news.bbc.co.uk/2/hi/americas/3710617.stm).

14   In many of her writings on photography, Sontag stresses that photography is a *way* of seeing. She makes this the first principle of her short piece "Photography: A Little Summa," writing: "1. Photography is, first of all, a way of seeing. It is not seeing itself" (*At the Same Time*, 124).

15   Sante, who was one of the first critics to comment on the Abu Ghraib photographs in "Tourists and Torturers," writes: "The first shot I saw, of specialist Charles A. Graner and Pfc. Lynndie R. England flashing a thumbs up behind a pile of their naked victims, was so jarring that for a few seconds I took it for a montage" (*New York Times*, May 11, 2004, Opinion section).

16   For details on the circumstances under which one such photograph was taken, see Allen, *Without Sanctuary*, 175–76. He writes: "Lawrence Beitler,

a studio photographer, took this photo. For ten days and nights he printed thousands of copies, which sold for fifty cents apiece."

17   Crile, *Abu Ghraib*, 27.

18   Ibid.

19   Ibid., 28.

20   Eisenman addresses this structure in *The Abu Ghraib Effect*, 60–72.

21   For two different perspectives on this issue, see Barbara Ehrenreich, "The Uterus Is No Substitute for a Conscience," *Arts and Opinion* 4, no. 1 (2005); and Timothy Kaufman-Osborn, "Gender Trouble at Abu Ghraib?" *Politics and Gender* 1 (2005): 597–619.

22   This fact comes out in Errol Morris's *Standard Operating Procedure*.

23   Crile, *Abu Ghraib*, 29.

8

SRI LANKA

Landscapes of Massacre

Suvendrini Perera

Shortly after the savage end to the savage thirty-year war in Sri Lanka in May 2009, a video filmed on a phone camera made global headlines. It showed the naked, blindfolded body of a man, hands bound, legs spread-eagled, being forced down into the ground in a marshy field, probably a paddy field. It is a healthy, whole body, muscled and well-fleshed, nothing like the wasted civilians who emerged from the war zone in their scraggly, broken groups night after night on our TV screens in the global north. This one is *fighting fit*: a soldier. There is a palpable squelch as the splayed body is violently pushed down into the mud. Seconds later, the man shudders, and we sense rather than hear the convulsive impact of bullet on flesh. This reflex of an imploding body, experts will later testify, is impossible to fake.

Another blindfolded and bound body buckles and falls on the marshy ground, next to the first. An unseen voice jeers, *like puppets*: this is easy work. The hand that holds the phone camera swivels slowly to show several more bodies, all naked, solid, prone on the ground, anomalously brown against the fresh green of the grass, the silver shimmer of water.

The video is replayed many times over the ensuing months on the BBC, CNN, and various Internet sites while the Lankan government persistently denies its veracity. Finally, the United Nations special rapporteur on extrajudicial, summary, or arbitrary executions declares that a succession of experts in forensics, photography, and the movement of the human body has determined that it cannot be other than authentic.[1]

Whenever I see this execution video (often in the months after it was first released), I think of some fragments from a poem that has been copied out on the door of a women's toilet stall at my university in Perth, Australia:

. . . Between the coconut palms the graves are full
of ruined bones, of speechless death-rattles
. . . the dead voices . . .
the blue mouths freshly buried . . .

What was going through her mind, the woman who carefully reproduced the twenty or so lines of a poem, word for word, standing in the unquiet anonymity of a toilet stall? What welling up of emotions, what compulsion of pain or outflow of rage, compelled her to copy out, or perhaps rewrite from memory, in deliberate black texta, these precise and terrible lines?

There are days when I scrutinize the faces of the students and coworkers who go in and out of our building. We are from many places here, other places of war and death, a community of elsewheres that we acknowledge only furtively in quick second glances and half smiles. Pablo Neruda wrote "Los Dictadores," published as part of his Latin American epic *Canto General*, in the 1930s and 1940s. It was published in Mexico in 1950. Anyone could have copied out this English translation from the Internet on a bathroom door sometime in 2008 or 2009. Is it the one place she feels free from observation, a survivor of some murderous quagmire? Or is she someone who coldly wills herself there, in a field of mud and coconut palms? Did her nostrils swell as she wrote, filling unbearably with that mix of "blood and body, a penetrating / petal that brings nausea"?

There are many places, too many to enumerate, poisoned by the penetrating petal that betrays the pervasive, unspoken presence of hidden graves. But Lankans make special claims on Neruda, Chile's consul in Ceylon from 1927 to 1929 (he was to describe it later as the place where he spent his bitterest hours and wrote many of his best poems). It is an intimate landscape that those lines call up, one unseen, unspoken, yet too well known:

The weeping cannot be seen, like a plant
whose seeds fall endlessly on the earth,
whose large blind leaves grow even without light.
Hatred has grown scale on scale,
blow on blow, in the ghastly water of the swamp,
with a snout full of ooze and silence.[2]

A Topography of Slaughter

In *Living with Torturers*, Sasanka Perera writes succinctly: "The Sri Lankan countryside is scattered with unmarked mass graves, not to mention sites where torture and violent death took place. Many of these locations are clearly known to local people. Such places are spatially marked as they are clearly identified in the local discourses and narratives of terror."[3] Few places on the island are free from the rot and ooze of silence. A local topography of massacres and mass graves can be plotted alongside the archaeological marvels of the heritage trail. Like the dim contours of some village drowned in the name of progress with the aid of a loan from the International Monetary Fund, hidden shapes float just under the shimmer of postcard-perfect paddy fields crowned by white-domed dagobas and temples, or else branch out beneath the sand of a surf beach on the distant eastern coast. Even if they remain unrecorded on any map or atlas, such subterranean topographies of slaughter, as Perera points out, are no secret to those who live here.

The dimensions of this local knowledge, its substrata of non-places and its unmapped courses marked by silent complicities and refusals, its web of wordless inflections and infinite lexicon of silences, are sounded in Michael Ondaatje's poem "The Distance of a Shout":

. . .
Monks from the north came
down our streams floating—that was
the year no one ate river fish.

There was no book of the forest,
no book of the sea, but these
are the places people died.

Handwriting occurred on waves,
on leaves, the scripts of smoke,
a sign on a bridge along the Mahaweli River.

A gradual acceptance of this new language.[4]

No book nor map but an ephemeral tracing by voice or hand registers the places where people died. Ondaatje's poem is contemporaneous with his novel of the war-ravaged 1990s, *Anil's Ghost*. Both texts are preoccupied by the relations of violence, body, and landscape: the language in which massacres are written on leaves and rivers, or in the smoke of burning villages and crops. The historic Mahaweli, the largest of the country's rivers, flowing from the central highlands into the ethnically mixed territory of the eastern province, is an artery of violence, ancient and recent. The Mahaweli was the site of one of the most ambitious and politically charged development projects of the 1980s and 1990s. In these decades leading up to the war, the attempt to remake the country starting with this riparian environment mobilized core identifications and ideologies of modernity, history, race-ethnicity, religion, culture, and nation.[5] Ondaatje's poem taps the anxieties and phobias unleashed by these events, revealing how violence, history, and landscape write themselves in and through one another. This is a co-implication in which the poem, too, finally participates and colludes.

This essay situates itself at the intersection of body, landscape, and violence, the forms of their inscription on and by one another, and our readings of those inscriptions. It maps multiple discourses—historiographic, testimonial, literary, political—that in their very plurality are fundamentally constitutive of the landscapes of massacre: they represent it, enable it, are inscribed by it, and denounce it—often simultaneously. At the same time, these discourses effect their own particularities of violence.

The war in Lanka, as a clash of incompatible nationalisms or competing homeland imaginaries, at its most elemental level pits one "territorial ego" against another.[6] The essay explores lines of connection between political violence and nationalized landscape as an artifact or text organized through historically embedded and ideologically loaded rhetorics and tropes.[7] Such mythopoeic, nationalized landscapes work hand in hand with ontologized regimes of territoriality. Land functions at once as object, scene, and medium of violence. It is the source, surrogate, and repository for the violences visited on bodies.

Mapping Terror 1: South and North

As Øivind Fuglerud points out, the exclusionary geographies of Sinhala and Tamil nationalism are characterized by a spatial framework broadly comparable to the one Allen Feldman identifies in the context of Northern Ireland.[8] It consists of three main zones: "sanctuary," "targeting community" (both imagined as the home ground of a single ethnic group), and "interface."[9] Although the main focus of this essay is the interface of the multiethnic regions of the east and the border areas between the north and south, I begin with a brief attempt—necessarily discontinuous, partial—to plot the multiple forms of violence, visible and invisible, enacted throughout the land.

The sudden revulsion against river fish described in "The Distance of a Shout" resonates with a memory dating back to the 1971 insurgency in southern Lanka when young Sinhala men and women, followers of the Janata Vimuki Peramuna (JVP), a group reputedly inspired by Ernesto "Che" Guevara's writings, took up arms against the state. The mostly rural uprising was as sudden as it was quickly overcome. Captured JVP members and suspected sympathizers were brutally tortured and murdered by army and police who had been initially caught off guard. The bodies of young men and women were heaped in mass graves or flung into the many deep-flowing rivers of the south.

I experienced the time of the insurgency mainly as a period of dragging, silent days when school was indefinitely suspended. At regular intervals, the radio assured us that order had been restored and "mopping-up" operations were in progress, a new term whose meaning unfolded only gradually in adult conversations overheard through closed doors. Among scores of horrific stories exchanged between my mother and her friends, I remember several about a woman washing clothes, or maybe bathing in a river, who glimpses an unusual movement of the current, a patch of wild color, out of the corner of her eye. Looking up, she sees the mangled body of her daughter or brother floating past. So, under conditions of official silence and censorship, we learned of the sullied, swollen rivers and fish engorged with human flesh.

We didn't know then that the 1971 insurgency was only a grim prelude, a bloodletting that inaugurated an era of terror to come. Eruptions of episodic violence during the 1970s culminated in full-blown war a decade later. Between 1983 and 2009, civilians of all ages and ethnicities would become targets of unimaginable, multipronged violence as a necropolitical order became normalized. "Necropolitics" is the term coined by Achille Mbembe as a counterpart to Michel Foucault's "biopolitics." Foucault posits that whereas in medieval times sovereign power was manifested through the prerogative to take life, in modern times, sovereignty is exercised through the "management of life rather than the menace of death."[10] An order in which "power spoke through blood" was supplanted by an order in which control over health, hygiene, population, race, and "the future of the species" became the dominant means of exercising sovereign authority.[11] In response to Foucault, Mbembe questions whether biopolitics is "sufficient to account for the contemporary ways in which the political, under the guise of war, resistance or of the fight against terror, makes the murder of the enemy its primary and absolute objective? . . . Imagining politics as a form of war, we must ask what place is given to life, death and the human body (in particular the wounded and slain body)? How are they inscribed in the order of power?"[12]

Mbembe's question prompts me to reflect on how, while the spectacle of public execution or the theatrical exhibition of tortured and maimed bodies buttressed the medieval sovereign's claim to absolute authority, contemporary necropolitics functions through making the wounded, slain, or disappeared body simultaneously visible *and* invisible. The body flung into a marsh or vanished in an unmarked white van is governed by the chilling logic of the unseen yet known. These are the dirty little open secrets on which such an order relies. In Argentina in the 1980s, the triumph of the Mothers of Plaza de Mayo was precisely their ability to bring a system of midnight disappearances and invisibilized killings into the light of day, to *materialize* that which was hidden, had gone missing. The defiant clanging of pots and pans, the names lovingly embroidered on white scarves of mourning, the empty center at the heart of the immovable circle of women: all these made present the absent bodies of the wounded and slain. *Murder will out.* That which had been spoken of only in hushed voices, behind closed doors, was literally cried aloud in the marketplace. The women's public calling to account exposed the obscene power of the open secret that had underwritten this necropolitical regime.

The Embilipitiya massacre in southern Lanka in 1989–90 is perhaps the ultimate sign of the naturalization of a necropolitical order. Forty-seven schoolchildren were abducted, tortured, and murdered by the army for acts that would count as no more than adolescent pranks in any society that had not become unhinged by terror. The massacre had no obvious ethnic motivation: both the schoolboys and the army were solidly Sinhala and Buddhist. How to explain the actions of parents who took their children to the army camp when ordered to do so and returned them there even after it was evident they had been subjected to torture?[13] Their responses betoken a profound collapse in the face of pervasive violence and a reflex of sheer terror, terror all the more disabling because unacknowledged, unspoken, and camouflaged by denial: when asked why he had cooperated with the military, one of the parents in the case responded, "We had faith they would not do something like this."[14] "To us" remains unspoken but implicit in his answer, for by then it was well known what happened in these places. The army camp in Boosa was a notorious torture site where many were taken, some never to return. Another infamous torture chamber was located on the fourth floor of an innocuous-looking building in Colombo. "Being taken to the Fourth Floor" became well understood as a euphemism for torture from the 1980s onward.

The open secret of killing, wounding, and torturing worked hand in hand with public spectacles of "spontaneous" massacres, attacks, and pogroms. At the beginning of the war, the 1983 anti-Tamil pogroms saw the murders of thousands of Tamils in the space of a few days, most of them burned alive in houses or cars or beaten with sticks and stones. Others were massacred, with the complicity of the prison hierarchy, inside the Welikade jail. At the Bindunuwewa Rehabilitation Camp for those suspected of being fighters with the Liberated Tigers of Tamil Eelam (LTTE), twenty-five young men were murdered by a frenzied Sinhala crowd as police and military looked on. Throughout the 1980s and 1990s, LTTE bombs, in their own necropolitical display, killed and maimed thousands of passers-by at bus stops and on busy streets, in a relentless staging of terror. The assassination of each VIP was accompanied by the collateral killing of unknown numbers of obscure bystanders of all ethnicities and religions.

The resurgent JVP, too, carried out its own campaigns of terror throughout the late 1980s, killing civilians, government officials, teachers, politicians. Patients died in their hospital beds when doctors and nurses were forbidden, on pain of execution, to report for work. Bodies appeared on lampposts and at junctions, wearing crude posters that cataloged their supposed crimes of noncooperation. Scores of suspected JVP members also disappeared: thrown into rivers, flung into the sea from helicopters, or deliberately placed at junctions during the curfew hours to be found at daybreak by children on their way to school or the faithful bearing flowers to temple. The army, the JVP, as well as anonymous paramilitaries and thugs associated with various politicians bore responsibility for the epidemic of killings and disappearances.

All of this happened in the "peaceful" south, with its claims to something like normal life, and where, simultaneously, unprecedented levels of wealth and consumption were fed by expatriate remittances, free trade zones, and boutique tourism. In the official war zones of the north and east, the killing was unimaginably magnified. Tamil, Muslim, and Sinhala civilians (and many others whose ethnicity was not deliberately targeted) were slashed with machetes, shot at point-blank range, blown to pieces, burned, or hacked to death. Everyday places—mosques, temples, and churches; paddy fields, wells, beaches, and sleeping villages; ferries and boats, bus stops, and train stations—all were scenes of sudden terror where government and rebel soldiers, Indian "peacekeepers," armed "homeguards" and paramilitaries killed and raped with near impunity.

In the north, a veritable alphabet soup of Tamil rebel groups—EPRLF (Elam People's Revolutionary Liberation Front), PLOTE (People's Liberation Organization of Tamil Eelam), EROS (Eelam Revolutionary Organization of Students), TELO (Tamil Eelam Liberation Organization), ENLF (Eelam National Liberation Front)—almost all with the word "Liberation" or "Revolution" hopefully inscribed in their titles, had sprung up after the anti-Tamil pogroms of 1983. The Marxist-Leninist ideologies of 1970s third world liberationism and a fervent ethnonationalism were the twin forces animating Tamil separatism in these early years.

The contradictions between the two are summed up by A. Sivanandan as an "uneasy mating of bourgeois historicism [manifested in the harking back to the imagined glories of an ancient Tamil Jaffna Kingdom] with historical materialism," in which Tamil liberation was understood as a vanguard stage in a wider program of socialist revolution.[15] By the mid-1980s, any serious commitment to a socialist agenda had been discarded, and an exclusionary and reactionary Tamil nationalism with terror at its core had gained the upper hand. The various separatist groups clashed among themselves for supremacy, as well as with state forces, until they were all engulfed by the total violence of the most ruthless among them, the Liberation Tigers of Tamil Eelam.[16] By the mid-1980s, "internal terror and totalitarian methods had taken over," leaving the population of the northern capital of Jaffna stunned by the rapidity with which what was originally imagined as a popular war of Tamil liberation was transformed into an internal war for total control over the Tamil people.[17] At the same time, the north was subject to intensive attack by state forces: "Indiscriminate shooting, helicopter strafing, bombing, shelling from the land and sea, mass arrests and torture had become the order of the day. When petrol bombs (barrels of inflammable, napalm-like substance) began to be rolled out of Avro planes to fall where they would, we had reached the zenith of state terrorism."[18]

The direct entry of the Indian army in the role of peacekeepers in mid-1987 seemed at first to herald a quick end to this terror by the Lankan state. But in a rapid and deeply shocking twist, the Indian Peace Keeping Force (IPKF), later popularly referred to as the Innocent People Killing Force, went from "friend and protector to aggressor and enemy" within the space of weeks.[19] Intense fighting broke out between the LTTE and the IPKF for control of the north. The LTTE, at first implicitly aligned with the IPKF against the Lankan state, was later covertly armed by the latter in its warring against the IPKF. Smaller Tamil groups variously supported the Indian or Lankan army.

The city of Jaffna, the capital of the north, was a major battleground. Daya Somasundaram, a psychologist whose *Scarred Minds: The Psychological Impact of the War on Sri Lankan Tamils* at times recalls Frantz Fanon's *Studies in a Dying Colonialism* with its case histories of torture in the Algerian war, identifies the IPKF's indiscriminate shelling of the city as calculated to produce perhaps the most profound effects of a "psychological terror"

223

that pervaded the entire environment and "reflected the anguish of all living things": "Trembling dogs were seen scampering all over, rabbits dropped dead and wild birds vanished from the Jaffna peninsula."[20] The LTTE for its part made cynical use of the civilian population as cover for its attacks on Indian forces and subsequently ordered a brutal evacuation of Jaffna, leaving behind its weak and vulnerable, the latter an unbearable abandonment in a chain of betrayals. Later, the LTTE would drive the Muslim population out of the Jaffna Peninsula at gunpoint, giving them two hours to leave the homes they had lived in for centuries.

The Sri Lankan state, the Indian state, and now the LTTE, the self-appointed champion of the Tamils, had each broken an implicit compact with the peoples of the north and east, producing what Somasundaram describes as a profound "cognitive dissonance."[21] He concludes that the brutality with which the LTTE (once indulgently and hopefully referred to as "our boys" by the populace) imposed its will on the people, coupled with the bloody internecine conflict among the various Tamils groups, produced "a greater impact . . . than the direct war with the Sri Lankan state. The psychological trauma of the internal war went much deeper and was felt more keenly."[22]

The complicated and shifting alliances during this period resemble Mbembe's description, via Gilles Deleuze and Félix Guattari, of a war machine characterized by a seriality of "plural allegiances, asymmetrical suzerainties, and enclaves." As Mbembe writes: "The state may, of its own doing, transform itself into a war machine. It may moreover appropriate to itself an existing war machine or help to create one. War machines function by borrowing from regular armies while incorporating new elements well adapted to the principle of segmentation and deterritorialization. Regular armies, in turn, may readily appropriate some of the characteristics of war machines."[23] In Jaffna in the 1980s, the targeting of the civilian population by multipronged violence can only be described as an operation in which, as in Deleuze's and Guatarri's war machine, the state and the forces who opposed it each increasingly came to mimic the characteristics of the other in order to enact terror on the population. Thus women and girls were gang-raped in frightening numbers by the Indian army, whose government had entered the war in the guise of peacekeepers and protectors of Tamil civilians.[24] Noncombatants were trapped, at random and by design, in the crossfire between various armed groups as the Lankan and Indian state armies, as well as LTTE and other militia, adopted dramatically shifting alliances.

The de facto administration, whether the Lankan state, the IPKF, or the LTTE, effectively held the civilian population hostage for a period of almost thirty years through a variety of terror strategies.[25] By the end-game of the war in 2009, the LTTE had adopted many of the tactics and characteristics of a conventional army, while the final military victory of the Lankan army is attributed to the tactic of its commander, Sarath Fonseka, of breaking his forces into small groups that operated outside a centralized command structure, spread out over varied terrain. This strategy eliminated the key distinction that Deleuze and Guattari identify between the "striated" space of state machinery and the "smooth" space of a guerrilla movement, enabling the state to appropriate the mobility of an insurgent war machine.[26]

Mapping Terror 2: The Interface

As already mentioned, Fuglerud applies the three-zone spatial framework developed by Feldman in his work on Northern Ireland to the geography of the Lankan war: the "sanctuary" (the symbolic space of the imagined ethnic homeland); the "targeting community" (the imagined heartland identified with the enemy); and the "interface" or "topographical-ideological boundary sector," the border zone.[27] Although no part of the country is ethnically unmixed, in the Lankan war, the south and its capital, Colombo, symbolized the power of the Sinhala state, while Jaffna and the north were at the heart of the Tamil national imaginary. The multiethnic eastern coast, on the other hand, defied the simple polarizations that operated elsewhere. Here, questions of majority and minority could not be reduced to simple binaries: the population consisted of Tamils, Muslims (mostly Tamil-speaking), and an almost equal number of Sinhalese. Religious, linguistic, and ethnic markers and boundaries among the groups were both nebulous and shifting.

The violence in the east was most directly aimed at remaking this multiethnic society. Both the state and the LTTE set out, largely successfully, to destroy the fabric of coexistence whereby Muslim, Tamil, and Sinhala people had lived, farmed, fished, and traded in a network of interlinked villages and settlements. Ethnic cleansing, to use a term adapted from the war in Bosnia, provided the warring parties with a simple answer to the complex local system of interactions that had evolved over centuries. As in the boundary zones between north and south, there is much evidence that from about the 1980s, massacres were integral to a state agenda calculated to break down preexisting patterns of coexistence.[28] A program of massacres was carried out by both official and unofficial agents of the state against Tamils and Muslims and, in retaliation, by the LTTE and allied groups against Muslims and Sinhalese. To cite one of several such sequences described in Rajan Hoole's meticulous chronicling of these years: "at Vattakandal in the Mannar District 40 civilians were killed at an army post and other civilians were forced to drink the blood of the dead. The Anuradhapura massacre of about 150 Sinhalese civilians on 14th May followed the Army's killing of 70 civilians in the LTTE leader's village of Valvettithurai a few days earlier. This was followed by the Navy's massacre of 30 civilians in the Kurrikkadduvan ferry off Jaffna."[29]

These attempts to reshape the multiethnic character of the east by a program of murder and expulsion worked hand in hand with another attempt by the state to remake its physical environment. For decades before the war, the region had been the target of numerous "development" programs such as irrigation schemes designed to divert rivers and build tanks and dams coupled with agricultural projects aiming to substitute one kind of crop for another—for example, cadju (cashews) where rice had been grown previously. Such projects entailed no less than the introduction of a different ecological system, one that called for new infrastructure and technologies that would enable the production of cash crops for the urban and export markets rather than the localized cultivation of staple foods. In turn, this would necessitate new sources of labor, premised on "internal colonization" schemes from the south—a move that was, critically, coupled with the engineering of a shift in the ethnic mix of the population, from predominantly Tamil and Muslim to Sinhala.

Ambitious modernization and development projects, such as the Assam Dam in Egypt, were a feature of third world nationalism in the era of decolonization. Invariably, they were bound up with deeply emotive and politically charged historical claims. As Serena Tennekoon points out in one of the key essays of the early years of the war, in Lanka, development is a discourse that contains and mediates contradictions and encompasses a range of meanings "of modernization and tradition . . .

of history, colonialism and independence, national identity and culture, material and spiritual wellbeing."[30] The anxieties provoked by modernity, colonization, and the moral decline associated with the West were assuaged by framing postindependence irrigation and agricultural projects as a reclaiming of ancient glories. The building of dams, the diversion of rivers, and related agricultural projects were promoted by harking back to a past hydraulic civilization characterized by gigantic tanks and ample granaries.

This past was explicitly marked in ethnoreligious terms by reference to the Buddhist epic the *Mahawamsa*, essentially a text that naturalizes Lanka as the site for the protection and propagation of authentic Buddhism.[31] Beginning with the words of the dying Buddha nominating Lanka as the future domicile for the true faith, the *Mahawamsa* narrates the transfer of key artifacts that signify the origins of Buddhism — a branch of the tree under which Siddhartha Gautama attained nirvana (thus becoming the Buddha, or the Enlightened One), and a tooth, said to be his, smuggled in the hair of a princess — from the Indian mainland to Lanka. There these artifacts are emplaced at the very heart of the political and social order of the new chosen seat. As Buddhism literally takes root in the land, always under fear of incursions from India, the *Mahawamsa*'s chronicle of the reigns of individual monarchs plays out against the creation of a society marked by the construction of inland lakes, rock fortresses, and monumental statues of the Buddha. This is the mythic imaginary continually reproduced in the aggressive Sinhala Buddhist ethnonationalism of the postindependence era through school textbooks, political speeches, Buddhist sermons, and popular culture — and often uncritically recirculated transnationally through orientalist, tourist, development, and aid discourses. Thus landscapes marked by tank, temple, and paddy field came to function, Tennekoon writes, as "metonyms for material prosperity and spiritual wellbeing" as well as for ethnoreligious identity. As such, these are artifacts that "constitute an iconographic code . . . signify[ing] a particular type of past as well as the (desired) shape of the present and future."[32]

The past, present, and future are deliberately knit together in what Tennekoon describes, in an inspired phrase, as contemporary "rituals of development." Eschewing the more neutral word "ceremony," Tennekoon uses the term "ritual" to signify the blending of sacred and secular, myth and modernity, in the official inaugurations of development projects, usually involving national politicians, local dignitaries, and chanting Buddhist monks. The term also refers to less ephemeral manifestations such as the statues that once again attempt to reproduce the ethnoreligiously charged landscape of the past through the contemporary project of development:

> The Mahavali Ministry commissioned a 41 meter-high Buddha statue at the Maduru oya [river] dam and a dagaba named the Mahavali Maha Saya on the bank of the Kotmale hydropower reservoir. The Maduru oya Buddha deliberately recalls a well-known 5th-century parallel, the Aukana Buddha who gazes over the Kala vava reservoir built by King Datusena. The Kotmale dagaba attempts to reconstruct materially and symbolically—in a very different time and place—the nostalgic, nationalist landscape of Sri Lanka's ancient hydraulic culture.[33]

The discourse of development, then, was perversely bound up with a retrograde brand of ethnonationalism. Harnessed to the postindependence project of reclaiming a devalued history, it failed to produce a new, national, decolonizing consciousness, instead tapping into a nativist vein in which "the invader" was a nebulous, protean, and ahistorical figure, able to be conflated with the mythic enemies of the *Mahawamsa*. This strain of the anticolonial imaginary (as represented by the monk Angarika Dharmapala at the turn of the twentieth century, for example) fused successive European colonizers with incursions from India in antiquity. Conjoined with pro-development narratives, this imaginary worked to reinforce a favorite myth of Sinhala ethnonationalism, that of a Buddhist age of plenty before Tamils arrived on the scene—although to speak of Tamils as a distinct group of intruders or new arrivals is an anachronism. Sinhala and Tamil are both comparatively new administrative and ethnographic identities imposed on a far more fluid range of linguistic, religious, and place-based identifications and affiliations.[34] As Hoole writes, "It is futile to parcel out ancient South India and Sri Lanka into ethnic enclaves (Sinhalese, Tamil, Malayali). . . . All that we may say with certainty is that there was in this region a constant confluence of peoples, influences, ideas, words, technical terms, vocabularies and symbols, that were readily adapted to local needs."[35]

Regardless, textbooks and popular culture alike reproduce stories of farsighted Sinhala monarchs who built vast systems of tanks and lakes, irrigating plentiful fields, carving a civilization of palaces and delicate water gardens out of rock, and sustaining a pure and rare form of Buddhism. This golden age was held to have been brought to a rude end by the invasion of a foreign "race" from South India, the Dravidians, identified as the ancestors of the Tamils. The intruders were held to have devastated the tanks and ravaged the temples, driving the monks to flee with their sacred objects after first burying the giant statues of the Buddha that they could not carry. With the departure of the monks and the destruction of the tanks, the rice fields turned to wastelands, arid, fever-ridden, occupied by the invaders. Development was the project of redeeming this lost territory and heritage.

As Hoole tartly characterizes it, in the postindependence era, "Reviving the ancient glories of the Sinhalese with foreign loans and putting the Tamils in their place was the name of the game."[36] From the Padaviya scheme of the 1950s to the multimillion-dollar Mahaweli project of the 1980s and 1990s, the irrigation programs at Gal Oya, Weli Oya, and Maduru Oya all involved environmental and social engineering processes that were underpinned by the scholarship of conjectured heritage and the politics of invented homelands. Dubious etymologies provided the justification for changing ancient place-names in an attempt to expunge the historical presence of the ethnic other from the imagined national heartland. Historical and archaeological studies channeled anticolonial or anti-imperialist energies into a narrow and exclusionary Sinhala ethnonationalism that, paradoxically, was also informed by orientalist images and tropes. Thus, development and modernity were both harnessed to "the mythohistoriography of the Sinhalese [that] has become indispensable to the political order."[37]

At another level, the potent appeal of a dream of progress yoked to a mythical past owes much to the transnational circulation and global influence of the Zionist model in the post–World War II period. Both Sinhala and Tamil nationalism drew, in their different ways, on the ambiguous ideology of Zionism.[38] In the 1980s, an entire class of A-level students in Jaffna is said to have abandoned the university entrance exams to enlist in the Liberation Tigers of Tamil Eelam after reading *Exodus*, Leon Uris's stirring novel of the post-Holocaust years. In the case of Sinhala nationalism, the Lankan state's promise to transform the arid borderlands harnessed a sense of sacred mission to a new dawn of modernity, socialism, and nation building, drawing on discourses similar to those that animated the project of the kibbutzim in Israel. State-sponsored programs promised landless peasants and urban poor a new start in the border zone, purportedly with the aim of consolidating a genuinely national consciousness.[39]

In practice, the settlements and development projects in the interface zones actively undermined the multiethnic relations that already existed in these places. Valentine Daniel and Yuvaraj Thangaraj describe the progressive breakdown of these links in the areas around Batticaloa where Buddhists and Hindus had once shared religious and cultural practices:

> Along with each settlement . . . came the building of a local Buddhist temple and the presence of a Buddhist priest. With the latter also came a form of Buddhism that was committed to purge folk elements of Buddhism from local Buddhist practices. . . . The local Tamils who had hitherto partaken in what they . . . knew as common Buddhist-Hindu practices, were struck by the exclusivist self-definition of the new state Buddhism and reacted to it by withdrawing into an exclusive Hindu-Tamil definition of their own. The local Sinhalese, briefly caught in the middle, found the pressures of settler ridicule, on the one hand, and allures of state patronage, on the other, too much to resist, and their submission to and incorporation into a state-fabricated Sinhalese national culture was to be completed in short order.[40]

In the lead-up to war, settlers who attempted to depart the dangerous environment that they had unwittingly entered were refused permission to leave. Instead, they were given the role of "homeguards" and provided with guns to serve as a buffer between army and guerrillas. So the scene was set for some of the most tangled and vicious clashes of the war, in which a series of tortuous alliances and combinations attempted to reduce the complex multiethnicity of the region into the polarities of Sinhala versus Tamil and Tamil versus Muslim.

In Dark Places: *Anil's Ghost* and Landscape as Violence

The most common image used to describe the thirty-year war in Lanka is that of an endless circle of violence in which each party responds to, and mirrors, the violence of its enemy. The image draws attention to the war as a temporal unfolding, a twisted, crazy chronology of cause and effect. In focusing on the spatial and territorial dimensions of the war, I understand it rather as a palimpsest of violence, enacted not in a passive or static arena but on a topography crafted layer upon layer by war and exclusionary violence. The encrustations, excrescences, and hollowed-out places of this landscape form an inexorable record of the violent making and unmaking of homelands and the bodies they erase, expel, or exterminate in that process. The second part of my essay attempts to reveal the massacres described previously as complex historical palimpsests, events in which the past continues to write itself in the present, shadowing and reinscribing that present in ambiguous, unpredictable ways. My reading of Ondaatje's *Anil's Ghost* suggests that without a critical understanding of the past, as the very ground on which the present is enacted, denunciations of contemporary violence risk becoming complicit with that which they attempt to denounce.

The layered geological terrain of the palimpsest is explicitly invoked in *Anil's Ghost*. The narrative begins with the exhumation of a mass grave on a hillside in Guatemala, although the main action will take place in Lanka sometime in the late 1980s and early 1990s. The text here invokes a cosmopolitan vision of human rights and the machinery of global governance that labors to dispense justice to a disordered world. Throughout the text, a transnational, cosmopolitan imaginary (represented by jazz, lost Hollywood movies, and scientific labor) serves as a counterpoint to the fevered nationalisms of (third world) states and counterstates. The heroes of *Anil's Ghost* are an archaeologist, a miner, and an anatomical pathologist (as well as other assorted doctors), all people who labor with fierce determination beneath the surface of things—in caves, gem pits, or the dark places of the human body:

Amygdala.
     The name had sounded Sri Lankan. . . . Studying at Guy's Hospital in London, having cut tissue away to reveal a small knot of fibres made up of nerve cells. . . . The professor gave her the word for it. *Amygdala.*
     "What does it mean?"
     "Nothing. It's a location. It's the dark aspect of the brain. . . . A place to house fearful memories. . . . Anger too, we think, but it specializes in fear."

. . .

"It sounds Sri Lankan, the name."[41]

In a text full of place-names, amygdala is one more baleful location, the dark aspect of the brain, a knot of fibers and nerves where fears, and perhaps anger and bad memories, cluster and accumulate. As in Ondaatje's earlier Booker Prize–winning novel, *The English Patient, Anil's Ghost* has at its center a body stripped of its outermost layers of protection and identification — nationality, ethnicity, name, skin, flesh. The bodies are reduced by war and violence to the substrata of exposed nerve-ends and veins or to a constellation of bares bones: shards and fragments of text, shattered artifacts to be reconstructed or restored. In both novels, the plot hinges on the detection of the true identity of the unknown body— not simply by learning its name, but by its *emplacing*, or inscription, in a historical frame. In *The English Patient*, this involves the literal insertion of the patient's story into the minutes of the Geographical Society in London and the *Histories* of Herodotus. Together with Rudyard Kipling's *Kim*, a third key intertext, these are the founding narratives in which Europe compulsively stages and restages the ground of its "meeting" with Asia — a meeting that, in the second half of *The English Patient*, reaches one kind of culmination in the bombs unleashed over Hiroshima and Nagasaki.

In *Anil's Ghost*, the key intertexts include the rock inscriptions of the interface zone between north and south and the Sinhala chronicle the *Chulawamsa* (the sequel to the *Mahawamsa*) in addition to Amnesty International reports and hundreds of accounts of disappearances gathered by the Nadesan Centre for Human Rights in Colombo. In the novel, history and human rights meet in the form of an anomalous skeleton discovered on an ancient archaeological site guarded by the army: a body of evidence that turns out to be "something not prehistoric," but that of a man recently murdered and probably buried while still alive.[42] For Anil, the expatriate forensic specialist, the discovery presents a simple imperative in a time of mass murders and midnight disappearances: "The representative of all those lost voices. To give him a name would name the rest."[43]

The anonymous skeleton stands for the nameless dead and disappeared and for the unquiet remains of those who will not stay buried, the open secrets of a regime of terror. So the wounded, scattered, and fragmented bodies of the tortured and disappeared stage their reappearance in daily life, refusing their containment and incorporation by necro-power. The search for the skeleton's name leads Anil through many dark places—hidden rock inscriptions, obscure scientific texts, the hopelessly contaminated wards and corridors of the Colombo General Hospital, the technologies employed by ancient Buddhist sculptors—allowing the text an extended meditation on the relations among aesthetics, art, history, science, and terror.

But this unknown victim of present-day terror is not the only body uneremoniously buried in this landscape of graves and killing fields: a number of passages reveal that this buried skeleton has its ancient counterparts in the monumental statues of the Buddha hastily interred by monks fleeing (unnamed) invaders. Thus the ground on which the action takes place is one already organized and marked by the spatial tropes, iconographies, and ideologically charged rhetorics of a nation-alized and ontologized landscape. Such ethnoreligious mythohistories, lyrically invoked in descriptions of lotus-filled tanks and delicately carved stones, reflect, refract, and ultimately even serve to vindicate in strange and disquieting ways, the narrative of contemporary violence.

The hastily interred stone bodies in the landscape refer back to yet other symbolic and literal body parts that, together with their metonyms, function in the ethnonational imagination as potent political talismans of the contemporary state. The broken and dismembered bodies that represent the open secret of a necropolitical order find their most notable counterpart in another body part, the legendary tooth, held to be the left incisor of the Buddha, that publicly functions as the symbolic reposi-tory of state sovereignty in Lanka. In this ossified fragment, politics and religion fuse into one: the Buddha's corporeal remains are believed to embody the key to rulership and good governance of the land. In the colonial period, Portuguese, Dutch, and British authorities all sought custody of this brittle fragment in order to legitimize their rule. During the recent war, one of the most psychologically potent attacks by the Liberation Tigers of Tamil Eelam was its attempt to bomb the Temple of the Tooth in Kandy in 1998.

In *Anil's Ghost*, the Buddha's eyes are invested with a similar symbolic weight: at the culmination of the plot, the painting of the pupils onto the eyes of a repaired statue of the Buddha is the final act in the statue's (re)consecration, signifying the restoration of a social and cultural order rent apart by terror. In this moment, it may be said, two orders of sovereignty, the biopolitical and necropolitical, meet: the statue of the Buddha, violently broken apart to be smelted and reforged anew into a whole, alludes to the symbolic suturing back together of a body politic dismembered by terror. In the transformative moment of restoration, both state and religion become inexplicably remote from the violences perpetrated in their name, a dissociation made credible by the text's invocation of, and interpellation by, the mythic terrain on which the action is situated: a meeting ground between Western orientalism and Sinhala Buddhist ethnonationalism.

I read *Anil's Ghost* as a novel of the interface, located, in Feldman's words, at a "topographical-ideological boundary sector."[44] This interface is not that between ethnicities—as Qadri Ismail points out, almost all the characters in *Anil's Ghost* are Sinhala and Buddhist; Tamils, Muslims, and, indeed, other minorities barely exist within its pages.[45] Rather, the fraught "boundary sector" in the text is that between topography and ideology, that is, the relation between the lovingly depicted landscape of ruined rock temples, jungle monasteries, and ancient water tanks where much of the action takes place and the ideologies that are inseparable from them, like the inscriptions a blind hand has traced upon a stone buried under water.[46]

Radhika Coomaraswamy and Minoli Salgado, among others, have pointed out that the Buddhist texts and traditions invoked in *Anil's Ghost* represent a strain of Buddhism that is more humanist, ascetic, and inclusive than the militant and murderous ultranationalism that has played so destructive a role in Lanka's history.[47] Yet these critics do not address the mythohistories and symbolic landscapes against and upon which the action takes place: the dried-up water gardens and leaf-halls of besieged monks, the broken temples and the buried Buddhas that have rooted themselves deep into soil and stone. The terrain on which these ancient fragments are cohered into historical narrative are locatable in Derridean terms as a site of ontotopology, that is, an "axiomatics linking indissociably the ontological value of present being [*on*] to its *situation*, to the stable and presentable determination of a locality, the *topos* of territory, native soil, city, body in general."[48] It is here that *Anil's Ghost* reveals its deep implication (call it perilous fascination, seduction, intoxication) with the landscape of Buddhist ethnonationalism and its interpellation by them.

Here, the text functions to uncritically reproduce (with one exception, discussed below) the ontotheologies and ontotopologies indissociable from this territorialized and mythopoeticized landscape.[49]

At the topographical-ideological interface, history, archaeology, geography (earth-writing) are all implicated in the waging of the war, its ramifications and reproductions. Literary discourses are not exempt. In literary representations of the war, a mythic nationalist landscape is reproduced even as war's violence is humanistically deplored and rejected. Ondaatje's poem "The Distance of a Shout" cited earlier begins with the lines "We lived on the medieval coast / south of warrior kingdoms," a location that immediately references the paranoid geography of "Dravidian" invasion from the north. This geography is reinforced as the poem proceeds, weaving past into present (a bridge along the Mahaweli River, the floating bodies of monks murdered in the border territories of the north). So, too, in Jean Arasanayagam's volume of poems, *Reddened Water Flows Clear*, past and present, the rhythms of seasonal cultivation and the coming of the killing times, the landscape of ancient subsistence farming and the scene of contemporary mass murder merge and coalesce:

It is nothing new to prepare here for parting
Or departure as gunshot once more sweeps over
The fields and perhaps with the last pluck
The coconuts fall hard, body blows thudding
On the bare earth . . .
We remember the falling bodies wrapped
In mat flung into the trenches among
The teak trees while the echo of gunshot
Struck hard against the rock fortress of Yapahuwa.[50]

The reference to the citadel at Yapahuwa once again ties the killings of the present to an epic past, endlessly recycled both in nationalist rhetoric and historical fantasy. The following is from a tourist Web site:

In 1272, King Bhuvenakabahu transferred the capital to Yapahuwa from Polonnaruwa in the face of marauding Dravidian invasions from South India, bringing the Sacred Tooth Relic with him. The move proved to be of little avail. Following the death of King Bhuvenakabahu in 1284, the Pandyans of South India invaded Lanka once again, and succeeded in capturing Sacred Tooth Relic too. Following its capture, Yapahuwa was largely abandoned & inhabited by Buddhist monks & religious ascetics. The capital was moved to Kurunagala.[51]

Marauding Dravidians, the capture of the most potent of political objects, the tooth relic, and the destruction of temples and the Buddhist faithful dispossessed and driven ever farther south: these are the all-too-familiar tropes invoked by the mythic landscape of the border zone. Only a single passage in *Anil's Ghost* suggests a level of reflexivity that is alert to the ideological resonances of these tropes. In a passage at the end of the novel, there is an anecdote about an event in a region of "desperate farming": a group of three men break open a giant statue of the Buddha, hoping to find hidden treasure within. Their actions mimic the political disemboweling and smashing of bodies in jails and secret torture places throughout the land, yet:

> This for once was not a political act or an act perpetrated by one belief against another. The men were trying to find a solution for hunger. . . . And the "neutral" and "innocent" fields around the statue and the rock carvings were perhaps places of torture and burials. Since it was mostly uninhabited land, with only a few farmers and pilgrims . . . a place where trucks came to burn and hide victims who had been picked up. These were fields where Buddhism and its values met the harsh political events of the twentieth century.[52]

The scare quotes around the words "neutral" and "innocent" in the passage suggest the abrupt intrusion of a different authorial voice. The transition from a literary to an academic discourse is underlined by the rare tentativeness of the "perhaps" and incongruous phrases such as "Buddhism and its values" and "harsh political events of the twentieth century." Yet even the awkward concessions and small qualifications made here are nullified by the epic sweep of the novel in its last stages, when the shattered Buddha is reassembled and reconsecrated in a ritual harking back to the ancient times of Parakrama Bahu, the legendary ruler who built the giant inland lake grandly named Parakrama Samudra (Sea of Parakrama).

Is the recuperation and repair of the shattered body of the Buddha the text's gesture of consolation and closure in the face of the mystery of the broken skeleton and the tortured and maimed bodies of the necropolitical order that it represents? Does the restoration of this broken body politic perform a parallel, hopeful, ending to the bleak conclusion in which Anil, the expatriate forensic pathologist, barely escapes with her life, while her collaborator, the archaeologist Sarath, is murdered? Two shattered bodies, one stone, the other bone, are linked by the hand of the drunken sculptor-miner who paints in the statue's eyes at its consecration, as he had previously reconstructed the anonymous, severed skull into the semblance of a recognizable human face. In the last scene, the repaired Buddha, elevated to its proper place, recalls both ancient monuments and their replicas in the era of development, as it once more overlooks the land with an Olympian gaze: "When the sun rose it would appear that it rested on the giant figure's shoulders. . . . After this hour the statue would be able to witness figures only from a great distance."[53]

In this closing scene, divine and artistic vision momentarily coincide, rising far above the harrowed terrain of history. Ondaatje's twelve-foot-high Buddha, reconstituted and restored to splendid and serene detachment at the end of *Anil's Ghost*, is in stark contrast to the Buddha figure of M. A. Nuhman's poem "Murder," written, in Tamil, in response to the burning of the public library in Jaffna at the outbreak of the war:

Last night
I dreamt
Buddha was shot dead
by the police,
guardians of the law.
His body drenched in blood
On the steps
Of the Jaffna Library.

Under cover of darkness
Came the ministers,
"His name is not on our list,
why did you kill him?"
they ask angrily.

"No sirs, no
there was no mistake.
Without killing him
*It was impossible
to harm a fly—* "⁵⁴

238

Nuhman's Buddha, unlike the one in *Anil's Ghost*, represents a body politic damaged beyond any possibility of restoration or repair as, in a final
gesture of complicity between the political leaders and their enforcers,
the murdered body of the Compassionate One is burned to ashes on the
library steps upon a pyre of Tamil writings. The allusion is to two decisive
incidents at the beginning of the war: the burning of the irreplaceable
Tamil manuscripts and cultural artifacts assembled at the Jaffna library,
and the anti-Tamil pogroms of 1983, in which the attackers were supplied
with electoral lists identifying Tamil houses and businesses. Both acts, the
poem emphasizes, far from being deeds of protecting or maintaining
Buddhism, are deeply inimical to it—so much so that they require these
champions of his religion to murder the Buddha himself before they can
put their program of ethnoreligious supremacy in place.

At the end of *Anil's Ghost*, the hand of a drunken master craftsman,
momentarily steadied, and invested with ritual authority, turns blind
stone into divinity, confers the talent of transcendence. God's-eye vision
is revealed as fallible and fragile, no heavenly gift but the product of
human care and skill. Yet the grand, telescopic gaze of the statue restored,
the flourish of chants and drums, the celebratory renewal of tradition,
cannot but trump the vitiated imaginary of transnational human rights
with which the novel began: a gouged-out mass grave in Guatemala, an
assorted cast of technocrats and experts, the salvaging of an incriminating
audiotape that Anil, presumably, will take back to the United Nations as
an indictment of another murderous third world regime.

Rereading the last pages of *Anil's Ghost* the day after the first postwar election in Sri Lanka, I cannot but see, superimposed on Ondaatje's
transcendent scene of the restoration of the statue's eyes, the Netra
Mangala, yet another "ritual of development": the enactment of the celebratory recirculation of a poisonous ethnonational mythology. In the
months since the war ended, the interface zones and border regions of

the divided country are once again being knit back together. Major roads have been reopened, mines are being cleared from fields, and airspace has been secured, enabling all sorts of movement into the interface zones: government officials and workers from nongovernmental organizations heading north and east, day-trippers in hired buses surveying the ruins old and new, the faithful making pilgrimages to sacred sites long inaccessible behind enemy lines.[55] Exiles and expatriates follow, as do journalists and missionaries. And it wasn't many months after the war ended that Sri Lanka made the list of top tourist destinations in the *New York Times*.[56]

At last, refugees released from government internment camps and other internally displaced persons are also being allowed to return to the houses and fields from which they fled or were expelled. Some find destruction and dereliction, or perhaps strangers in possession. With rudimentary supplies — a bag of cement, canvas for roofing — others get ready to start again. In this postwar landscape, "development" and "settlement" are once again loaded words. A BBC report observes that "Sinhalization" of the east and border zones is a major concern, as settlers from the south arrive, with the sanction of military, government, and religious leaders. In a Muslim quarter of Batticaloa, members of the police build a Buddhist temple. New settlers from the south tell the journalist that they have been given their land by the army who will soon come to register their title to it.[57] Meanwhile, the victorious president, Mahinda Rajapakse, is lauded as a hero king on the verge of ushering in a new golden age of Sinhala Buddhist rule over the reunified land.[58]

The counternarratives to these territorial myths are, by contrast, more elusive: local, fragile, tentative. They lack both the institutional patronage that has embedded the former deeply in national consciousness and the cultural cachet, the orientalist heritage gloss, that attaches to them abroad. There are strange conjunctions between state-sanctioned attempts to "Sinhalize" the interface zones and neoliberal, human rights and globalization rhetorics of equal mobility and openness for all; between the ethnonationalist Sinhala-Buddhist imaginary and the orientalist promotion of heritage landscapes and cultural sites for the tourist market; between dominant aid agendas and essentialist models of agrarian and rural development: all these suggest how transnational discourses collude with the victorious ethnocratic reclaiming of the "*topos* of territory, native soil, city, body in general."[59] Against these strange conjunctions, what of the nameless bodies of the wounded and slain? Of the disappearances and hidden graves whose scandalous, invisible presence, as an open secret, continues to buttress the sinister triumph of a necropolitical body politic?

NOTES

1   UN News Center, "Deeming Sri Lanka Execution Video Authentic, UN Expert Calls for War Crimes Probe," January 7, 2010, http://www.un.org/apps/news/story.asp?NewsID=33423&Cr=sri+lanka&Cr1=.

2   Pablo Neruda, "The Dictators," in *Neruda and Vallejo: Selected Poems*, trans. and ed. Robert Bly (Boston: Beacon Press, 1993), 93.

3   Sasanka Perera, *Living with Torturers* (Colombo, Sri Lanka: International Centre for Ethnic Studies, 1995), 3.

4   Michael Ondaatje, "The Distance of a Shout," in *Handwriting* (Suffolk, U.K.: Bloomsbury, 1998), 6.

5   See Serena Tennekoon, "Rituals of Development: The Accelerated Mahaväli Development Program of Sri Lanka," *American Ethnologist* 15, no. 2 (1988): 294–310.

6   Rajan Hoole, *Sri Lanka: The Arrogance of Power; Myths, Decadence and Murder* (Colombo, Sri Lanka: University Teachers for Human Rights [Jaffna], 2001), 342.

7   James S. Duncan, *The City as Text: The Politics of Landscape Interpretation in the Kandyan Kingdom* (Cambridge: Cambridge University Press, 1990), 19.

8   Øivind Fuglerud, *Life on the Outside: The Tamil Diaspora and Long Distance Nationalism* (London: Pluto Press, 1999), 44–45.

9   Allen Feldman, *Formations of Violence: The Narrative of the Body and Political Terror in Northern Ireland* (Chicago: University of Chicago Press, 1991), 28.

10 Michel Foucault, *The Foucault Reader*, ed. Paul Rabinow (London: Penguin, 1984), 268.

11 Ibid., 268–69.

12 Achille Mbembe, "Necropolitics," trans. Libby Meintjes, *Public Culture* 15, no. 1 (2003): 12.

13 Basil Fernando, "Tales of Two Sri Lankan Massacres: The Relevance of Embilipitiya to Bindunuwewa," *Asian Legal Resource Centre Bulletin* 4, no. 3 (2005).

14 Ibid.

15 A. Sivanandan, "Sri Lanka: Racism and the Politics of Underdevelopment," *Race & Class* 26, no. 1 (1984): 23.

16   See R. Cheran, introduction to *Pathways of Dissent: Tamil Nationalism in Sri Lanka* (New Delhi: Sage, 2009), xxxiv–xl.

17   Daya Somasundaram, *Scarred Minds: The Psychological Impact of War on Sri Lankan Tamils* (Colombo, Sri Lanka: Vijitha Yapa Publishers, 1998), 61. See also Sivamohan Sumathy, *Militants, Militarism and the Crisis of (Tamil) Nationalism* (Colombo, Sri Lanka: Marga Institute, 2001).

18   Somasundaram, *Scarred Minds*, 61.

19   Ibid., 224

20   Ibid., 230–31.

21   Ibid., 224–25.

22   Ibid., 175.

23   Mbembe, "Necropolitics," 32.

24   The best account of this period is in Rajan Hoole et al., *The Broken Palmyrah* (Claremont, Calif.: Sri Lanka Studies Institute, 1990).

25   See ibid.; and Somasundaram, *Scarred Minds*.

26   Gilles Deleuze and Felix Guattari, "Nomadology or the War Machine," in *A Thousand Plateaus: Capitalism and Schizophrenia*, trans. Brian Massumi (Minneapolis: University of Minnesota Press, 1987). On a similar transition by the Israeli army, see Eyal Weizman, "The Art of War: Deleuze, Guattari, Debord and the Israeli Defence Force," *Mute*, August 3, 2006, http://www.metamute.org/?q=en/node/8192.

27   Feldman, *Formations of Violence*, 28.

28   Hoole, *Sri Lanka*.

29   Ibid., 214.

30   Tennekoon, "Rituals of Development," 295.

31   Although some might describe Buddhism as a philosophy rather than a religion, in Lanka, Buddhism is institutionalized as the official religion of the ethnocratic state and was declared as such in the constitution of 1972.

32   Tennekoon, "Rituals of Development," 297.

33   Ibid.

34   There are several studies contesting the validity of the categories Aryan and Dravidian. See, for example, Kumari Jayawardena, "Class and Ethnic Consciousness 2," *Lanka Guardian* 6, no. 6 (1983): 17–20; and Arjun Guneratne, "What's in a Name? Aryans and Dravidians in the Making of Sri Lankan Identities," in *The Hybrid Island*, ed. Neluka Silva (London: Zed Books, 2002), 20–40.

35   Hoole, *Sri Lanka*, 198.

36   Ibid., 203.

37   Margo Kleinfeld, "Destabilizing the Identity-Territory Nexus: Rights-Based Discourse in Sri Lanka's New Political Geography," *GeoJournal* 64 (2005): 289.

38 The history of Israeli involvement with both the Sri Lankan government and the Tamil separatist groups remains to be fully explored. See Hoole, *Sri Lanka*, 312.

39 R. Cheran points out that, as a solution to the problem of landless Sinhala peasantry, internal colonization was preferable to either industrialization or reorganization of landownership, especially as the latter posed a threat to the giant land holdings of the Sinhala elite in southern and central Lanka (introduction to *Pathways of Dissent*, xxv).

40 E. Valentine Daniel and Yuvaraj Thangaraj, "Forms, Formations and Transformations of Tamil Refuge," in *Mistrusting Refugees*, ed. E. Valentine Daniel and John Chr. Knudsen (Berkeley: University of California Press, 1995), 232–33.

41 Michael Ondaatje, *Anil's Ghost* (London: Bloomsbury 2000), 134–35.

42 Ibid., 50

43 Ibid., 56.

44 Feldman, *Formations of Violence*, 28.

45 Qadri Ismail, "A Flippant Gesture towards Sri Lanka: A Review of Michael Ondaatje's *Anil's Ghost*," *Pravada* 6, no. 9-10 (2000): 24–29. The peopling of Sri Lanka in the body of Ondaatje's text is very different from the multiethnic society casually revealed in the Acknowledgments at the end of the book. To me, this suggests, rather than a refusal of the fact of multiethnicity, a deliberate simplification or stripping back to perceived essentials. The question that this poses, slightly different from the one Ismail asks, is about the ideological-aesthetic choice to isolate violence as a "dark aspect of the brain" rather than, say, considering it in sociopolitical and historical terms.

46 Sankaran Krishna's *Postcolonial Insecurities: India, Sri Lanka, and the Question of Nationhood* (Honolulu: University of Hawaii Press, 1999) offers perhaps the best analysis of the linkage between Buddhist ideologies and state policies in this period.

47 Radhika Coomaraswamy, "In Defense of Humanistic Ways of Knowing: A Response to Qadri Ismail," *Pravada* 6, no. 9-10 (2000): 29–30; and Minoli Salgado *Writing Sri Lanka* (New York: Routledge, 2006).

48 Jacques Derrida, *Spectres of Marx: The State of the Debt, the Work of Mourning, and the New International*, trans. Peggy Kamuf (New York: Routledge, 1994), 82.

49 On ontotheologies, see Jacques Derrida, *Rogues*, trans. Michael Naas (Stanford, Calif.: Stanford University Press, 2005), 157.

50 Jean Arasanayagam, "Canto 1," in *Reddened Water Flows Clear* (London: Forest Books 1991), 9–10.

51 Riolta Lanka Holidays Ltd., "Yapahuwa (Fire Rock) Fortress," Sri Lanka Holidays, http://www.mysrilankaholidays.com/yapahuwa.html.

52 Ondaatje, *Anil's Ghost*, 300.

53 Ibid., 305–6.

54 M. A. Nuhman, "Murder," trans. S. Pathmanathan, quoted in Sivamohan Sumathy, "Is There War in Your Ur?" *Himal Southasian*, October 2008, http://www.himalmag.com/Is-there-war-in-your-ur_nw1976.htm.

55 Jehan Perera, "Rapid Increase of Southern Tourists to Jaffna Has Positive and Negative Impact," *Transcurrents*, March 9, 2010, http://transcurrents.com/tc/2010/03/rapid_increase_of_southern_tou.html.

56 Lionel Beehner, "Sri Lanka: Checkpoints in Paradise," *New York Times*, March 14, 2010, http://travel.nytimes.com/2010/03/14/travel/14next.html.

57 BBC, "Crossing Continents: Sri Lanka's Troubled Peace," BBC News, BBC iPlayer file, 28 minutes, http://www.bbc.co.uk/iplayer/episode/p005nhvg/Crossing_Continents_Sri_Lankas_fragile_peace/.

58 See Eric Ellis, "Sri Lanka: A One-Family State," interview by Phillip Adams, *Late Night Live*, ABC Radio National, February 1, 2010, MP3 audio file, http://www.abc.net.au/rn/latenightlive/stories/2010/2807163.htm; and Tisaranee Gunasekara, "Towards a Rajapakse Future," *Himal Southasian*, February 2010, http://www.himalmag.com/Towards-a-Rajapakse-future_nw4195.html.

59 Derrida, *Spectres of Marx*, 82. On the convergence between neoliberalism and human rights, see John Nguyet Erni, "Human Rights in the Neoliberal Imagination," *Cultural Studies* 23, no. 3 (2009): 417–36.

BIBLIOGRAPHY

Agamben, Giorgio. *Homo Sacer: Sovereign Power and Bare Life*. Translated by
    Daniel Heller-Roazen. Stanford, Calif.: Stanford University Press, 1998.
———. *Remnants of Auschwitz*. Translated by Daniel Heller-Roazen. New York:
    Zone Books, 1999.
———. *State of Exception*. Translated by Keven Attell. Chicago: University of
    Chicago Press, 2005.
Alexander, Matthew. *How to Break a Terrorist*. New York: Free Press, 2008.
———. "Torture's Loopholes." *New York Times*, January 21, 2010, section A.
Allen, James. *Without Sanctuary: Lynching Photography in America*. Santa Fe,
    N.Mex.: Twin Palms Publishers, 2003.
Allen, James, Hilton Als, John Lewis, and Leon F. Litwack. *Without Sanctuary:
    Lynching Photography in America*. Santa Fe, N.Mex.: Twin Palms, 2005.
Alter, Jonathan. "Time to Think about Torture." *Newsweek*, November 5, 2001, 45.
Amin, Shahid. "Remembering the Muselman." In *Fussing Modernity: Appro-
    priation of History and Political Mobilization in South Asia*, edited by Kotani
    Hiroyuki, Fujii Takeshi, and Oshikawa Fumiko. Osaka, Japan: Japan Center
    for Area Studies and National Museum of Ethnology, 2000.
Amnesty International. "'Not Part of My Sentence': Violations of the Human

Rights of Women in Custody." March 1999. http://www.amnestyusa.org/
document.php?id=D0F5C2222D1AABEA8025690000692FC4&lang=e
(accessed December 21, 2009).

Apel, Dora. "Torture Culture: Lynching Photographs and the Images of Abu
Ghraib." *Art Journal* 64, no. 2 (Summer 2005): 88–100.

Arasanayagam, Jean. "Canto 1." In *Reddened Water Flows Clear.* London: Forest
Books, 1991.

Arendt, Hannah. "Collective Responsibility." In *Responsibility and Judgment,*
edited by Jerome Kohn, 147–158. New York: Schocken Books, 2003.

Argetsinger, Amy. "At Colleges, Students Are Facing a Big Test." *Washington
Post,* September 17, 2001, section B.

"Article 15-6 Investigation of the 800th Military Police Brigade." In *The Torture
Papers: The Road to Abu Ghraib,* edited by Karen J. Greenberg and Joshua L.
Dratel, 405–557. New York: Cambridge University Press, 2005.

Athey, Stephanie. "The Terrorist We Torture: The Tale of Abdul Hakim
Murad." In *On Torture,* edited by Thomas C. Hilde, 87–104. Baltimore:
Johns Hopkins University Press, 2008.

Avelar, Idelber. "Five Theses on Torture." *Journal of Latin American Cultural
Studies* 10, no. 3 (2001): 253–271.

Bakare-Yusuf, Bibi. "The Economy of Violence: Black Bodies and the Unspeakable Terror." In *Feminist Theory and the Body: A Reader,* edited by Janet Price
and Margrit Shildrick, 311–23. New York: Routledge, 1999.

Baker, Al. "For Emergency Official Touched by 9/11's Horrors, Fears of Complacency." *New York Times,* May 21, 2002, section A.

Banksy. *Wall and Piece.* London: Century, 2005.

BBC. "Crossing Continents: Sri Lanka's Troubled Peace." BBC News. BBC
iPlayer file. http://www.bbc.co.uk/iplayer/episode/p005nhvg/Crossing_
Continents_Sri_Lankas_fragile_peace/.

Beehner, Lionel. "Sri Lanka: Checkpoints in Paradise." *New York Times,* March
14, 2010. http://travel.nytimes.com/2010/03/14/travel/14next.html.

Begg, Moazzam. *Enemy Combatant: A British Muslim's Journey to Guantánamo and
Back.* London: Free Press, 2006.

Benjamin, Mark. "Navy Supervisor Doctored Whistleblower's Records." Salon,
February 1, 2010. http://www.salon.com/news/feature/2010/01/31/
camp_lejeune.

———. "Soldier Suicides Rocket." Salon, March 19, 2009. http://www.salon.
com/news/feature/2009/03/19/army_suicides/index.html.

Bennett, Drake. "The War in the Mind." *Boston Globe,* November 27, 2005,
section K.

Bernstein, Nina. "U.S. Is Settling Detainee's Suit in 9/11 Sweep." *New York
Times,* February 28, 2006.

Blake, John. "Seeking a Moral Compass While Chasing Terrorists: How to React to Enemies Raises Tough Issues for People of Faith." *Atlanta Journal Constitution*, September 22, 2001, section B.

Blanchot, Maurice. *The Infinite Conversation*. Translated by Susan Hanson. Minneapolis: University of Minnesota Press, 2003.

Boltanski, Luc. *Distant Suffering: Media, Morality, and Politics*. New York: Cambridge University Press, 1999.

Borradori, Giovanna, ed. *Philosophy in a Time of Terror: Dialogues with Jürgen Harbermas and Jacques Derrida*. Chicago: University of Chicago Press, 2003.

Bourdieu, Pierre. *Outline of a Theory of Practice*. Translated by Richard Nice. Cambridge: Cambridge University Press, 1989.

Bourdieu, Pierre, and Loïs Wacquant. *An Invitation to Reflexive Sociology*. Chicago: University of Chicago Press, 1992.

Bourke, Joanna. "Sexy Snaps." *Index on Censorship* 1 (2005): 39–45.

Bowden, Mark. "The Dark Art of Interrogation." *Atlantic Monthly*, October 2003, 51–70.

Bradbury, Steven G. Memorandum to John A. Rizzo. "Re: Application of 18 U.S.C. §§ 2340-2340A to the Combined Use of Certain Techniques in the Interrogation of High Value al Qaeda Detainees." U.S. Department of Justice, Office of Legal Counsel. May 10, 2005. http://luxmedia.vo.llnwd.net/o10/clients/aclu/olc_05102005_ bradbury46pg.pdf.

———. Memorandum to John A. Rizzo. "Re: Application of United States Obligations Under Article 16 of the Convention Against Torture to Certain Techniques that May be Used in the Interrogation of High Value al Qaeda Detainees." U.S. Department of Justice, Office of Legal Counsel. May 30, 2005. http://luxmedia.vo.llnwd.net/ o10/clients/aclu/olc_05302005_ bradbury.pdf.

Bravin, Jess. "Interrogation School Tells Army Recruits How Grilling Works— 30 Techniques in 16 Weeks, Just Short of Torture; Do They Yield Much?" *Wall Street Journal*, April 26, 2002, section A.

Brecher, Bob. *Torture and the Ticking Time Bomb*. Malden, MA: Blackwell, 2007.

Brison, Susan J. "The Torture Connection: When Photographs from Abu Ghraib Can't Be Distinguished from 'Good Old American Pornography,' It's Not Just the Torture We Should Be Questioning." *San Francisco Chronicle*, July 25, 2004.

Judd. Review of *Torture and Democracy*. BrothersJudd, March 4, 2008. http://brothersjudd.com/index.cfm/fuseaction/reviews.detail/book_ id/1642/Torture%20and%20.htm.

Brown, Wendy. "Neo-liberalism and the End of Liberal Democracy." *Theory & Event* 7, no. 1 (2003).

Bush, George W. "Detention, Treatment, and Trial of Certain Non-Citizens in the War against Terrorism." In *Torture and Truth,* edited by Mark Danner, 78–82. New York: New York Review of Books, 2004.

———. "President Bush Delivers Graduation Speech at West Point." Office of the Press Secretary, The White House. June 1, 2002. http://georgewbush whitehouse.archives.gov/news/releases/2002/06/20020601-3.html.

———. "President Bush Discusses Homeland Security at the FBI Academy." Office of the Press Secretary, The White House. September 10, 2003. http://georgewbushwhitehouse.archives.gov/news/releases/2003/09/20030910-6.html.

———. "President Bush's Address on Terrorism before a Joint Meeting of Congress." *New York Times,* September 21, 2001, section B, late edition.

———. "President Outlines Steps to Help Iraq Achieve Democracy and Freedom." October 24, 2004. http://www.whitehouse.gov/news/releases/2004/05/20040524-10.html (accessed October 3, 2007).

Butler, Judith. *Excitable Speech: The Politics of the Performative.* London: Routledge, 1997.

———. *Frames of War.* London: Verso, 2009.

———. "Photography, War, Outrage." *PMLA: Theories and Methodologies* (2005): 822–27.

———. *Precarious Life: Powers of Mourning and Violence.* London: Verso, 2004.

Bybee, Jay S. "Re: Standards of Conduct for Interrogation under 18 U.S.C. §§ 2340-2340A (August 1, 2002)." In *The Torture Papers: The Road to Abu Ghraib,* edited by Karen J. Greenberg and Joshua L. Dratel, 172–217. New York: Cambridge University Press, 2005.

Carby, Hazel. "A Strange and Bitter Crop: The Spectacle of Torture." Open-Democracy, October 11, 2004. http://www.opendemocracy.net/media-abu_ghraib/article_2149.jsp (accessed June 28, 2010).

Castañeda, Antonia I. "Sexual Violence in the Politics and Policies of Conquest: Amerindian Women and the Spanish Conquest of Alta California." In *Building with Our Hands: New Directions in Chicana Studies,* edited by Adela de la Torre and Beatríz M. Pesquera, 15–33. Berkeley: University of California Press, 1993.

Cavarero, Adriana. *Horrorism: Naming Contemporary Violence.* Translated by William McCuaig. New York: Columbia University Press, 2009.

Chandrasekaran, Rajiv, and Peter Finn. "U.S. Behind Secret Transfer of Terror Suspects." *Washington Post,* March 11, 2002, section A.

Chapman, Steve. "No Tortured Dilemma." *Washington Times,* November 5, 2001, section A.

Cheran, R., ed. *Pathways of Dissent: Tamil Nationalism in Sri Lanka.* New Delhi: Sage, 2009.

Cole, David, ed. *The Torture Memos.* New York: New Press, 2009.

Comaroff, Joshua. "Terror and Territory: Guantánamo and the Space of Contradiction." *Public Culture* 19, no. 2 (2007): 381–405.

Conrad, Courtenay Ryals, and Will H. Moore, "What Stops the Torture?" *American Journal of Political Science* 54, no. 2 (April 2010): 459–76.

Conroy, John. "Annals of Police Torture: What Price Freedom?" *Chicago Reader*, March 2, 2001, 1.

———. "Tools of Torture." *Chicago Reader*, February 4, 2005.

———. *Unspeakable Acts, Ordinary People: Dynamics of Torture*. New York: Knopf, 2000.

Coomaraswamy, Radhika. "In Defense of Humanistic Ways of Knowing: A Response to Qadri Ismail." *Pravada* 6, no. 9-10 (2000): 29–30.

Cranny-Francis, Anne. "Sonic Assault to Massive Attack: Touch, Sound and Embodiment." *SCAN: Journal of Media, Arts, Culture* 5, no. 3 (2008). http://scan.net.au/scan/journal/display.php?journal_id=124.

Crile, Susan. *Abu Ghraib: Abuse of Power*. Rome: Gangemi Editore, 2007.

Daniel, E. Valentine, and Yuvaraj Thangaraj. "Forms, Formations and Transformations of Tamil Refuge." In *Mistrusting Refugees*, edited by E. Valentine Daniel and John Chr. Knudsen, 225–56. Berkeley: University of California Press, 1995.

Danner, Mark. *Stripping Bare the Body: Politics Violence War*. New York: Nation Books, 2009.

———. *Torture and Truth: America, Abu Ghraib, and the War on Terror*. New York: New York Review of Books, 2004.

———. "US Torture: Voices from the Black Sites." *New York Review of Books* 56, no. 6 (April 9, 2009).

———. "We Are All Torturers Now." *New York Times*, January 6, 2005, section A, late edition.

Debord, Guy. *Society of the Spectacle*. Translated by Ken Knabb. London: Rebel Press, 2006.

Deleuze, Gilles, and Felix Guattari. *A Thousand Plateaus: Capitalism and Schizophrenia*. Translated by Brian Massumi. Minneapolis: University of Minnesota Press, 1987.

Derrida, Jacques. *Rogues*. Translated by Michael Naas. Stanford, Calif.: Stanford University Press, 2005.

———. *Spectres of Marx: The State of the Debt, the Work of Mourning, and the New International*. Translated by Peggy Kamuf. New York: Routledge, 1994.

Dershowitz, Alan. "Want Torture? Get a Warrant." *San Francisco Chronicle*, January 22, 2002, section A.

Desch, Michael. "The More Things Change, the More They Stay the Same: The Liberal Tradition and Obama's Counterterrorism Policy." In *PS Symposium: "Torture and the War on Terror,"* edited by Jim Piazza and Jim Walsh (July 2010): 425–29.

249

Dodds, Paisley. "FBI Letter Alleged Abuse." *Boston Globe*, December 7, 2004, section A.

Dolbee, Sandi. "Agonizing Over Torture: Can Deliberate Hurt Be Justified in Times of Terror?" *San Diego Union-Tribune*, November 23, 2001, section D.

Dorf, Michael C. "Renouncing Torture." In *The Torture Debate in America*, edited by Karen J. Greenberg. New York: Cambridge University Press, 2006.

Doss, Erika. "Making the Imagination Safe in the 1950s: Disneyland's Fantasy Art and Architecture." In *Designing Disney's Theme Parks*, edited by Karal Ann Marling, 179–89. Paris and New York: Flammarion, 2006.

Dow, Mark. *American Gulag: Inside U.S. Immigration Prisons*. Berkeley: University of California Press, 2004.

Dray, Philip. *At the Hands of Persons Unknown: The Lynching of Black America*. New York: Modern Library, 2003.

Dubois, Page. *Torture and Truth*. New York: Routledge, 1991.

Duncan, James S. *The City as Text: The Politics of Landscape Interpretation in the Kandyan Kingdom*. Cambridge: Cambridge University Press, 1990.

Dyzenhaus, David. "Schmitt v. Dicey: Are States of Emergency Inside or Outside the Legal Order?" *Cardozo Law Review* 27 (March 2006): 2005–39.

Ebony, David. *Botero: Abu Ghraib*. Munich: Prestel Verlag, 2006.

Eggan, Dan, and Griff Witte. "The FBI's Upgrade That Wasn't: $170 Million Bought an Unusable Computer System." *Washington Post*, August 18, 2006, section A.

Ehrenreich, Barbara. "The Uterus Is No Substitute for a Conscience." *Arts and Opinion* 4, no. 1 (2005).

Eisenman, Stephen F. *The Abu Ghraib Effect*. London: Reaktion Books, 2007.

Eisgruber, Christopher, and Lawrence Sager. "Civil Liberties in the Dragons' Domain: Negotiating the Blurred Boundary between Domestic Law and Foreign Affairs after 9/11." In *September 11 in History*, edited by Mary Dudziak, 163–79. Durham, N.C.: Duke University Press, 2003.

Ellis, Eric. "Sri Lanka: A One-Family State." Interview by Phillip Adams. *Late Night Live*, ABC Radio National, February 1, 2010. MP3 audio file. http://www.abc.net.au/rn/latenightlive/stories/2010/2807163.htm.

Erni, John Nguyet. "Human Rights in the Neo-liberal Imagination." *Cultural Studies* 23, no. 3 (2009): 417–36.

Esposito, Richard, and Brian Ross. "CIA's Harsh Interrogation Techniques Described." *ABC News*, November 18, 2005.

Evans, Michael. "Bagram Prison in Afghanistan May Become the New Guantá-namo." *Times Online*, March 22, 2010. http://www.timesonline.co.uk/tol/news/world/us_and_americas/article7070460.ece.

Fein, Helen. "More Murder in the Middle: Life-Integrity Violations and Democracy in the World, 1987." *Human Rights Quarterly* 17, no. 1 (1995): 170–91.

Feldman, Allen. "Abu Ghraib: Ceremonies of Nostalgia." *OpenDemocracy*, October 18, 2004. http://www.opendemocracy.net/media-abu_ghraib/article_2163.jsp (accessed June 28, 2010).

———. *Formations of Violence: The Narrative of the Body and Political Terror in Northern Ireland*. Chicago: University of Chicago Press, 1991.

Fernando, Basil. "Tales of Two Sri Lankan Massacres: The Relevance of Embilipitiya to Bindunuwewa." *Asian Legal Resource Centre Bulletin* 4, no. 3 (2005).

Findlay, John M. *Magic Lands: Western Cityscapes and American Culture after 1940*. Berkeley: University of California Press, 1993.

Finn, Peter, and Joby Warrick. "In 2002, Military Agency Warned Against 'Torture.'" *Washington Post*, April 25, 2009. http://www.washingtonpost.com/wp-dyn/content/article/2009/04/24/AR2009042403171.html.

Fletcher, George F. "Black Hole in Guantánamo Bay." *Journal of International Criminal Justice* 2 (2004): 121–32.

Foucault, Michel. *The Birth of Biopolitics: Lectures at the Collège de France*. Translated by Graham Burchell Basingstroke. Hampshire: Palgrave Macmillan, 2008.

———. *Discipline and Punish: The Birth of the Prison*. Translated by Alan Sheridan. New York: Vintage Books, 1979.

———. *The Foucault Reader*. Edited by Paul Rabinow. London: Penguin, 1984.

———. *The History of Sexuality: Volume 1: An Introduction*. Translated by Robert Hurley. New York: Random House, 1978.

———. *Security, Territory, Population: Lectures at the Collège de France, 1977–78*. Translated by Graham Burchell Basingstroke, Hampshire: Palgrave Macmillan, 2007.

———. *"Society Must Be Defended": Lectures at the Collège de France*. Translated by David Macey. New York: Picador, 2003.

Fox, Ben. "Guantánamo Hunger Strikers Say Feeding Tubes Employed as Punishment." *Associated Press*, October 20, 2005.

Freeze, Colin. "What Would Jack Bauer Do?" In *Secrets of "24,"* edited by Dan Burstein and Arne J. de Keijzer, 144–46. New York: Sterling, 2007.

Fuglerud, Øivind. *Life on the Outside: The Tamil Diaspora and Long Distance Nationalism*. London: Pluto Press, 1999.

Galtung, Johann. "Violence, Peace and Peace Research." *Journal of Peace Research* 6, no. 3 (1969): 167–91.

Gilroy, Paul. *Postcolonial Melancholia*. New York: Columbia University Press, 2005.

Glaberson, William. "6 at Guantánamo Said to Face Trial in 9/11 Case." *New York Times*, February 8, 2008. http://www.nytimes.com/2008/02/09/us/09gitmo.html.

Glaberson, William, and Margot Williams. "Officials Report Suicide of Guantánamo Detainee." *New York Times.* June 3, 2009. http://www.nytimes.com/2009/06/03/us/politics/03gitmo.html.

Glanz, James. "Torture is Often a Temptation and Almost Never Works." *Washington Post,* May 9, 2004. http://www.nytimes.com/2004/05/09/weekinreview/the-world-torture-is-often-a-temptation-and-almost-never-works.html.

Golden, Tim. "Guantánamo Detainees Stage Hunger Strike." *New York Times,* April 9, 2007.

http://www.nytimes.com/2007/04/09/us/09hunger.html.

———. "Tough U.S. Steps in Hunger Strike at Camp in Cuba." *New York Times,* February 9, 2006. http://www.nytimes.com/2006/02/09/politics/09gitmo.html.

———. "Years After Two Afghans Died, Abuse Case Falters." *New York Times,* February 13, 2006, section A.

Gourevitch, Philip, and Errol Morris. "Exposure: The Woman Behind the Camera at Abu Ghraib." *New Yorker,* March 24, 2008.

Graham, Elaine L. *Representations of the Post/Human.* Manchester, U.K.: Manchester University Press, 2002.

Greenberg, Karen J., and Joshua L. Dratel, eds. *The Torture Papers: The Road to Abu Ghraib.* New York: Cambridge University Press, 2005.

Gregory, Derek. "The Black Flag: Guantánamo Bay and the State of Exception." *Geografiska Annaler: Series B, Human Geography* 88, no. 4 (2006): 405–27.

Gronke, Paul, and Darius Rejali. "U.S. Public Opinion on Torture, 2001–2009." In *PS Symposium: "Torture and the War on Terror,"* edited by Jim Piazza and Jim Walsh (July 2010).

Gross, Oren, and Fionnuala Ní Aoláin. *Law in Times of Crisis.* Cambridge: Cambridge University Press, 2006.

"Guantanamo Gets Worse." *Sydney Morning Herald,* March 9, 2009.

Gunasekara, Tisaranee. "Towards a Rajapakse Future." *Himal Southasian,* February 2010. http://www.himalmag.com/Towards-a-Rajapakse-future_nw4195.html.

Guneratne, Arjun. "What's in a Name? Aryans and Dravidians in the Making of Sri Lankan Identities." In *The Hybrid Island,* edited by Neluka Silva, 20–40. London: Zed Books, 2002.

Gurstein, Rochelle. "The Triumph of the Pornographic Imagination." *Arts and Opinion* 7, no. 1 (2008).

Hafner-Burton, Emilie, and James Ron. "Seeing Double: Human Rights Impact through Qualitative and Quantitative Eyes." *World Politics* 61, no. 2 (April 2009): 370–73.

Hafner-Burton, Emilie, and Jacob N. Shapiro. "Tortured Relations." In *PS Symposium: "Torture and the War on Terror,"* edited by Jim Piazza and Jim Walsh (July 2010).

Hannah, Matthew. "Torture and the Ticking Time Bomb: The War on Terrorism as a Geographical Imagination of Power/Knowledge." *Annals of the Association of American Geographers* 96, no. 3 (2006): 622–40.

Harris, Neil. "Expository Expositions: Preparing for the Theme Parks." In *Designing Disney's Theme Parks,* edited by Karal Ann Marling, 19–27. Paris and New York: Flammarion, 2006.

Henderson, Conway. "Conditions Affecting the Use of Political Repression." *Journal of Conflict Resolution* 35, no. 1 (1991): 120–42.

Henderson, Schuyler W. "Disregarding the Suffering of Others: Narrative, Comedy, and Torture." *Literature and Medicine* 24, no. 2 (Fall 2005): 181–208.

Herbert, Bob. "Who We Are." *New York Times.* August 1, 2005. http://www.nytimes.com/2005/08/01/opinion/01herbert.html (accessed December 27, 2009).

Hersh, Seymour M. "The General's Report: How Antonio Taguba, Who Investigated the Abu Ghraib Scandal, Became One of Its Casualties." *New Yorker,* June 25, 2007.

Hesford, Wendy S. "Staging Terror." *TDR: The Drama Review* 50, no. 3 (Fall 2006): 29–31.

Hirsch, Michael. "Truth about Torture: A Courageous Soldier and a Determined Senator Demand Clear Standards." *Newsweek,* November 7, 2005.

Hoffman, Bruce. "Nasty Business." *Atlantic Monthly,* January 2002, 49–52.

Holtzman, Elizabeth. "Torture and Accountability." *The Nation* 281, no. 3 (July 18, 2005).

Hoole, Rajan. *Sri Lanka: The Arrogance of Power; Myths, Decadence and Murder.* Colombo, Sri Lanka: University Teachers for Human Rights [Jaffna], 2001.

Hoole, Rajan, Daya Somasundaram, K. Sritharan, and Rajani Thiranagama. *The Broken Palmyrah.* Claremont, Calif.: Sri Lanka Studies Institute, 1990.

Horton, Scott. "The Guantánamo 'Suicides': A Camp Delta Sergeant Blows the Whistle." *Harper's,* January 18, 2010. http://harpers.org/archive/2010/01/hbc-90006368.

Howell, Allison. "Victims or Madmen? The Diagnostic Competition over 'Terrorist' Detainees at Guantánamo Bay." *International Political Sociology* 1, no. 1 (2007): 29–47.

Huggins, M. K., M. Haritos-Fatouros, and P. G. Zimbardo. *Violence Workers: Police Torturers and Murderers Reconstruct Brazilian Atrocities.* Los Angeles: University of California Press, 2002.

Human Rights Clinic of Columbia Law School. "In the Shadows of the War on Terror: Persistent Police Brutality and Abuse in the United States." Report prepared for the United Nations Human Rights Committee on the occasion of its review of the United States of America's second and third periodic report to the Human Rights Committee, May 2006.

Human Rights First. "Torture: Quick Facts." www.humanrightsfirst.org/us_law/ etn/misc/factsheet.aspx (accessed December 7, 2009).

Human Rights Watch. "Leadership Failure: Firsthand Accounts of Torture of Iraqi Detainees by the U.S. Army's 82nd Airborne Division." September 22, 2005. http://hrw.org/reports/2005/uso905.

Humphreys, Macartan, and Jeremy M. Weinstein. "Handling and Manhandling Civilians in Civil War." *American Political Science Review* 100, no. 3 (2006): 429–47.

Intelligence Science Board. "Educing Information: Interrogation; Science and Art." Washington, D.C.: Center for Strategic Intelligence Research, National Defense College, December 2006. Available online at Federation of American Scientists, http://www.fas.org/irp/dni/educing.pdf.

Ismail, Qadri. "A Flippant Gesture towards Sri Lanka: A Review of Michael Ondaatje's *Anil's Ghost*." *Pravada* 6, no. 9-10 (2000): 24–29.

Jayawardena, Kumari. "Class and Ethnic Consciousness 2." *Lanka Guardian* 6, no. 6 (1983): 17–20.

Jenkins, Philip. "Fighting Terrorism As If Women Mattered: Anti-abortion Violence as Unconstructed Terrorism." In *Making Trouble: Cultural Constructions of Crime, Deviance, and Control*, edited by Jeff Ferrell and Neil Websdale, 319–46. Hawthorne, N.Y.: Aldine De Gruyter, 1999.

Johnson, Carrie, and Walter Pincus. "Supermax Prisons in the US Already Hold Terrorists." *Washington Post*, May 22, 2009. http://www.washingtonpost. com/wp-dyn/content/article/2009/05/21/AR2009052102009.html.

Johnston, David, and Neil A. Lewis. "US Will Give Qaeda Suspect a Civilian Trial." *New York Times*, February 26, 2009.

"Joint Resolution to Authorize the Use of United States Armed Forces Against Iraq." Public Law 107-243 (October 10, 2002).

Joint Task Force Guantánamo. *Camp Delta Standard Operating Procedures*, 28 March 2003.

"Judge Throws Out Terror Convictions." *USA Today*, September 1, 2004. http://www.usatoday.com/news/washington/2004-09-01-terror-doj_x.htm.

Kahn, Paul W. *Sacred Violence: Torture, Terror and Sovereignty*. Ann Arbor: University of Michigan Press, 2008.

Kantorovich, E. V. "Make Them Talk." *Wall Street Journal*, June 18, 2002, section A.

Kaplan, Amy. "Homeland Insecurities: Transformations of Language and Space." In *September 11 in History*, edited by Mary Dudziak, 55–69. Durham, N.C.: Duke University Press, 2003.

———. "Violent Belongings and the Question of Empire Today: Presidential Address to the American Studies Association, October 17, 2003." *American Quarterly* 56, no. 1 (2004): 1–18.

Kaufman, Michael T. "What Does the Pentagon See in 'Battle of Algiers'?" *New York Times*, September 7, 2003.

Kaufman-Osborn, Timothy. "Gender Trouble at Abu Ghraib?" *Politics and Gender* 1 (2005): 597–619.

Khan, Mahvish Rukhsana. *My Guantánamo Diary: The Detainees and the Stories They Told Me*. Carlton North, Australia: Scribe, 2008.

Kirkpatrick, David D. "Senators Laud Treatment of Detainees in Guantánamo." *New York Times*, June 28, 2005. http://query.nytimes.com/gst/fullpage.htm l?res=9C01EED6143AF93BA15755C0A9639C8B63.

Kleinfeld, Margo. "Destabilizing the Identity-Territory Nexus: Rights-Based Discourse in Sri Lanka's New Political Geography." *GeoJournal* 64 (2005): 287–95.

Knight, Danielle. "Trade in Tools of Torture." *U.S. News and World Report*, November 24, 2003.

Kooijmans, Pieter H. "Torturers and Their Masters." In *The Politics of Pain: Torturers and Their Masters*, edited by Ronald Crelinsten and Alex P. Schmid, 13–17. San Francisco: Westview Press, 1995.

Koppelman, Alex. "Obama Reframes the Torture Debate." *Salon*, April 29, 2009. http://www.salon.com/politics/war_room/2009/04/29/obama_torture/index.html.

Krech, David, and Richard S. Crutchfield. *Theory and Problems of Social Psychology*. New York: McGraw-Hill, 1948.

Krishna, Sankaran. *Postcolonial Insecurities: India, Sri Lanka, and the Question of Nationhood*. Honolulu: University of Hawaii Press, 1999.

Kurnaz, Murat. *Five Years of My Life: An Innocent Man in Guantánamo Bay*. New York: Palgrave Macmillan, 2007.

Kurtz, Christopher. *Complicity: Ethics and Law for a Collective Age*. Cambridge: Cambridge University Press, 2000.

LaCapra, Dominick. *Writing History, Writing Trauma*. Baltimore: Johns Hopkins University Press, 2001.

Lagouranis, Tony, and Allen Mikaelian. *Fear Up Harsh: An Army Interrogator's Dark Journey through Iraq*. New York: New American Library, 2007.

Lelyveld, Joseph. "Interrogating Ourselves." *New York Times Magazine*, June 12, 2005. http://www.nytimes.com/2005/06/12/magazine /12TORTURE. html (accessed June 15, 2005).

Leonnig, Carol. "More Join Guantánamo Hunger Strike." *Washington Post*, September 13, 2005, section A.

"L'essor inquiétant du 'supplice propre' en démocratie." *Libération*, December 16, 2008. http://www.liberation.fr/sciences/0101305811-l-essor-inqui-etant-du-supplice-propre-en-democratie.

Levi, Primo. *The Drowned and the Saved*. Translated by Raymond Rosenthal. London: Abacus, 1998.

———. *Survival in Auschwitz.* Translated by Stuart Wolfe. New York: Summit
   Books, 1985.

Levinas, Emmanuel. *Collected Philosophical Papers.* Translated by Alphonso
   Lingis. Dordrecht, Netherlands: Martinus Nijhof, 1987.

Levinson, Sanford. "Contemplating Torture." In *Torture*, 23–43. New York:
   Oxford University Press, 2004.

Lewis, Anthony. "A Different World." *New York Times*, September 12, 2001,
   section A, late edition.

Lobel, Jules. "Emergency Powers and the Decline of Liberalism." *Yale Law Journal* 98 (May 1989).

Locke, John. *Two Treatises on Government.* Edited by Peter Laslett. New York:
   Cambridge University Press, 1965.

Londregan, John B., and Keith T. Poole. "Poverty, the Coup Trap, and
   the Seizure of Executive Power." *World Politics* 42, no. 2 (January 1990):
   151–83.

Luban, David. "Liberalism, Torture and the Ticking Bomb." In *The Torture
   Debate in America*, edited by Karen J. Greenberg, 35–83. New York: Cambridge University Press, 2006.

Maas, Peter. "Torture, Tough or Lite: If a Terror Suspect Won't Talk, Should
   He Be Made To?" *New York Times*, Week in Review, March 9, 2003.

Mackey, Chris [pseud.]. *Interrogator's War: Inside the Secret War on Al Qaeda.*
   Boston: Little Brown, 2004.

Manzoor, Parvez S. "Turning Jews into Muslims: The Untold Saga of the
   Muselmänner." *Islam21*, no. 28 (2001): 1–7.

Marling, Karal Ann. "Imagineering the Disney Theme Parks." In *Designing Disney's Theme Parks*, 29–177. Paris and New York: Flammarion, 2006.

Marx, Leo. *The Machine in the Garden.* Oxford: University of Oxford Press, 2000.

Maxwell, Anne. *Colonial Photography and Exhibitions.* London: Leicester University Press, 1999.

Mayer, Jane. "A Deadly Interrogation." *New Yorker*, November 15, 2005.

———. "Whatever It Takes: The Politics of the Man Behind *24.*" In *Secrets of
   "24,"* edited by Dan Burstein and Arne J. de Keijzer, 22–36. New York:
   Sterling, 2007.

Mazzetti, Mark. "U.S. Army Says Prison Deaths Are Homicides." *Los Angeles
   Times*, March 26, 2005.

Mbembe, Achille. "Necropolitics." Translated by Libby Meintjes. *Public Culture*
   15, no. 1 (2003): 11–40.

McCoy, Alfred W. "The Punishment of David Hicks." *The Monthly* (June 2006):
   20–29.

———. *A Question of Torture: CIA Interrogation, from the Cold War to the War on
   Terror.* New York: Metropolitan Books, 2006.

McLaughlin, Abraham. "How Far Americans Would Go to Fight Terror." *Christian Science Monitor*, November 14, 2001.

Melia, Michael. "More Gitmo Detainees Join Hunger Strike." *Associated Press*, January 8, 2007. http://www.sfgate.com/cgi-bin/article.cgi?f=/n/a/2007/01/08/international/i1152839S55.DTL.

———. "Yemeni Official: Gitmo Inmate Died of Asphyxiation." *Associated Press*, August 1, 2009.

Miles, Steven H. *Oath Betrayed: Torture, Medical Complicity, and the War on Terror.* New York: Random House, 2006.

Miller, Jason. "FBI's Case Management Project Remains on Shaky Ground." *Federal News Radio*, November 11, 2009. http://federalnewsradio.com/index.php?sid=1809819&nid=35&_hw=FBIs+Case+Management+Project+Remains+on+Shaky+Ground%94 (accessed December 7, 2009).

Mitchell, Andrew. "Torture and Photography: Abu Ghraib." Unpublished monograph.

Mitchell, Luke. "Six Questions for Cynthia Smith on the Legality of Force-feeding at Guantánamo." *Harper's*, June 4, 2009. http://harpers.org/archive/2009/06/hbc-90005110 (accessed June 22, 2009).

Modell, David. "Viewpoint: The Power of Abuse Pictures." *BBC News*, May 13, 2004. http://news.bbc.co.uk/2/hi/americas/3710617.stm.

Moore, Will H. "Incarceration, Interrogation and Counterterror: Do (Liberal) Democratic Institutions Constrain Leviathan?" In *PS Symposium: "Torture and the War on Terror,"* edited by Jim Piazza and Jim Walsh (July 2010).

Morris, Errol. *Standard Operating Procedure.* DVD. Sony Pictures Classic and Participant Media, 2008.

Nacos, Brigitte. *Mass-Mediated Terrorism: The Central Role of the Media in Terrorism and Counterterrorism.* New York: Rowman and Littlefield, 2002.

Nancy, Jean-Luc. *The Ground of the Image.* Translated by Jeff Fort. New York: Fordham University Press, 2005.

Nanji, Ayaz. "Report: 108 Died in U.S. Custody." *CBS News*, March 16, 2005. http://www.cbsnews.com/stories/2005/03/16/terror/main680658.shtml.

Neruda, Pablo. "The Dictators." In *Neruda and Vallejo: Selected Poems*, translated and edited by Robert Bly, 93. Boston: Beacon Press, 1993.

Nicholl, David. "Guantánamo and Medical Ethics." *Jurist*, June 13, 2006.

Nicholl, David, Holly Atkinson, John Kalk, William Hopkins, Elwyn Elias, Adnan Siddiqui, Ronald Cranford, and Oliver Sacks. "Forcefeeding and Restraint of Guantánamo Bay Hunger Strikers." *Lancet* 367 (March 11, 2006): 811.

Nietzsche, Friedrich. *On the Genealogy of Morals and Ecce Homo.* Translated by Walter Kaufmann. New York: Random House, 1989.

Nuhman, M. A. "Murder." Translated by S. Pathmanathan, 1981. Quoted in

Sivamohan Sumathy, "Is There War in Your Ur?" *Himal Southasian,* October 2008. http://www.himalmag.com/Is-there-war-in-your-ur_nw1976.html.

Olsberg, Nicholas. Foreword to *Designing Disney's Theme Parks,* edited by Karal Ann Marling. Paris and New York: Flammarion, 2006.

Ondaatje, Michael. *Anil's Ghost.* London: Bloomsbury, 2000.

———. "The Distance of a Shout." In *Handwriting.* Suffolk, U.K.: Bloomsbury, 1998.

———. *The English Patient.* New York: Vintage, 1992.

Ortíz, L. Ricardo. "On (Our) American Ground: Caribbean-Latino-Diasporic Production and the Postnational 'Guantanamera.'" *Social Text* 26, no. 1 (2008): 3–28.

Pawelczynska, Anna. *Values and Violence in Auschwitz.* Translated by Catherine S. Leach. Berkeley: University of California Press, 1979.

Pease, Donald. "The Global Homeland State: Bush's Biopolitical Statement." *Boundary* 2 30, no. 3 (2003): 1–18.

Perera, Jehan. "Rapid Increase of Southern Tourists to Jaffna Has Positive and Negative Impact." *Transcurrents,* March 9, 2010. http://transcurrents.com/tc/2010/03/rapid_increase_of_southern_tou.html.

Perera, Sasanka. *Living with Torturers.* Colombo, Sri Lanka: International Centre for Ethnic Studies, 1995.

Perera, Suvendrini. "What Is a Camp . . . ?" *Borderlands* 1, no. 1 (2002). http://www.borderlands.net.au/vol1no1_2002/perera_camp.html.

Phillips, Joshua E. S. *None of Us Were Like This Before: American Soldiers and Torture.* New York: Verso, 2010.

Physicians for Human Rights. *Break Them Down: Systemic Use of Psychological Torture by US Forces.* Cambridge, Mass.: Physicians for Human Rights, 2005. http://physiciansforhumanrights.org/library/documents/reports/break-them-down-the.pdf.

———. "Forced Feeding of Gitmo Detainees Violates International Medical Codes of Ethics." September 16, 2005. http://physiciansforhumanrights.org/library/news-2005-09-16.html.

Piazza, James A., and James Igoe Walsh. "Physical Integrity Rights and Terrorism." In *PS Symposium: "Torture and the War on Terror"* (July 2010).

Priest, Dana. "CIA Holds Terror Suspects in Secret Prisons." *Washington Post,* November 2, 2005. http://www.washingtonpost.com/wpdyn/content/article/2005/11/01/AR2005110101644.html.

Priest, Dana, and Barton Gellman. "U.S. Decries Abuse But Defends Interrogations; 'Stress and Duress' Tactics Used on Terrorism Suspects Held in Secret Overseas Facilities." *Washington Post,* December 26, 2002, section A.

Prokosch, Eric. "Amnesty International's Anti-torture Campaigns." In *A Glimpse of Hell: Reports on Torture Worldwide,* edited by Duncan Forrest, for Amnesty International, 26–35. New York: New York University Press, 1996.

Puar, Jasbir K. *Terrorist Assemblages.* Durham, N.C.: Duke University Press, 2007.

Pugliese, Joseph. "Abu Ghraib's Shadow Archives." *Law and Literature* 9, no. 2 (2007): 247–76.

———. "Geocorpographies of Torture." *Australian Critical Race and Whiteness Studies Association Journal* 3, no. 1 (2007).

———. "Necroethics of Terrorism." *Law and Critique* 21 (2010): 213–31.

Radack, Jesselyn. "When Whistle-Blowers Suffer." *Los Angeles Times,* April 27, 2010. http://www.latimes.com/news/opinion/la-oe-radack-20100427,0,754088.story.

Raju, Mana. "Graham: Detainees Get Better Treatment Than Nazis." *The Hill,* June 12, 2008. http://thehill.com/leading-the-news/graham-gitmo-detainees-get-better-treatment-than-nazis-2008-06-12.html.

Rasul, Shafiq, Asif Iqbal, and Rhuhel Ahmed. "Detention in Afghanistan and Guantánamo Bay." Center for Constitutional Rights, July 26, 2004. http://ccrjustice.org/files/report_tiptonThree.pdf.

Ratner, Michael. "The Guantánamo Prisoners." In *America's Disappeared,* edited by Rachel Meeropol, 31–59. New York: Seven Stories Press, 2005.

Ratner, Michael, and Ellen Ray. *Guantánamo: What the World Should Know.* White River Junction, Vt.: Chelsea Green Publishing, 2004.

Reid, Tim. "One in Five Guantánamo Bay Detainees Is on Hunger Strike." *Times* (London), January 15, 2009. http://www.timesonline.co.uk/tol/news/world/us_and_americas/article5518812.ece.

Reid-Henry, S. "Exceptional Sovereignty? Guantánamo Bay and the Re-colonial Present." *Antipode* 39, no. 4 (2007): 627–48.

Rejali, Darius. "Modern Torture as a Civic Marker: Solving a Global Anxiety with a New Political Technology." *Journal of Human Rights* 2, no. 2 (2003), 153–71.

———. *Torture and Democracy.* Princeton, N.J.: Princeton University Press, 2007.

———. *Torture and Modernity: Self, Society and the State in Modern Iran.* San Francisco: Westview Press, 1994.

———. "Torture's Dark Allure." *Salon,* June 18, 2004. http://dir.salon.com/story/opinion/feature/2004/06/18/torture_1/index.html.

Ricchiardi, Sherry. "Missed Signals." *American Journalism Review* 26, no. 4 (August/September 2004): 22–29.

Rich, Frank. "The 'Good Germans' Among Us." *New York Times,* October 14, 2007, section 4, late edition.

Riolta Lanka Holidays Ltd. "Yapahuwa (Fire Rock) Fortress." Sri Lanka Holidays. http://www.mysrilankaholidays.com/yapahuwa.html.

Rivera-Fuentes, Consuela, and Lynda Birke. "Talking with/in Pain: Reflections on Bodies Under Torture." *Women's International Studies Forum* 24, no. 6 (2001): 653–68.

Rodley, Nigel. Foreword to *The Politics of Pain: Torturers and Their Masters*, edited by Ronald Crelinsten and Alex P. Schmid. San Francisco: Westview Press, 1995.

Rose, David. *Guantánamo: The War on Human Rights*. New York: New Press, 2004.

Ross, Lee, D. Greene, and P. House. "The False Consensus Phenomenon: An Attributional Bias in Self-Perception and Social Perception Processes." *Journal of Experimental Social Psychology* 13, no. 3 (1977): 279–301.

Rothman, Hal K. *Devil's Bargain: Tourism in the Twentieth-Century American West*. Lawrence: University of Kansas Press, 1998.

Russell, Lynette. *Savage Imaginings*. Melbourne: Australian Scholarly Publishing, 2001.

Rutenberg, Jim. "Torture Seeps into Discussion by News Media." *New York Times*, November 5, 2001, section C.

Saar, Erik, and Viveca Novak. *Inside the Wire: A Military Intelligence Soldier's Eyewitness Account of Life at Guantánamo*. New York: Penguin, 2005.

Salgado, Minoli. *Writing Sri Lanka*. New York: Routledge, 2006.

Sante, Luc. "Tourists and Torturers." *New York Times*, May 11, 2004, Opinion section.

Savage, Charlie. "Split Seen on Interrogation Techniques: Navy Official Says Many Back Stance against Coercion." *Boston Globe*, March 31, 2005, section A.

Scarry, Elaine. *The Body in Pain: The Making and Unmaking of the World*. New York: Oxford University Press, 1985.

Scheppele, Kim. "Law in a Time of Emergency: States of Exception and the Temptations of 9/11." *University of Pennsylvania Journal of Constitutional Law* 6, no. 5 (May 2004): 1001–83.

Schmitt, Eric. "Iraq Abuse Trial Is Again Limited to Lower Ranks." *New York Times*, March 23, 2006, section A, late edition.

Schmitt, Eric, and Carolyn Marshall. "In Secret Unit's 'Black Room' a Grim Portrait of U.S. Abuse." *New York Times*, March 19, 2006. http://www.nytimes.com/2006/03/19/international/middleeast/19abuse.html.

Scott, Andrea K. "Susan Crile––Abuse of Power." Art in Review, *New York Times*, October 13, 2006.

Seelye, Katharine Q. "Some Guantánamo Detainees Will be Freed, Rumsfeld Says." *New York Times*, October 23, 2002. http://www.nytimes.com/2002/10/23/world/threats-responses-detainees-some-Guantánamo-prisoners-will-be-freed-rumsfeld.html?pagewanted=1.

Serwer, Adam. "Tortured Talking Points." *Guardian*, December 30, 2009.

http://www.guardian.co.uk/commentisfree/cifamerica/2009/dec/30/torture-bomb-flight-253.

Sharrock, Justine. "Am I a Torturer?" *Mother Jones*, March/April 2008.

Shklar, Judith N. "The Liberalism of Fear." In *Political Thought and Political Thinkers*, edited by Stanley Hoffman, 3–20. Chicago: University of Chicago Press, 1998.

Shue, Henry. "Torture." *Philosophy and Public Affairs* 7, no. 2 (1978): 124–43.

Sifton, John. "The Bush Administration Homicides." *The Daily Beast*, May 5, 2009. http://www.thedailybeast.com/blogs-and-stories/2009-05-05/how-many-were-tortured-to-death/full/.

Simeone, Nick. "Terror-Indictment." GlobalSecurity.org, August 28, 2002. http://www.globalsecurity.org/security/library/news/2002/sec-020828-2f5d9e89.htm (accessed June 28, 2010).

Simons, Marlise. "Spanish Court Weighs Inquiry on Torture for 6 Bush-Era Officials." *New York Times*, March 28, 2009. http://www.nytimes.com/2009/03/29/world/europe/29spain.html.

Sivanandan, A. "Sri Lanka: Racism and the Politics of Underdevelopment." *Race & Class* 26, no. 1 (1984): 1–37.

Smith, Andrea. *Conquest: Sexual Violence and American Indian Genocide*. Cambridge, Mass.: South End Press, 2005.

Sökmen, Müge Gürsoy. *World Tribunal on Iraq: Making the Case Against War*. Northampton, Mass.: Olive Branch Press, 2008.

Somasundaram, Daya. *Scarred Minds: The Psychological Impact of War on Sri Lankan Tamils*. Colombo, Sri Lanka: Vijitha Yapa Publishers, 1998.

Sontag, Susan. *At the Same Time: Essays and Speeches*. New York: Farrar, Straus and Giroux, 2007.

———. *On Photography*. New York: Farrar, Straus and Giroux, 1977.

———. *Regarding the Pain of Others*. New York: Farrar, Straus and Giroux, 2003.

———. "Regarding the Torture of Others." *New York Times Magazine*, May 23, 2004.

Staub, Ervin. "Torture: Psychological and Cultural Origins." In *The Politics of Pain: Torturers and Their Masters*, edited by Ronald Crelinsten and Alex P. Schmid, 99–112. San Francisco: Westview Press, 1995.

Stimson, James A., Michael B. MacKuen, and Robert S. Erikson. "Dynamic Representation." *American Political Science Review* 39, no. 3 (September 1995): 543–65.

Sumathy, Sivamohan. *Militants, Militarism and the Crisis of (Tamil) Nationalism*. Colombo, Sri Lanka: Marga Institute, 2001.

Suskind, Ron. *The One Percent Doctrine: Deep Inside America's Pursuit of Its Enemies Since 9/11*. New York: Simon and Schuster, 2006.

Sussman, David. "Defining Torture." *Case Western Reserve Journal of International Law* 37 (2005): 225–30.

———. "What's Wrong with Torture." In *The Phenomenon of Torture*, edited by William Schulz, 178–79. Philadelphia: University of Pennsylvania Press, 2007.

Teitel, Ruti. "Empire's Law: Foreign Relations by Presidential Fiat." In *September 11 in History*, edited by Mary Dudziak, 194–211. Durham, N.C.: Duke University Press, 2003.

Tennekoon, Serena. "Rituals of Development: The Accelerated Mahaväli Development Program of Sri Lanka." *American Ethnologist* 15, no. 2 (1988): 294–310.

Thomas, Evan. "'24' versus the Real World." *Newsweek*, September 20, 2006. http://www.newsweek.com/id/45788.

Toliver, Raymond. *The Interrogator*. Fallbrook, Calif.: Aero Publishers, 1978.

Tolnay, Stewart E., and E. M. Beck. *A Festival of Violence: An Analysis of Southern Lynchings, 1882–1930*. Urbana: University of Illinois Press, 1995.

"Torture and Democracy." *The Nation* 279, no. 1 (July 5, 2004).

Umansky, Eric. "Failures of Imagination." *Columbia Journalism Review* 45, no. 3 (September/October 2006): 16–31.

UN News Center. "Deeming Sri Lanka Execution Video Authentic, UN Expert Calls for War Crimes Probe." January 7, 2010. http://www.un.org/apps/news/story.asp?NewsID=33423&Cr=sri+lanka&Cr1.

U.S. Senate Armed Services Committee. "Inquiry into the Treatment of Detainees in U.S. Custody." November 20, 2008. http://armed-services.senate.gov/Publications/Detainee%20Report%20Final_April%2022%202009.pdf (accessed June 23, 2010).

von Zielbauer, Paul. "Army Colonel Is Acquitted in Abu Ghraib Abuse Case." *New York Times*, August 29, 2007, section A, late edition.

Waldron, Jeremy. "Torture and Positive Law: Jurisprudence for the White House." *Columbia Law Review* 105, no. 6 (2005): 1681–1750.

———. "Torture on Trial: Morality, Law and the Utility of Torture." Presentation at Columbia Law School, New York, April 14, 2006.

Weiser, Benjamin. "Asserting Coercion, Embassy Bombing Suspect Tries to Suppress Statements." *New York Times*, July 13, 2000, section B.

———. "U.S. Faces Tough Challenge to Statements in Terrorism Case." *New York Times*, January 25, 2001, section B.

Weizman, Eyal. "The Art of War: Deleuze, Guattari, Debord and the Israeli Defence Force." *Mute*, August 2006. http://www.metamute.org/?q=en/node/8192.

White, Josh. "Guantánamo Force-Feeding Tactics Are Called Torture." *Washington Post*, March 1, 2006, section A.

White, Robert Joseph. "IG Auschwitz: The Primacy of Racial Politics." PhD diss., University of Nebraska, 2000.

262

Williams, Kristian. *American Methods: Torture and the Logic of Domination.* Cambridge, Mass.: South End Press, 2006.

Williams, Rudi. "Detainees Eat Well, Gain Weight on Camp Delta's Muslim Menu." Press release. *American Forces Press Service,* July 3, 2002. http://www.defenselink.mil/nedws/newsarticle.aspx?id=43686.

Winik, Jay. "Security Comes Before Liberty." *Wall Street Journal,* October 23, 2001, section A.

Wittes, Benjamin. "Checks, Balances, and Wartime Detainees." *Policy Review* 130 (April and May 2005): 3–22.

Wolin, Sheldon. "Collective Identity and Constitutional Power." In *The Presence of the Past,* 8–31. Baltimore, Md.: Johns Hopkins University Press, 1989.

Woodward, Bob. "Cheney Says War against Terror 'May Never End.'" *Washington Post,* October 21, 2001, section A, final edition.

———. "Detainee Tortured, Says U.S. Official." *Washington Post,* January 14, 2009, section A.

"Word for Word: Psychology and Sometimes a Slap; The Man Who Made Prisoners Talk." Week in Review, *New York Times,* December 12, 2004.

Worthington, Andy. *The Guantánamo Files: The Stories of the 774 Detainees in America's Illegal Prison.* London: Pluto Press, 2007.

Yee, James. *For God and Country: Faith and Patriotism under Fire.* New York: Public Affairs, 2005.

Yoo, John C. Memorandum to Alberto Gonzales. U.S. Department of Justice, Office of Legal Counsel. August 1, 2002. http://www.usdoj.gov/olc/docs/memo-gonzales-aug1.pdf.

———. Memorandum to William Haynes II. January 9, 2002. In *The Torture Papers: The Road to Abu Ghraib,* edited by Karen Greenberg and Joshua Dratel. Cambridge: Cambridge University Press, 2005.

Young, Iris Marion. "The Logic of Masculinist Protection: Reflections on the Current Security State." *Signs* 29, no. 3 (Autumn 2003): 1–25.

———. "Responsibility, Social Connection, and Global Labor Justice." In *Global Challenges,* 159–86. Cambridge: Polity Press, 2007.

Zagorin, Adam. "At Guantánamo, Dying Is Not Permitted." *Time,* June 30, 2006. http://www.time.com/time/nation/article/0,8599,1209530,00.htm.

Žižek, Slavoj. "From Homo Sucker to Homo Sacer." In *Welcome to the Desert of the Real,* 83–111. New York: Verso, 2002.

———. *Iraq: The Borrowed Kettle.* New York: Verso, 2004.

———. "Knight of the Living Dead." *New York Times,* March 24, 2007.

———. *The Parallax View.* Cambridge, Mass.: MIT Press, 2006.

———. "24, Or Himmler in Hollywood." In *Secrets of "24."* edited by Dan Burstein and Arne J. de Keijzer, 202–6. New York: Sterling, 2007.

NOTES ON CONTRIBUTORS

Stephanie Athey is Associate Professor of English and Director of the Honors program at Lasell College in Newton, Massachusetts. She has received appointments as Visiting Scholar at Columbia University's Center for the Study of Human Rights (2006) and Research Associate of the William Monroe Trotter Institute for the Study of Black Culture at the University of Massachusetts-Boston, and she directs the Mexico Shoulder to Shoulder Service-Learning Partnership. Her primary research and teaching interests are race, gender, and literary studies, and the relationship between human rights, gender, and economic development in transnational contexts. She is editor of *Sharpened Edge: Women of Color, Resistance and Writing* (2003) and author of several articles on the public discourse of torture, including "The Terrorist We Torture: The Tale of Abdul Hakim Murad" (2007) and "Dark Chamber, Colonial Scene: Post-9/11 Torture and Representation" in *Theoretical Perspectives on Human Rights and Literature*, edited by Alexandra Schultheis and Swanson Goldberg (2011). She is currently working on a book, *Torture's Echo*, that explores U.S. representations of torture in print journalism, memoir, and fiction since September 11, 2001.

Shampa Biswas is Associate Professor of Politics at Whitman College in
Walla Walla, Washington. Her research interests include issues of nationalism, sovereignty, globalization, global development, postcolonial theory,
and South Asian politics. She is coeditor of *Margins, Peripheries and Excluded
Bodies: International Relations and States of Exception* (2010) and author of
several articles on postcolonial international relations, race in international
relations, and the nation-state in the context of globalization.

Mark Danner has written about foreign affairs, political conflict, human rights,
and war for three decades, covering Central America, Haiti, the Balkans,
Iraq, and many other stories. Among his books are *The Massacre at El Mozote:
A Parable of the Cold War* (1994), *Torture and Truth: America, Abu Ghraib and
the War on Terror* (2004), and *Stripping Bare the Body: Politics Violence War*
(2009). Danner is Chancellor's Professor of English, Journalism and Politics at the University of California, Berkeley, and James Clarke Chace Professor of Foreign Affairs, Politics and the Humanities at Bard College. His
work has been honored with a National Magazine Award, three Overseas
Press Awards, an Emmy, and a MacArthur fellowship.

Julia Ireland is Assistant Professor of Philosophy at Whitman College in Walla
Walla, Washington. She is currently completing a book on the political
implications of Martin Heidegger's interpretation of the German Romantic
poet Friedrich Hölderlin. She also teaches aesthetics and is particularly
interested in the interpretative dimension of the act of seeing.

Timothy V. Kaufman-Osborn is the Provost and Dean of the Faculty as well
as the Baker Ferguson Professor of Politics and Leadership at Whitman
College in Walla Walla, Washington. He is the author of several books and
numerous articles on capital punishment, the discipline of political science,
feminist theory, and American pragmatism, among other topics. He has
served as president of the Western Political Science Association as well as
the American Civil Liberties Union of Washington, and he recently completed a term on the Executive Council of the American Political Science
Association.

Suvendrini Perera completed her PhD degree at Columbia University, New
York, and her BA degree at the University of Sri Lanka, Kelaniya, and
is Professor of Cultural Studies at Curtin University in Perth, Australia. She
has published widely on topics related to race, ethnicity, multiculturalism,
and refugees. Her latest books include *Australia and the Insular Imagination:
Beaches, Borders, Boats and Bodies* (2009) and *Living Through Terror* (2010),

coedited with Antonio Traverso. Histories of coexistence in multiethnic societies, state violence, and diaspora cultural studies are among her current research interests.

Joseph Pugliese is Associate Professor in the Department of Media, Music, Communication and Cultural Studies at Macquarie University, Sydney, Australia. His most recent publications include a monograph, *Biometrics: Bodies, Technologies, Biopolitics* (2010), shortlisted for the Surveillance Studies Book Prize 2010, and an edited collection of essays, *Transmediterranean: Diasporas, Histories, Geopolitical Spaces* (2010).

Darius Rejali is Chair and Professor of Political Science at Reed College in Portland, Oregon. He is the author of *Torture and Democracy* (2007), winner of the 2007 Human Rights Book of the Year Award from the American Political Science Association and the 2009 Raphael Lemkin Award for the best biennial book on genocide-related materials. Rejali is a 2003 Carnegie Scholar and recipient of the 2009 Danish Distinguished Chair in Human Rights and International Studies, awarded by the Fulbright Scholar Program.

Lauren Wilcox is a PhD candidate in Political Science at the University of Minnesota, Minneapolis. Her work examines how the body has been theorized in international relations and the various constructions of bodies found in practices related to international security.

Zahi Zalloua is Associate Professor of French and General Studies at Whitman College and editor of *The Comparatist.* He is the author of *Montaigne and the Ethics of Skepticism* (2005) and editor of *Montaigne after Theory/Theory after Montaigne* (2009). He has also edited issues of *L'Esprit Créateur* (2006) and *SubStance* (2009) and coedited, with Nicole Simek, a special issue of *Dalhousie French Studies* on representations of trauma in French and Francophone literature (2007). His other publications address globalization, literary theory, interdisciplinary approaches to philosophy and literature, experimental fiction, and gender studies. He is currently writing a study on unruly fictions in modern French texts.

INDEX

A

Abdulmutallab, Umar Farouk, 108

abortion clinic bombings, 124n17

Abu Ghraib: Abuse of Power (Crile),
190–92, 211n6, 212n8

The Abu Ghraib Effect (Eisenman),
212n9

Abu Ghraib prison abuses: accountability for, 17, 67–73, 91–97;
camera as instrument of torture,
188–89, 190, 213n13; enhanced
interrogation techniques, 9,
53–57; festivals of violence,
164; fictionalizing, 8; group
identity formation through,
146; humiliation, 7–8, 13, 191,
202–5, 213n13; photography as
a component of, 188–89, 190,

213n13; prosecution timeline,
31; psychic violence of, 203–4;
spectators role in, 146, 191, 199;
torture, gratuitous use of, 9, 13;
women's role in, 210n2

Abu Ghraib prisoners: demographics, 9; humanity, restoring
through art, 18, 190–91; survivor accounts, 53–56

Abu Ghraib prison interrogators,
53, 57

Abu Ghraib torture photographs:
complicit seeing enacted in,
189–99, 213n13; depoliticizing
by Bush, 17, 68; disorientation
of the uncanny on viewing,
212n9; framing to obscure suffering, 194; hierarchical power

Abu Ghraib torture photographs (cont.)
relations in, 205–9; humiliation
in, 202–9; intimacy in, 207–9;
lynching postcards compared,
192, 194; in the media, 7–8;
photographers' role, 210n1,
211n4; pornography connection,
189, 210n2; purpose of, 188–89;
sympathy response to, 189–90,
211n3
Abu Ghraib torture photographs,
artistic response to: eliciting
sympathy, 192, 198, 205, 211n3;
evoking sound, 199; hierarchical power relations, 199–202,
205–9, 206*f*; humiliation, 191,
200*f*, 202–5, 203*f*; introduction,
191–92; responsive touch of the
viewer in, 199–202; restoring
affective connection, 18, 191–92,
194–98, 199–202, 205; restoring
humanity through, 18, 190–91;
space in, 201
accountability: borders of, 96; criminal liability protections, 21n6,
155n32; military, post-9/11,
83–84; Mothers of Plaza de Mayo,
220–21; political, 9–10; post–Abu
Ghraib, 17, 67–73, 91–97, 102;
rule of law for, 82; of the security
state, 87–93
Addington, David, 62
Agamben, Giorgio, 16, 165, 169,
176–77, 178, 180–81
al-Dossary, Jumah, 175
Alexander, Matthew, 25, 27, 33
al Hanashi, Mohammad Ahmed
Abdullah Saleh, 115
alibi, 132, 133, 139, 146–47
Ali et al. v. Rumsfeld, 69–70
Al-Jamadi, Manadel, 142–43

allegations of torture, validating, 31
al-Marri, Ali Saleh Kahlah, 46–47
Al Qaeda, 21n7
Alter, Jonathan, 138
al-Zarqawi, Abu Musab, 25, 33
American Civil Liberties Union,
69–70
American Gothic (Laing), 191, 194
American Gothic (Wood), 194
Amin, Shahid, 177–78
amnesia, 46. *See also* forgetfulness
Amnesty International, 139, 232
Anglo Saxon Modern torture technique, 30
Anil's Ghost (Ondaatje), 18, 218,
230–38
animalization of detainees, 162–64,
180, 205–9, 206*f. See also* dehumanizing the enemy
antiterrorism techniques, effective,
32–33
Anuradhapura massacre, 226
apostrophe: Banksy's doll as figure of,
165, 168–69, 182; the rhetorical
figure of the, 159
Arasanayagam, Jean, 235
archetype of torture: alibi in the,
132–33, 146; in anti-torture
scholarship, 138–41; features of,
137; the group in, 142–46; in
the law, 131–32, 141; limiting/
obscuring function of, 142–46,
148–49; in the media, 131–32,
136–38; reality vs. the, 141–43; in
torture debate, 12
Arendt, Hannah, 72
Argentinian dirty war, 60, 62, 220
Army Field Manual 34-52, 8, 39, 48
art: Banksy's doll as apostrophic figure, 165, 168–69, 182; politics
and ethics relation to, 18, 191;

restoring humanity through, 18, 191. *See also* Abu Ghraib torture photographs, artistic response to; *specific artists*

Athey, Stephanie, 6–8, 9, 11–12, 14, 19

atrocity-related trauma, 39–40

attention grab, 59

attention slap, 59

Auschwitz prisoners, 16

authoritarian regimes: Disneyland as, 169–70; torture in, 9, 35–36

Avelar, Idelbar, 148

B

Bagram Airbase detention center, 142, 143–44, 183

Bagram Airfield, 111

Banksy, 17, 158, 160–70, 181, 182. *See also* doll installation at Disneyland

Batticaloa, 230, 239

beatings, coordinated, 129

Begg, Moazzam, 163, 164, 167

belly slap, 59

Bindunuwewa Rehabilitation Camp, 221

bin Laden, Osama, 23n18

biopolitics, 220, 234

biopower, 102, 103–9, 114–22, 182

black sites (CIA), 58–61, 111–12, 135

Blanchot, Maurice, 174, 175

the body: in fiction, 232–34, 236–37; language of, 109–10, 172–73; of the *Muselmann*, 176–82; permeable boundary of, 199, 202; psychic withdrawal of, 173–75; silencing the voice of, 139–40; slave vs. citizen, 109; sovereign made present in, 110–11. *See also* victims of torture

body cavity searches, 130–31, 133, 142

The Body in Pain (Scarry), 109–10, 132, 139–40

Boltanski, Luc, 149

Boosa army camp, 221

boot camps for juveniles, 29

border fortification, 85–86

borders: of accountability, 96; ideological, Sri Lankan war, 225–30, 234–36

Botero, Fernando, 191, 212n8

Botero Abu Ghraib (Botero), 191, 212n8

Bowden, Mark, 138

British antiterrorism techniques, 33

British intelligence, 58

Brown, Wendy, 81–82

Buddha, 227, 233–34

Buddha statues, 227, 228, 233–34, 236–38

Buddhism, 227–29, 230, 239

Bunning, Jim, 116

Burge, Jon, 27, 29, 150

Bush, George W.: on Abu Ghraib photos, 17, 68; addressing the threat of terrorism, 121; enhanced interrogation techniques speech, 61; mentioned, 74; on 'Wanted, Dead or Alive' poster, 167; "we do not torture," 112

Bush, George W., administration: Army Field Manual 34–52 changes, 39; eavesdropping authorization, 77–78; enhanced interrogation technique policy, 113; executive power expansion and, 82–83; indictments for torture of detainees, 102; Iraq War, 76; mentioned, 90; security

Bush, George W. (cont.)
　　state creation, 10, 82–87; torture
　　policy, 5–6, 21n6, 40–41, 149–50,
　　190; on treatment of Guantá-
　　namo Bay detainees, 101, 102;
　　truth commission demand of
　　Leahy, 47
Butler, Judith, 4, 10, 11, 120
Bybee, Jay, 21n7, 113

C

camera as instrument of torture,
　　188–89, 190, 213n13
Camp Delta. *See* Guantánamo Bay
　　detention center
Camp Iguana, 171
Camp Nama, 142, 143, 145
Canto General (Neruda), 216
Castañeda, Antonia, 166–67
Central Intelligence Agency, 47,
　　57–61, 76–77, 111–12, 135,
　　155n32
Chandrasekaran, Rajiv, 135
checks and balances, 75
Cheney, Dick, 13, 40–41, 49, 62, 63,
　　82, 149
Chicago Police Department, 27, 29,
　　150
child detainees, 160, 171–75
children, abduction, torture and mur-
　　der of, 221
Chulawamsa, 232
citizen detention, 85–86
clean torture techniques, 30, 113
close confinement, 39
Cold War era, 76, 77, 80
Colombo, 225
Colombo torture chamber, 221
colonialism, US, 166–68
command dynamic of torture, 145
command responsibility doctrine, 70

communal nature of torture, 12,
　　142–46
complicitous accountability, 93–97
complicity doctrine, 94, 96
Congressional representatives
　　denouncing torture, 50–51,
　　64–65
Conroy, John, 150
Conyers, John, 47
Coomaraswamy, Radhika, 234
corruption, governmental, 27
Crapo, Michael D., 116
Crile, Susan: *Abu Ghraib: Abuse of
　　Power*, 190–92, 194–98, 199–202,
　　211n6, 212n8; *Crouching in Ter-
　　ror*, 191, 194–99, 195f, 205, 207;
　　Erotic Humiliation, 191, 202–5,
　　203f; *Panties as Hood*, 191, 199–
　　202, 200f; *Private England, with
　　Prisoner on a Leash*, 205–9, 206f
criminal complicity, 94, 96
Crouching in Terror (Crile), 191, 194–
　　99, 195f, 205, 207
cruel, inhuman, and degrading acts,
　　21n6
cuffed high technique, 54
culture of torture, US, 40, 42–43
Curda, Karel, 33
Czech resistance, 32–33

D

Daniel, Valentine, 230
Danner, Mark, 6, 7, 9, 19, 41, 67, 91,
　　94, 95
"The Dark Art of Interrogation"
　　(Bowden), 138
the dead: in fiction, 232–34; *Figuren*
　　figure, 181, 182; measuring ter-
　　rorism through numbers of, 4
death: in detention, 114, 115, 143,
　　153n7, 155n32, 175, 182; team-

272

work required for, 143; as theatre, 220, 222; unseen yet known, 217–21

death, preventing: force-feeding of detainees, 4–6, 102, 103–9, 114–22; medicalization of torture for, 112–14

debate on torture. *See* torture debate

dehumanizing the enemy, 11, 160, 163, 166–67, 172, 180, 202. *See also* animalization of detainees

Deleuze, Gilles, 224, 225

democracy, torture and, 4–11, 25–29, 35–38, 40, 48–50, 61. *See also specific administrations*

Dershowitz, Alan, 138, 150

detainee designation, 86

detainees, high-value, 58–61

Detainee Treatment Act, 50–51

detention, originating torture in, 147

Detroit terror cell, 170

devices of torture, exporting, 145

Dharmapala, Angarika, 228

"Los Dictadores" (Neruda), 216

dictatorship, Disneyland as, 170

dignity: force-feeding as an assault on, 119; vocabulary of, 202

Dirty Harry Effect, 52

the disappeared, 220–21, 232–34

disciplinary punishment, 104–9

Discipline and Punish (Foucault), 103, 112

Disney, Walt, 166

Disneyland: Banksy's doll installation at, 158, 159–60, 181, 182; Guantánamo Bay vs., 17, 160–70

"The Distance of a Shout" (Ondaatje), 217–18, 219, 235

distancing, geographical and geopolitical, 111–12, 135, 183

doctrine of emergency and executive power, 77–87

dogs, intimidation by, 48, 113, 191, 194–99, 195*f*, 205, 207

doll installation at Disneyland (Banksy), 158, 159–60, 181, 182

Dorf, Michael, 23n17

Doss, Erika, 162

Dravidians, 229, 235, 236

Dubois, Page, 151

Durand, Robert, 118

Durbin, Richard, 116

Dyzenhaus, David, 87

E

economics of torture, 35, 145

Edmonson, John, 101

Eelam National Liberation Front (ENLF), 222

Eelam People's Revolutionary Liberation Front (EPRLF), 222

Eelam Revolutionary Organization of Students (EROS), 222

Eighth Amendment to the Constitution, 69

Eisenman, Stephen R., 212n9

Eisgruber, Christopher, 86

electrotorture, 30

Elmaghraby, Ehab, 130, 131, 133, 142, 151

Embilipitiya massacre, 220–21

empathy, 192

enemy combatant category, 84

England, Lynndie R., 8, 69, 70, 191–92, 194, 205–9, 206*f*, 213n15

The English Patient (Ondaatje), 232

enhanced interrogation techniques: Bush defense of, 61, 113; public exposure of, anticipating, 58; public position on, 51; Senate Armed Services Committee

enhanced interrogation techniques (cont.)
report, 61; survivor accounts,
53–56, 57, 170–75. *See also specific
techniques*

Erotic Humiliation (Crile), 191, 202–5,
203*f*

eroticism, 145

Esposito, Richard, 58–59, 61

ethics: art's relation to, 18, 191; of
force-feeding, 119–20; of self-
sacrifice, 14–15; of war photography, 189–90

ethnic cleansing in Sri Lanka, 225–26

execution as theatre, 192, 194, 215–
16, 220

executive power, expansion of:
doctrine of emergency to justify, 77–81; historically, 75–77;
legislating, 80, 83; for national
security, 77–78; security state and,
10, 81–87

executive power, restraining, 75, 80,
84, 85, 87

Exodus (Uris), 229

expressive violence, 103

extraordinary rendition practice, 86

F

the face, 181–82

false consensus, 41

Fanon, Frantz, 223

Fay, George R., 143

FBI, 77, 83

fear: hooding and, 55; politics of, 52,
88; submission and, 88, 95–96

fearful public theory, 36–37

Feed and Forage Act, 80

Feldman, Allen, 219, 225, 234

fiction: human rights in, 232–33,
238; torture justified in, 12,
14, 15, 23nn23-24, 24n30, 50,

51–52. *See also specific subjects; specific works*

Fifth Amendment to the Constitution, 69

Figuren, 160, 181, 182

Finn, Peter, 135

Finnegan, Patrick, 23n24

forced standing, 39, 59–60

force-feeding detainees: justification
for, 114, 117, 118, 120–21; medical monitoring of, 117–18, 119;
morality of, 117, 118, 121–22;
normalization through, 116–17;
physician protests, 119–20;
restraint chairs for, 117, 120; as
sovereign power through biopolitics, 102, 103–4, 114–22; statistics, 102

Foreign Intelligence Surveillance Act,
76, 83

foreign nationals detention rights,
85–86

forgetfulness: historical, 27, 166–67;
political, 25, 38–40; pursuit of,
46; social, 27, 40–42

Forward Operating Base Mercury,
142

Foucault, Michel, 5, 102, 103, 105,
112, 220

Frederick, Ivan Chip, 150

free choice, hunger striking as, 119

French in Algeria, 60

French Modern torture technique, 30

Freud, Sigmund, 212n9

Fuglerud, Øivind, 219, 225

future torture, predicting, 38

G

Galtung, Johan, 4

Gautama, Siddhartha. *See* Buddha

Gellman, Barton, 135

Geneva Convention, 21n7, 22n9, 69, 84, 106, 118

geographic distancing, 58–61, 135, 183

geopolitical distancing, 111–12

Gestapo (Nazi) antisabotage unit, 32–33, 34

Gonzales, Alberto, 21n7

good and evil, 11–12, 162, 165

graffiti, 158

Graham, Lindsay, 116

Graner, Charles A., 69, 70, 94, 95, 150, 194, 207, 213n15

gratuitous torture, 8

Greece, 109

grey holes, 87

Gronke, Paul, 40

group dynamics of torture, 142–44

group identity formation, 145

Guantánamo Bay detainee abuses: Bush administration policy on, 101, 102; distancing the sovereign from, 111–12; enhanced interrogation techniques, 55, 57, 60; humiliation, 8; Initial Reaction Force (IRF) rituals, 156n39; prisoner accounts, 57, 167, 171–75; psychic violence, 173–74; purpose, 104, 105–6

Guantánamo Bay detainees: Banksy's iconic depiction of, 158, 159–60, 181, 182; citizenship of, 111; deaths of, 114, 115, 123n11, 126n52, 175; dehumanizing, 160, 162–64, 166–67, 172, 180; demographics, 9; disciplinary power over, 104–9; domestic housing of, 111, 122; extralegal status, 106, 163; *homo sacer* status, 16, 163, 180; hunger strikes by, 101–4, 114–22; iconic function of, 165;

juridical protections for, 84; juvenile, 160, 171–75

Guantánamo Bay detainees, hunger strikers: characterization as insane, 120–21; force-feeding, 101–4, 114–22; purpose of, 101, 114, 115; statistics, 101–2

Guantánamo Bay detention center: closing of, 102, 112, 122, 183; disciplinary power at, 104–9; Disneyland compared, 17, 160–70; hunger strikes at, 101–4, 114–22; Nazi concentration camps compared, 16–17, 176–82; Obama administration policies, 38–39, 102, 112, 122, 183; penalogical entertainment in, 164; purpose of, 104; souvenir shop, 164; statistics, 101; surveillance environment of, 143

Guattari, Félix, 224, 225

guerrilla art, 158. *See also* doll installation at Disneyland

Guevara, Ernesto "Che," 219

guilt, collective, 72–73

H

Hamdan v. Rumsfeld, 85, 106

Hamilton, Alexander, 75

Harman, Sabrina, 210n1, 211n4

Harris, Harry, 115, 118

Harry Callahan, 52

Herodotus, 232

Hersh, Seymour, 55

Heydrich, Reinhard, 32

High Five Paintball Club, 142

Himmler, Heinrich, 14–15

Histories (Herodotus), 232

Hobbes, Thomas, 88, 89

Hoffman, Bruce, 138

Holocaust Jews, 16

Holtzman, Elizabeth, 70–71
Homeland Security Department, 85
homo sacer, 16, 163
hooding, 54–56, 202–5, 203*f*
Hoole, Rajan, 226, 228, 229
humanity: art in restoring, 18, 190; the body as a site of common, 202
human rights: of detainees, 163; in fiction, 232–33, 238; intervention success factors, 37; respect for, 35
Human Rights First, 69–70
humiliation, infliction of: artistic response to, 191, 200*f*, 202–5, 203*f*, 206*f*; detainee accounts of, 171–72; disguised as security, 130–31, 133, 142; for intelligence gathering, 8; as not-torture, 102, 113; purpose of, 8, 13; separating torture from, 8; standard practice of, 55
hunger strikers: characterization as insane, 120–21; force-feeding of, 101–4, 114–22; statistics, 101–2
hunger strikes: as acts of war, 115, 118, 121; beginnings, 114; purpose of, 101, 114, 115
hypothetical torture, 134–35

I

Ibrahim, Mukhtar Said, 33
Immigration and Naturalization detention centers, 29
imprisonment, US historical use of, 166–68
Indian Peace Keeping Force (IPKF), 222, 223, 224
Initial Reaction Force (IRF) rituals, 156n39
injustice, responsibility in relation to, 96
Inside the Wire (Saar), 129

intelligence gathering via torture, 7–9, 22n12, 31–33, 40, 102–3, 107–8, 133, 147–48
International Emergency Economic Powers Act, 80
international law, following, 39
interrogation: alibi of, 133, 139, 146–47; Army Field Manual 34-52 policy, 8, 39, 48; a false motive for torture, 133; Obama administration policies, 39; ritual of violence in, 139–40. *See also specific practices*
interrogational torture, 22n12, 31–33, 40, 107–8, 133, 147–48
interrogators, female, 55
intimacy: of perpetrators and spectators, 145; in torture photographs, 207–9
Iqbal, Jvail, 130, 133
Iran-Contra scandal, 76
Iraq, US war in, 76
Iraq Special Forces, 60
Ireland, Julia A., 18, 19, 20
Irish Republican Army prisoners, 58
Ismail, Qadri, 234
Israeli domestic intelligence, 59

J

Jack Bauer, 12, 14, 23n23, 40, 50, 51–52, 64
Jackson, Robert, 19
Jaffna, 223–24, 225
Jaffna library, 237–38
Janata Vimuki Peramuna (JVP), 219, 222
Japan's torture crisis, 28
Jefferson, Thomas, 79, 87
Jew-become-Muslim, 176–82
Johnson, Lyndon B., administration, 76

Joint Chiefs of Staff, 76
Jones, Anthony R., 143
judicial systems, permissive, 27
judicial torture, 109
Justice Department, 83
justified torture: fictionalizing, 12, 14, 15, 23nn23–24, 24n30, 50, 51–52; good and evil narrative for, 11–12; for intelligence gathering, 7–9, 22n12, 31–33, 40, 102–3, 107–8, 133, 147–48; security rationale, 7, 8, 12, 13, 28, 32–33, 101–4, 106–8, 114–22, 138; war on terror in justifying, 7, 102–4, 109, 121, 134, 145, 149. *See also* utilitarian torture
juvenile boot camps, 29
juvenile detainees, 160, 171–75

K

Kahn, Paul, 109–10
Kaplan, Amy, 85, 167
Karpinski, Janis, 69
Kaufman-Osborn, Timothy V., 10, 19
Khadr, Omar, 160, 171–75
Kim (Kipling), 232
Kipling, Rudyard, 232
Kurnaz, Murat, 163, 180
Kurrikkadduvan massacre, 226
Kutz, Christopher, 94

L

Lagouranis, Tony, 143, 145
Laing, Gerald, 191, 194
landscape of violence. *See* Sri Lankan landscape of violence
language: disciplinary, violence in, 173–74; ritualized, 132; of the tortured body, 109–10, 172–73; of violence, 172–73, 218; of violence on the landscape, 218;

voice of the detainee, artistic response to, 199
Leach, Catherine, 177
Leahy, Patrick, 26, 47, 61
legal torture: Bush administration sanctions, 5–6; criminal liability protections, 21n6, 155n32; legislating, 6–7, 39, 50–51; memos on, 6, 21nn6–7, 22n8, 57–58, 71, 113. *See also* enhanced interrogation techniques
Levi, Primo, 176, 177
Levinas, Emmanuel, 181–82
Levinson, Sanford, 138
Lewis, Anthony, 74
Liberated Tigers of Tamil Eelam (LTTE), 221, 223–25, 233
Lincoln, Abraham, 79
Living with Torturers (Perera), 217
Lobel, Jules, 78, 80–81
Locke, John, 78–79, 87, 88, 89
logic of masculinist protection, 90
long-time standing, 59–60
Louima, Abner, 150
Louisiana Purchase, 79
Luban, David, 140, 145, 151
lynching, 150, 164
lynching postcards, 192, 194

M

Maas, Peter, 138
Mackey, Chris, 142, 143
Madison, James, 75
Mahavish Khan, Rukhsana, 176
Mahawamsa, 227–29, 232
Mahaweli River, 218, 229, 235
Mahvish Khan, Rukhsana, 163, 182
Manifest Destiny, 159, 166
Manzoor, Parvez, 178–79
marking techniques of torture, 30, 113
Marling, Karal Ann, 165

masculinist protection, logic of, 90
Mbembe, Achille, 18, 220
McCain, John, 122
the media: Abu Ghraib prison abuses and, 7–8; fearful public theory promulgated by, 36; public debate on torture, shaping the, 6–7, 41, 42; speculation on torture, 134–38, 151; torture archetype in the, 136–38
medical ethics of force-feeding, 119–20
medicalization of torture, 112–14, 117–20
mental patients, indefinite detention of, 120
Metropolitan Detention Center, Brooklyn, New York, 130
Mickey Mouse, 162
military command structure, 76
Military Commissions Act, 6, 39, 50–51, 61, 62, 85, 149
military tribunals, 84
Modell, David, 193, 213n13
Mohamed, Binyam, 101
Mohammed, Khalid Sheikh, 8–9, 53, 112
morality of torture, 33, 117, 118, 121–22
Morris, Errol, 210n1
Mothers of Plaza de Mayo, 220–21
motives for torture, 9
"Murder" (Nuhman), 237–38
Muselmann, 16, 160, 176–82
Muslims: at Guantánamo, 179–82; of the Holocaust, 176–79; in Sri Lanka, 224, 225–30, 239

N
Nadesan Centre for Human Rights, 232

Nancy, Jean-Luc, 163, 169
"A Nasty Business" (Hoffman), 138
National Emergencies Act, 80
national security, 77–78. *See also* war on terror
National Security Act, 76
National Security Agency, 77, 81
National Security Council, 76
Native Americans, 166–67
Nazi concentration camps, 16, 174, 176
Nazi Party, heroic ethics of self-sacrifice, 14–15
necropolitics, 18, 220, 233–34
Neruda, Pablo, 216–17
neutralizing violence, 174
New York Times Magazine, 7–8
Nietzsche, Friedrich, 3
Nixon, Richard, administration, 58, 76, 80
noise-induced stress, 39, 56
not-torture. *See* enhanced interrogation techniques
nudity, forced: human pyramids, 48; as not-torture, Bush administration on, 60; photographs of, artistic response to, 188, 191, 194–209; prisoner accounts, 54; purpose of, 55; standard practice of, 48, 57
Nuhman, M. A., 237–38

O
Obama, Barack, 51
Obama, Barack, administration: Guantánamo Bay policy, 48, 102, 112, 122, 183; interrogation policies, 25, 48; political forgetfulness, 38–40; torture policy, 40–41, 112
observer witness and victim gap,

17–18. *See also* archetype of torture

Ondaatje, Michael, 18, 217–18, 219, 230–38

othering, 11, 16, 177–78, 181–82. *See also* animalization of detainees

P

pain: empathy vs. sympathy for, 192; language disintegration with, 109–10; quantifying and controlling, 108; sleep deprivation and tolerance of, 30

Pannwitz, Heinz von, 32–33

Panties as Hood (Crile), 191, 199–202, 200*f*

Pappas, Thomas, 69

Parakrama Samudra, 236

partisanship, torture as symbolic of, 41

Pawelczynska, Anna, 177, 180

Pease, Donald, 88

penalogical entertainment, 164

People's Liberation Organization of Tamil Eelam (PLOTE), 222

Perera, Sasanka, 217

Perera, Suvendrini, 18–19, 20, 163

pluralistic ignorance, 41

poetry about torture, 216–18, 235

police torture, 27, 29, 150

policy, torture as, 26–28, 48–50, 61

political violence, torture as, 4–11

politics of torture: challenging the, 11–19; criminal liability protections, 21n6, 155n32; inviolability of governmental accountability, 70–71; Leahy's demand for tribunal, 26, 47, 61; legislating, 6–7, 39, 50–51. *See also specific administrations*

Posner, Richard, 138

prerogative power doctrine, 78–79

prevention of torture, 26, 27, 34–40

Priest, Dana, 135

Private England, with Prisoner on a Leash (Crile), 205–9, 206*f*

pro-torture majorities, existence of, 36

psychological torture, 108, 145

Puar, Jaspar, 163

the public: complicity in use of torture, 6–7, 9–10, 27, 62–65, 93–97; concept of torture, 129; debate on torture, shaping the, 6–7, 41–42, 134–38; fictionalized torture, response to, 50, 51–52; Holtzman's appeal to, 71; position on torture, 35–38, 40–41, 47–48; validating torture, 31

Pugliese, Joseph, 16–17, 19, 20

R

racialization of space, 170

racism, *Muselmann* figure in the camps, 176–82

Rajapakse, Mahinda, 239

rape: as torture, 13–14, 130–31, 142, 151, 153n6; as an unnecessary body cavity search, 130–31, 133, 142

rapists, peacekeepers as, 224

Rasul v. Bush, 85

Ratner, Michael, 171

Reagan, Ronald, administration, 75, 76

reality: of the body, rupturing, 54, 113, 173–75; of torture, mediating, 11–12

recreational tourism, 166

Reddened Water Flows Clear (Arasanayagam), 235

Rejali, Darius, 9–10, 19, 147–48

Remnants of Auschwitz (Agamben), 176

restraint chairs for force-feeding, 117, 120

rituals: of development, 227–28, 238–39; of torture, 132–33; of violence, 147, 156n39

Rodley, Nigel, 147

Romper Room, 142–43

Roosevelt, Franklin, 79

Roosevelt, Theodore, 79

Ross, Brian, 58–59, 61

Rothman, Hal, 166

rule of law, 82–83, 85, 87

Rumsfeld, Donald, 21n6, 59–60, 69, 91, 94, 95

Rumsfeld, Hamdan v., 85, 106

S

Saar, Erik, 129

Sager, Lawrence, 86

Salgado, Minoli, 234

Sanchez, Ricardo, 68, 69

Sante, Luc, 192, 194

Scalia, Antonin, 23n23

Scarred Minds (Somasundaram), 223

Scarry, Elaine, 9, 109–11, 132, 133, 139–40, 141, 145, 147, 173

Scheppele, Kim, 76, 80

Schonhoff, Colleen M., 116

security state: characteristics of, 81–82; consent of the governed in, 88–92; creation of, 10, 74, 81–87; Disneyland as a, 170; dissent in the, 90; equality in the, 89; freedom in the, 89; illusion of national unity, 92

Senate Armed Services Committee, 61

Senate Intelligence Committee, 61

Senate Judiciary Committee, 61

Senate Select Committee on Intelligence, 47

Senate Select Committee on Watergate, 64

sensorium of the body, disrupting, 54, 113, 173–75

separation of powers, 75

Serra, Richard, 191

sexual assault, 113, 142. *See also* rape

shame interrogation practice, 55

Shin Beit, 59

shock photography, 189–90

Sinhala, 219, 221–22, 225–30, 232, 234, 239

Sivanandan, A., 223

60 Minutes II, 7, 55

sleep deprivation: Army Field Manual 34-52 on, 39; as not-torture, 102, 113; pain tolerance and, 30; Spanish Inquisition use of, 33–34; standard practice of, 9, 59, 129

Smith, Andrea, 166

social contract: prisoner exception to the, 111, 117, 121–22; in the security state, 81, 87–94

social contract theory, 68, 71–73

social forgetfulness, 40–42

social hierarchy, torture to produce and sustain, 109

social practice legitimizing torture, 27

soldiers: in Iraq, position on torture, 40; returning, atrocity-related trauma, 39–40

Solzhenitsyn, Alexander, 169

Somasundaram, Daya, 223

Sontag, Susan, 7, 189, 192, 198

South Africa, Truth and Reconciliation Commission, 62

sovereign power, 102, 103–9, 114–22, 220

Soviet Union, 59

space: distancing the sovereign, 111–12, 135, 183; of exception, 169; of leisure and recreation, 161–62, 165–70; racialization of, 170; of suffering without a future, 174–75; of torture, Crile's work on, 197

Spanish Inquisition, 33–34, 60

Specter, Arlen, 62

Sri Lanka: economic development in, postwar, 226–28, 238–39; ethnonationalism, postwar, 225–29, 239; modernity, 228–30

Sri Lankan landscape of violence: execution video, 215–16; in fiction, 218; ideological boundary sector, 225–30, 234–36; in literature, 18, 230–38; necropolitical order, 18, 220–22; in poetry, 216–18; regimes of territoriality, 18, 219–25; state as war machine, 224–25; unseen yet known, 217–21, 232–34

Standard Operating Procedure (Morris), 210n1, 211n4

Staub, Ervin, 149

stealthy torture, 30–31, 113

Stop Bush (Serra), 191

Strauss, Marcy, 130

stress positions: Abu Ghraib use of, 189, 199, 201; Army Field Manual 34-52 on, 39; artistic response to, 199, 200*f*, 201; Guantánamo Bay use of, 129; as not-torture, 102, 189, 199, 201; prisoner accounts, 54–57

structure of torture, 139, 173–74

Studies in a Dying Colonialism (Fanon), 223

suffering without a future, 174–75

suicide, 115, 118, 175, 182

Sussman, David, 140–41

Swanner, Mark, 143

sympathy, 192, 198, 202, 205, 211n3

T

Taguba, Antonio M., 143

Taliban, 211n7

Tamil, 154, 219, 221–30, 233–34, 237–38

Tamil Eelam Liberation Organization (TELO), 222

Tancredo, Tom, 12

teamwork for torture, 142–44

techniques of torture: 1950s–1970s, 54; changes in, 29–30; contagion effect, 30–31; medicalization of, 112–14; types of, 30–31, 113. *See also* enhanced interrogation techniques; *specific techniques*

technology of torture, exporting, 145

Teitel, Ruti, 83–84

temperature-induced stress, 39, 57, 60, 106, 113, 129

Temple of the Tooth, 233

Tennekoon, Serena, 226, 227

terrorism link to torture, 36–37

terrorist videos, amateur, 160–61, 170

Thangaraj, Yuvaraj, 230

theatre, death and torture as, 132, 139, 164, 189, 220, 222

theory of the uncanny, 212n9

ticking-time-bomb scenario, 7, 8, 12, 13, 28, 32–33, 103, 138–39, 140

"Time to Think about Torture" (Alter), 138

time without respite, 174–75

Tomorrowland, Disneyland, 159

tooth, Buddha's, 227, 233, 235–36

torture: defined, 3–4, 26, 39, 51,

281

torture (cont.)
113, 130–31, 138–41; drivers of, 36–37; iconic scenario of, 138; logic of, 105; normalizing, 13–14, 151; origin of, 147; purposes alleged, 13, 105–6; structure of, 139, 173–74; symbolic elements, 132; unseen yet known, 217–21, 232–34. *See also* enhanced interrogation techniques; interrogational torture; justified torture
"Torture" (Strauss), 130
torture crisis, 42–43
torture debate: in the media, 6–7; normalizing torture through, 13–14, 151; shaping the, 41–42, 134–38; torturer-tortured dyad in, 12
torture memos, 6, 21nn6–7, 22n8, 57–58, 71, 113
torturers: attributes when choosing, 29; characteristics of, 34; fictionalizing, 14; fiction of the power of, 132; Nazi Party, 14–15; protecting, 51, 62–63; psychology of, 29; as spectators, 146, 191, 199
torturer-tortured dyad. *See* archetype of torture
torture threshold, 21n6
"Torture Tough or Lite" (Maas), 138
touch, 201–2
trials, 38–39, 69
Truman, Harry, administration, 77
Truth and Reconciliation Commission, 62
truth commission, US, 47, 61–62
"Turning Jews into Muslims" (Manzoor), 178
24 (television), 12, 14, 15, 23nn23–24, 24n30, 50, 51–52
"*24, Or Himmler in Hollywood*" (Žižek), 14

U

undocumented/illegal residents, 86
United Nations Convention Against Torture and Other Cruel, Inhuman, or Degrading Treatment or Punishment, 21n6, 70
United Nations Convention on the Rights of the Child, 171
United States: acknowledging use of torture, 62–65; colonialism, 166–68; culture of torture, 40, 42–43; exceptionality conviction, 19; exporting torture, 145, 150; history of torture, 27, 29, 149–52, 166–68; mythic landscapes of, 166–67; newness of torture to, fiction of, 13, 14, 149; policy on torture, official, 48–50, 61; threshold for torture defined, 21n6. *See also specific administrations*
Universal Declaration of Human Rights, 27
Uris, Leon, 229
USA PATRIOT ACT, 83
"US Behind Secret Transfer of Terror Suspects" (Chandrasekaran and Finn), 135
"U.S. Decries Abuse but Defends Interrogations" (Priest and Gellman), 135
utilitarian torture, 5, 7–9, 23n18, 102. *See also* justified torture

V

Valvettithurai massacre, 226
victims of torture: communal assault on, 145–46; giving voice to, 18–19; medical monitoring of, 112–14; observer-witness of the, 17–18; othering, 11, 16, 177–78,

181–82; psychic withdrawal of, 173–75. *See also* archetype of torture; the body

Vietnam conflict, 29

Vietnam War, 76, 80

violence: expressive, 103–4; festivals of, 164; historical, forgetting, 166–67; language of, 172–73, 218; neutralizing, 174; psychic, 173–74, 203–4; ritual of, 147, 156n39; sociality of, 104; against women, 211n4, 224. *See also* rape

violence workers, training, 145

voice of the detainee: artistic response to, 199; speech-body rift, 172–73. *See also* language

voyeurism, 22n13

W

Waldron, Jeremy, 141, 147, 151

war, hunger strikes as acts of, 115, 118, 121

War Crimes Act, 22n9, 51, 62–63

war machines, 224–25

war on terror: colonialism's intersection, 167–68; dehumanizing the enemy in the, 11; Holocaust compared, 15; justifying torture through, 7, 10, 102–4, 109, 121, 134, 145, 149; the law, impact on, 86; mobilizing support for, 92; prisoner deaths during, 114; torture as practiced during the, 13, 46, 53, 65; torture debate and, 6; Wild West symbolism in the, 167

war-on-terror detainees, 130–31, 133, 135, 136. *See also* Guantánamo Bay detainees

war-on-terror prison camps, 150

war photography, 189–90

War Powers Resolution, 76

waterboarding, 8–9, 28–29, 47, 53, 60–61, 112

Watergate, 58, 80

"We are all torturers now" (Danner), 67

Welikade jail, 221

the West, 166–67

whistle-blowers, 39

Wilcox, Lauren, 4–6, 19

Willet, Sabin, 181

Winkenwerder, William, 118

witness-victim relationship. *See* archetype of torture

Wittes, Benjamin, 84

Wolin, Sheldon, 75

women, violence against, 211n4, 224. *See also* rape

Wood, Grant, 194

World War II antiterrorism techniques, 33

Worthington, Andy, 171

wrongdoing, punishable, 69

Wyden, Ron, 116

Y

Yapahuwa, 235–36

Yee, James, 143

Yergin, Daniel, 77

Yoo, John, 21n7, 38, 50

Young, Iris Marion, 10, 74, 88, 90, 95–96

Z

Zionist ideology, 229–30

Žižek, Slavoj, 13–14, 16, 17, 151

Zubaydah, Abu, 112, 114